Discovering
Jesus

Harsh Mahan Cairae is a student of religion and philosophy. He has been studying the scriptures of several religions for many years. His first book, *An Aryan Journey*, was a research based primarily on Vedic and Zoroastrian texts.

Discovering Jesus

HARSH MAHAAN CAIRAE

RUPA

Published by
Rupa Publications India Pvt. Ltd 2022
7/16, Ansari Road, Daryaganj
New Delhi 110002

Sales centres:
Allahabad Bengaluru Chennai
Hyderabad Jaipur Kathmandu
Kolkata Mumbai

Copyright © Harsh Mahaan Cairae 2022

All rights reserved.
No part of this publication may be reproduced, transmitted,
or stored in a retrieval system, in any form or by any means,
electronic, mechanical, photocopying, recording or otherwise,
without the prior permission of the publisher.

The views and opinions expressed in this book are
the author's own and the facts are as reported by her
which have been verified to the extent possible,
and the publishers are not in any way liable for the same.

ISBN: 978-93-91256-33-3

Second impression 2022

10 9 8 7 6 5 4 3 2

The moral right of the author has been asserted.

Printer in India

This book is sold subject to the condition that it shall not,
by way of trade or otherwise, be lent, resold, hired out, or otherwise
circulated, without the publisher's prior consent, in any form of
binding or cover other than that in which it is published.

Dedicated to my guru, His Divine Grace
Sri Swatmaramji, the author of
Hatha Yoga Pradeepika

CONTENTS

Preface — ix

1. The Apostles and Paul — 1
2. The Myths Created — 51
3. Acquiring Apostolic Authority — 129
4. The March to Supremacy — 205
5. Retrieving the Lost Teachings — 255
6. The Further Question — 345

Bibliography — 377

Index — 379

This is not anti-Christian propaganda but a work in search of the truth, addressed to other seekers of truth, without questioning anybody's faith or intending to hurt anyone's sentiments or feelings.

PREFACE

The message of Jesus is of interest to every student of religion. This, as a normal course, should have been found in the Bible. A study of the same, however, reveals that very little is mentioned therein as his teachings, and Paul appears as the predominant figure with more than half of the New Testament attributed to him. In his writings, Paul does not propound anything to be the teachings of Jesus but lays stress on what the conduct of a Christian should be. He also admits that he had never met Jesus in his lifetime but claims that he received his message when he appeared to him much after his death. Paul has also claimed that he neither received anything from the Apostles who had accompanied Jesus in his lifetime and should be believed to be conveying Jesus's message nor was appointed an apostle by them. Though several passages of the New Testament convey the impression that Paul and the Apostles preached the same thing, a closer inspection reveals that this impression had been deliberately created by the Pauline Church to make the Pauline teachings credible. The present work unearths evidence from the Bible and other Christian sources to show that Paul was in conflict with the Apostles. He was not considered to be an apostle by the Church of James, which was the church to which all the Apostles owed allegiance. His works were not accepted as a part of the scriptures by the followers of this Church, which was initially headed by Saint James, the Apostle and brother of Jesus.

With Paul being in conflict with the Apostles, his links to the teachings of Jesus get snapped, making it essential to know what Paul established as a theology and how his theology succeeded in overriding what the Apostles were preaching. A study of what has been written by the Church Fathers, the great bishops and other eminent Christian theologians in the early centuries, is the basis of the story that has been presented in this book. In contrast to Paul, who wrote prolifically, the Apostles wrote virtually nothing. The Apostles' teachings were conveyed orally and were then documented by their disciples. With time, when the two theologies came in conflict, the teachings of the Apostles were ascribed to the persons who had recorded them. As these were contradictory to what Paul, who had by then been acknowledged as an apostle, had written, the Pauline Church declared the teachings heretical and their followers, heretics. It started from the West, but soon, the Pauline writings found their way into the scriptures of the East as well. Thus began the changeover of the East too. Left to itself, the process would have taken a little longer and would have gone unnoticed, but due to historical factors, an attempt was made to force it on the East, which led to a myriad of controversies and, finally, a split between the Eastern and the Western Church.

In the given situation, the teachings of Jesus need to be searched for in the beliefs of the Christians who were declared heretics by the Pauline Church. A study of this in isolation presents a lot of difficulties, as what is known about these beliefs can only be found in what has been recorded by the Church Fathers who were their critics. It is, thus, not only disjointed, but is presented in a manner in which the Apostles could be proved to be illogical. Fortunately, it closely resembles Vedic beliefs, because of which their entire belief system can be brought out by understanding the Vedic beliefs and looking for each element of this belief system in what has been recorded by the Christian Fathers about the heretics and their beliefs. This is what the book has done.

Though unrelated to the subject, several findings emerged in the study that suggest that the Jews had their origin from the Vedic Aryans. As this is very important, a chapter on it has been added at the end. It has been done with the full understanding that something emerging only from literary sources cannot be the final word on a subject like this but can only be a pointer for other sources of history to look for its confirmation or rejection.

1

THE APOSTLES AND PAUL

The study of Christianity is of immense interest to a student of religion, as its followers constitute the highest numbers in the world today. In doing so, the basic urge is to look for the teachings of Jesus Christ. This is impeded by the fact that the Bible has recorded more of his life than his teachings. Any attempt to look for them in the present followers is met with difficulty by the fact that the religion is split into a very large number of sects, which are called Churches, each of which claims to be following the authentic version of the religion.

References from the Bible show that Jesus had 12 prominent disciples, who were called Apostles. One of them had betrayed him, which had led to his crucifixion. This Apostle was replaced by another with the common consent of the remaining 11. These Apostles had accompanied Jesus in his lifetime and are to be trusted for knowing what his real teachings were. Christianity today, in all the Churches, however, is what Paul laid down. Paul had emerged shortly after the death of Jesus and had never met him in his lifetime. He has claimed that he did not receive the teachings from the Apostles who had accompanied the living Jesus but had received them directly from Christ, who had appeared to him after his death and had imparted the real secrets to him. He also claimed that he was an apostle, though not appointed so by the other Apostles. In addressing some of his epistles, while introducing himself as an apostle, he has stated the authority by which he was so appointed.

> Paul, a servant of Jesus Christ, called to be an apostle, separated unto the Gospel of God.
>
> (Romans 1:1)
>
> Paul, called to be an apostle of Jesus Christ through the will of God.
>
> (1 Corinthians 1:1) (2 Corinthians 1:1) (Ephesians 1:1)
>
> Paul, an apostle (not of men, neither by man, but by Jesus Christ, and God the Father, who raised him from the dead).
>
> (Galatians 1:1)
>
> Paul, an apostle of Jesus Christ by the commandment of God our saviour, and Lord Jesus Christ, which is our hope.
>
> (1 Timothy 1:1)
>
> Paul, an apostle of Jesus Christ by the will of God, according to the promise of life which is in Christ Jesus.
>
> (2 Timothy 1:1)
>
> Paul, a servant of God, and an apostle of Jesus Christ, according to the faith of God's elect, and the acknowledging of the truth which is after godliness.
>
> (Titus 1:1)

It can be seen from these that Paul claimed to be an apostle 'by the will of God' or 'by commandment of God'. He is emphatic in the Galatians, where he stresses 'not of men, neither by man, but by Jesus Christ, and God the Father'. As Paul had never met Jesus in his lifetime, it is evident that this was only a claim on his part for which, he insisted, there was divine sanction. Paul's claim of being an apostle seems to have been questioned during his lifetime by the other Apostles and by some groups of Christians. Paul appears to have had serious doctrinal differences with the other Apostles and appears to have struggled all his life against them to establish his form of Christianity over what they were propounding. In the Bible, the conflict between the Apostles and Paul has been played down and concealed to whatever extent was possible. This was necessary as showing Paul to be teaching the same things as the Apostles was a basic requirement for the Pauline Church. Glimpses of this conflict, however, do emerge in the Bible. Since only Pauline Christianity has survived, the scriptures and other religious literature have come to us through the traditions of the Pauline Church alone. In this, though the doctrinal differences between Paul and the other Apostles were far more fundamental, the major point of difference that has been projected, is that the other Apostles insisted on following all the precepts of Judaism in their Christianity, while Paul preached the religion in a purer form from which the elements of Judaism had been purged. In his epistles, Paul has, at times, referred to the other Apostles as 'Judaizers' and 'of the circumcision'. It would be of interest to trace this conflict between the two sides as it emerges from the Bible.

To begin with, Paul was with the Apostles and was at Antioch with Barnabas. As per the Pseudo-Clementine literature in *The Writings of Early Church Fathers*, Barnabas is another name of Apostle Mathias. The beginning of the separation appears to have been over Judaizing the Gentiles who were being converted to Christianity. Though the occasion when the Apostles and Paul parted ways is not clearly evident, it appears to be the one mentioned in the following passages. This can be said because this event seems to have been very significant for Paul, as he has mentioned it twice but has changed the version on the second occasion to express his independence from the Apostles and, to a certain extent, his superiority over them. An attempt has been made in the Bible to show it to be a difference not between Paul and the Apostles, but with 'certain men which came down from Judea'. The references from the Bible regarding this incident are given below.

> And certain men which came down from Judea taught the brethren, and said, Except ye be circumcised after the manner of Moses, ye cannot be saved.
>
> When therefore Paul and Barnabas had no small dissension and disputation with them, they determined that Paul and Barnabas, and certain other of them, should go up to Jerusalem unto the apostles and elders about this question.
>
> (The Acts 15:1–2)

Though 'certain men' have been stated to have raised the issue of circumcision and following the Law of Moses, while Paul and Barnabas have been reported to be jointly disputing with them, the circumstances and the events that followed show that this is not true. This was evidently a dispute between Paul and Barnabas. If it had been some other persons preaching differently, the authority of the two apostles together would have been sufficient to end the dispute. What followed confirms the same. When the two reached Jerusalem, it has been reported, that some Christians who were from the sect of the Pharisees stated that the new converts should be circumcised and commanded to follow the Law of Moses. Though it is reported that after much consideration it was decided that the Gentiles converted to Christianity should not be circumcised and the Law of Moses should not be imposed on them, again the events that followed show this reporting to be untrue. The Apostles are reported to have sent letters, along with two brethren, Judas and Silas, to accompany Paul and Barnabas to Antioch. The fact that these two were sent at all is an indication that the differences were between Paul and Barnabas, otherwise just the letters should have been sufficient. The significant portions of the letter are given below.

> For as much as we have heard, that certain which went out from us have troubled you with words, subverting your

souls, saying, Ye must be circumcised, and keep the law: to whom we gave no such commandment.

(The Acts 15:24)

For it seemed good to the Holy Ghost, and to us, to lay upon you no greater burden than these necessary things; That ye abstain from meats offered to idols, and from blood, and from things strangled, and from fornication: from which if ye keep yourselves, ye shall do well. Fare ye well.

(The Acts 15:28–29)

Here a specific statement has been made that no commandment had been given for circumcising the new converts or for requiring them to keep the Law of Moses. This is an untrue reporting of the event not only because, as would emerge ahead, Peter would, throughout his life, insist on following the Law of Moses but also because on return from Jerusalem, Paul circumcised Timothy while converting him (The Acts 16:3). This, he is reported to have done, because of 'the Jews'. The reference cannot be to those Jews who were not Christian because it would have been immaterial to them how the Gentiles were being converted to a religion that was alien to them. It is obvious that he did so to comply with the directions of the Apostles. That there was no departure from the Law of Moses on the part of the Apostles in their response, is also indicative in the above reference wherein a direction has been given to abstain from 'blood, and from things strangled.' This was a very important part of the Jewish traditions in which the animals to be eaten were slaughtered in a particular manner, called the *shechita*, in which the blood was drained out. The meat was considered to be kosher and fit to be eaten only after that. Later Christians have not followed this. As would emerge ahead, Paul's hostility to the Apostles and Jewish practices increased gradually. At this stage, the stipulation of following this practice of the Jews has been retained by Paul.

The same incident has been reported in the Galatians. By the time this epistle was written, Paul was asserting his independent authority and was not looking to the Apostles for clarification and support as was reported in the Acts. The relevant extracts are below.

> But I certify you, brethren, that the gospel which was preached of me is not after man.
> For I neither received it of man, neither was I taught it, but by the revelations of Jesus Christ.
> (Galatians 1:11–12)

> Neither went I up to Jerusalem to them which were apostles before me; but I went into Arabia and returned again unto Damascus.
> (Galatians 1:17)

> Then fourteen years after I went up again to Jerusalem with Barnabas, and took Titus with me also.
> And I went up by revelation, and communicated unto them that gospel which I preach among the Gentiles, but privately to them which were of reputation, lest by any means I should run, or had run, in vain.
> But neither Titus, who was with me, being a Greek, was compelled to be circumcised:
> And that because of false brethren unawares brought in, who came in privily to spy out our liberty which we have in Christ Jesus, that they might bring us into bondage:
> To whom we gave place by subjection, no, not for an hour; that the truth of the gospel might continue with you.
> But to those who seemed to be somewhat, (whatsoever they were, it maketh no matter to me: God accepteth no man's person:) for they who seemed to be somewhat in conference added nothing to me:
> But contrariwise, when they saw that the gospel of the

uncircumcision was committed unto me, as the gospel of the circumcision was unto Peter;

(For he that wrought effectually in Peter to apostleship of the circumcision, the same was mighty in me towards the Gentiles:)

And when James, Cephas and John, who seemed to be pillars, perceived the grace that was given unto me, they gave to me and Barnabas the right hands of fellowship; that we should go unto the heathen, and they unto the circumcision.

(Galatians 2:1–9)

Paul is unequivocal in his assertion here that he did not receive the teachings of Jesus from the Apostles but received them 'by the revelations of Jesus Christ'. After receiving the same, he did not go to Jerusalem to meet the persons who were Apostles before him to confer with them, and it was only 14 years later that he went to check with them the correctness of the gospel which he preached 'lest by any means I should run, or had run, in vain'. Though he has claimed that he went because of a revelation, it is evident that it was because there was a dispute whether the Law of Moses and other precepts of Judaism had to be followed or not, as he adds, 'but neither Titus, who was with me, being a Greek, was compelled to be circumcised'. Circumcision of the Gentiles being converted to Christianity was a pressing issue, as he has already mentioned that he circumcised Timothy. It was, evidently, for the resolution of this issue that he had gone to the Apostles. It is the same incident that has been mentioned in the Acts of the Apostles which has been paraphrased here. He further confirms this when he says 'that they may bring us into bondage'. In all Christian literature, following the Law of Moses has been called a bondage, from which Christ has been stated to have liberated the believers. The Acts of the Apostle, while recording this event, has reported Paul accepting the Law of Moses, at least for kosher meat, and further reported that he circumcised Timothy to satisfy the Jews. However, by the time the Galatians has been written, he had parted ways with the Apostles completely and taken an aggressive posture, as evidenced by his words, '...no, not for an hour, that the truth of the gospel might continue with you'. His reference to 'those who seemed to be somewhat', is a reference to the Apostles, who, he says, added nothing to him. The reference after that is very significant, as he names the Apostles and talks of two gospels, one of the 'uncircumcision' committed to him and the other of the circumcision to Peter. It is, thus, evident that Paul was preaching something totally different from what the Apostles were preaching, which he has termed as 'the gospel of the uncircumcision'. Though he has stated that James, Peter and John accepted this as correct and decided that Paul and Barnabas should preach amongst the heathens, while the Apostles should preach amongst the Jews, this is not true, as the Acts of the Apostles has correctly reported that Paul and Barnabas went back to Antioch with clarifications from the Apostles. Once separated from the Apostles, Paul harped on the theme that he was the Apostle of the Gentiles and had been entrusted to preach amongst them by God and Christ, just as the other Apostles had been entrusted to preach amongst the Jews, though Peter was the person declared by Jesus on whom the Church was to be built. He had been preaching amongst Jews and even non-Jews from a very early stage.

Peace at Antioch between Paul and Barnabas did not last long. Very soon, Paul parted ways with Barnabas and the rest of the Apostles. This final parting, too, has been reported in a different manner at two different places in the Bible. In the Acts of the Apostles it has been reported in the following manner.

> And some days after Paul said unto Barnabas, Let us go again and visit our brethren in every city where we have preached the word of the Lord, and see how they do.
>
> And Barnabas determined to take with them John, whose surname was Mark.
>
> But Paul thought not good to take him with them, who departed from them from Pamphylia, and went not with them to the work.
>
> And the contention was so sharp between them, that they departed asunder one from the other: and so Barnabas took Mark and sailed unto Cyprus;
>
> And Paul chose Silas, and departed, being recommended by the brethren unto the grace of God.
>
> (The Acts 15:36–40)

The reason given here for their separation is insignificant. No doctrinal point has been projected. It has been stated to be a personal issue that Barnabas wished to take John Mark along, while Paul disagreed because he had left them on a previous journey. They, however, parted ways and are not reported to have been ever reconciled. The reporting of this parting in the Galatians is different. The same is given below.

> But when Peter was come to Antioch, I withstood him to the face, because he was to be blamed.
>
> For before that certain came from James, he did eat with the Gentiles: but when they were come, he withdrew and separated himself, fearing them which were of the circumcision.
>
> And the other Jews dissembled likewise with him; in so much that Barnabas also was carried away with their dissimulation.
>
> But when I saw that they walked not uprightly according to the truth of the gospel, I said unto Peter before them all, If thou, being a Jew, livest after the manner of Gentiles,

and not as do the Jews, why compellest thou the Gentiles to live as do the Jews?

We who are Jews by nature, and not sinners of the Gentiles,

Knowing that a man is not justified by the works of the law, but by the faith of Jesus Christ.

(Galatians 2:11–16)

Paul's claim that he 'withstood Peter to the face' may or may not be true. How Peter reacted to it has not been stated, though an impression has been given that he admitted his guilt, which does not appear to be true because it is clear that the issue was of Peter requiring the Gentiles to live as the Jews did—something he continued to do till the end. Barnabas has been reported to have sided with Peter. This appears to have been the occasion for the separation of Paul and Barnabas. It appears that after the two had returned from Jerusalem, with the Apostles clarifying that the Law of Moses and the practices of Judaism had to be followed by the new converts to Christianity, Paul complied with it for some time (as we know, Timothy was circumcised by him), but very soon he resisted and developed differences with Barnabas, for which Peter came to Antioch personally to settle the issue. It seems Paul refused to agree on this occasion, because of which he was separated from the Apostolic Church by Peter. Barnabas, who was a fellow preacher with him for a long time, thus, was separated, never to be reconciled.

Though there were major doctrinal differences between Paul and the Apostles, as would emerge later, what has been stated here is the difference of opinion which Paul has repeatedly mentioned. His view was that faith in Jesus Christ is sufficient for the salvation of man, while the Apostles thought that many other things had to be done for the same, in which following the Law of Moses and all Jewish practices were fundamental. The views of the Apostles on Paul not observing the Law of

Moses emerge from the following passage also.

> And the day following Paul went in with us unto James; and all the elders were present.
> And when he had saluted them, he declared particularly what things God had wrought among the Gentiles by his ministry.
> And when they heard it, they glorified the Lord, and said unto him, Thou seest, brother, how many thousands of Jews there are which believe; and they are all zealous of the law:
> And they are informed of thee, that thou teachest all the Jews which are among the Gentiles to forsake Moses, saying that they ought not to circumcise their children, neither to walk after the customs.
>
> (The Acts 21:18–21)

In this passage, though it is the Apostles who are questioning Paul, they have imputed the objections to his opposing the Law, to the Jews who had become Christian. Their concurrence to this view is, however, evident.

A direct opposition to Paul's view that faith is sufficient and following the Law is not required comes from James in the following passages.

> If ye fulfil the royal law according to the scripture, Thou shalt love thy neighbour as thyself, ye do well.
>
> (Epistle of James 2:8)

> For whosoever shall keep the whole law, and yet offend in one point, he is guilty of all.
>
> (Epistle of James 2:10)

> What doth it profit, my brethren, though a man say he hath faith, and have not works? Can faith save him?
>
> (Epistle of James 2:14)

> Even so faith, if it hath not works is dead, being alone.
>
> Yea, a man may say, Thou hast faith, and I have works: shew me thy faith without thy works, and I will shew thee my faith by my works.
>
> Thou believest that there is one God; thou doest well: the devils also believe, and tremble.
>
> But wilt thou know, O vain man, that faith without works is dead?
>
> Was not Abraham our father justified by works, when he offered Isaac his son upon the alter?
>
> Seest thou how faith wrought with his works, and by works was faith made perfect?
>
> (Epistle of James 2:17–22)

> Ye see then how that by works a man is justified, and not by faith only.
>
> (Epistle of James 2:24)

> For as the body without the spirit is dead, so faith without works is dead also.
>
> (Epistle of James 2:26)

James is emphatic that the entire Law of Moses has to be followed. Even if offence is made on one point, it would amount to being guilty against the entire Law. He has also expressed the inadequacy of faith alone, in the absence of good deeds, which, for him, were intricately linked to obeying the Law. This epistle, which is addressed by James to the 'twelve tribes which are scattered abroad', has been written in direct opposition to what Paul was preaching. It has been written as a rebuttal of Paul's view that faith was enough and that there was no need of the Law.

The other doctrinal differences have not been brought out by Paul in his writings, but his conflict with the Apostles is visible at several places in his epistles. The first epistle is to the Romans, in which he builds up his case on how faith alone is sufficient for salvation and the Law is no longer required. He has also responded to the types of objections that have been raised by James, that faith without works is useless, by stressing that good conduct would remain a prerequisite for a faithful. It is, however, not clear to whom the epistle was sent, as there could not have been a Church at Rome at that time because the Emperor Claudius had expelled all Jews from Rome (The Acts 18:2), and Paul, who preached amongst the Gentiles, had not gone there yet (Romans 1:10–15). Despite the Jews' absence and the fact that Paul was yet to preach in Rome, the opening sentences and the greetings give an impression that there were a large number of Christians there. He has mentioned both Jews and Gentiles and has stressed on faith with righteousness. To the Jews, he has pointed out that their custom of circumcision is relevant, only if the Law was properly obeyed. This, too, was only for the past, as now God had shown a way to be made right with Him without keeping the requirements of the Law—by having faith in Jesus Christ. He holds that only when this faith is there, is the Law truly fulfilled. Paul's attitude towards Jewish practices and the Apostles can be seen to have gradually hardened in the Bible. This may have been with the gradual strengthening of his position as a preacher in the area of his influence. In the Romans, he is tolerant towards Jewish practices and advises his followers not to dispute over such issues as can be seen below.

> He that regardeth the day, regardeth it unto the Lord; and he that regardeth not the day, to the Lord he doth not regard it. He that eateth, eateth to the Lord, for he giveth God thanks; and he that eateth not, to the Lord he eateth not, and giveth God thanks.
>
> (Romans 14:6)

> But why dost thou judge thy brother? Or why dost thou set at nought thy brother? For we shall all stand before the judgement seat of Christ.
>
> (Romans 14:10)

> I know, and am persuaded by the Lord Jesus, that there is nothing unclean of itself; but to him that esteemeth anything to be unclean, to him it is unclean.
>
> But if thy brother be grieved with thy meat, now walkest thou not charitably. Destroy not him with thy meat, for whom Christ died.
>
> (Romans 14:14–15)

In the Epistle to the Romans there are also signs of Paul having lost ground in the area where he had been preaching till then, because of which he wished to move West to Spain and Italy. This is reflected in the following passages.

> But now having no more place in these parts, and having a great desire these many years to come unto you.
>
> (Romans 15:23)

> That I may be delivered from them that do not believe in Judea; and that my service which I have for Jerusalem may be accepted of the saints.
>
> (Romans 15:31)

> Now I beseech you, brethren, mark them which cause divisions and offences contrary to the doctrine which ye have learned; and avoid them.
>
> (Romans 16:17)

> Now to him that is of power to stablish you according to my gospel, and the preaching of Jesus Christ, according to the revelation of the mystery, which was kept secret since the world began.
>
> (Romans 16:25)

After the Epistle to the Romans, the First Epistle to the Corinthians also shows signs of differences between Paul and the Apostles, which can be seen from the passages below.

> Now I beseech you, brethren, by the name of our Lord Jesus Christ, that ye all speak the same thing, and that there be no divisions among you; but that ye be perfectly joined together in the same mind and in the same judgement.
>
> For it hath been declared unto me of you, my brethren, by them which are of the house of Chloe, that there are contentions among you.
>
> Now this I say, that every one of you saith, I am of Paul; and I of Apollos, and I of Cephas; and I of Christ.
>
> Is Christ divided? Was Paul crucified for you? Or were ye baptized in the name of Paul?
>
> (1 Corinthians 1:10–13)

> For while one saith, I am of Paul; and another, I am of Apollos; are ye not carnal?
>
> Who then is Paul, and who is Apollos, but ministers by whom ye believed, even as the Lord gave to every man?
>
> I have planted, Apollos watered; but God gave the increase.
>
> (1 Corinthians 3:4–6)

> For we are labourers together with God: ye are God's husbandry, ye are God's building.
>
> According to the grace of God which is given unto me, as a wise master- builder, I have laid the foundation, and another buildeth thereon. But let every man take heed how he buildeth thereupon.
>
> (1 Corinthians 3:9–10)

Paul is conciliatory in his approach here. Cephas is another name of Peter. The believers apparently claimed themselves to be followers of Peter and Apollos, to whom he is trying to preach unity in the name of Christ. Paul claims that he had been the person who had introduced Christianity in Corinth, perhaps when he was with the Apostles, as he has said that he laid the foundation, but now it was Apollos who was their guide and Paul, while saying we are 'labourers together', cautions them to 'take heed how he buildeth thereupon'. He seems to have been rejected by the believers, who appear to have gone over to the Apostles, to whom Paul is making an appeal to return to him, as reflected in the following passages.

> But with me it is a small thing that I should be judged of you, or of man's judgement: yea, I judge not mine own self.
> (1 Corinthians 4:3)

> For who maketh thee to differ from another? And what hast thou that thou didst not receive? Now if thou didst receive it, why dost thou glory, as if thou hadst not received it?
> (1 Corinthians 4:7)

> For though ye have ten thousand instructors in Christ, yet have ye not many fathers: for in Christ Jesus I have begotten you through the gospel.
> Wherefore I beseech you, be ye followers of me.
> (1 Corinthians 4:15–16)

It appears that Paul was not acknowledged as an apostle, perhaps by the other Apostles and their followers, for which he reinforces his claim in the following passages.

> Am I not an apostle? am I not free? have I not seen Jesus Christ our Lord? are not ye my work in the Lord?
> If I be not an apostle unto others, yet doubtless I am to you: for the seal of mine apostleship are ye in the Lord.
> (1 Corinthians 9:1–2)

He has proceeded to show that the Apostles accepted money for preaching while he did it for free, though Christ had allowed the preachers to live off their ministry. He has blamed such preachers of seeking worldly rewards in the following passage.

> And every man that striveth for the mastery is temperate in all things. Now they do it to obtain a corruptible crown; but we an incorruptible.
>
> (1 Corinthians 9:25)

The following passages are of interest for understanding the points on which Paul differed from the Apostles other than the question of Judaizing.

> Moreover, brethren, I declare unto you that gospel which I preached unto you, which also ye have received, and wherein ye stand;
>
> (1 Corinthians 15:1)

> For I delivered unto you first of all that which I also received, how that Christ died for our sins according to the scriptures;
>
> And that he was buried and that he rose again the third day according to the scriptures.
>
> (1 Corinthians 15:3–4)

> Therefore whether it were I or they, so we preach, and so ye believed.
>
> Now if Christ be preached that he rose from the dead, how say some among you that there is no resurrection of the dead?
>
> But if there be no resurrection of the dead, then is Christ not risen:
>
> And if Christ be not risen, then is our preaching vain, and your faith is also vain.
>
> Yea, and we are found false witnesses of God; because we have testified of God that he raised up Christ: whom he raised not up, if so be that the dead rise not.

> For if the dead rise not, then is not Christ raised:
> And if Christ be not raised, your faith is in vain; ye are yet in your sins.
>
> (1 Corinthians 15:11–17)

Paul begins by saying that this was the gospel that he had preached, which, in turn, he had received. It has been claimed at several places by Paul that he received the message directly from Jesus Christ and that the Apostles did not impart anything to him. It is evident that the gospel, which he has mentioned, is not the gospel of the Apostles but the one Paul claimed he received from Jesus Christ. He proceeds to say that, as per this, Christ was buried and he rose again the third day. Accordingly, the claim of the resurrection of Christ is based on the gospel of Paul and not on what the Apostles preached. In the next few lines after these passages, he has listed out the people who saw Jesus after he rose from the dead. The last among them was Paul himself, though his claim to have seen Jesus has to be on a different footing from the rest because the time when he claims he saw him is much after Jesus had ascended to heaven. He has proceeded to say that he as well as the Apostles preached the same thing. The statement does not appear to be true, as he has stated that some Christians did not believe in the resurrection of the dead. He has linked the belief in the theory of resurrection to Christ's rising from the dead. This counter belief that Christ did not rise from the dead could have come among these Christians only from the Apostles. He has stressed on this issue and has stated that the belief in Christ rising from the dead was fundament to their faiths. As will emerge ahead, the Apostles do not appear to be subscribing to this view.

Paul's rivalry with the Apostles emerges further in his Second Epistle to the Corinthians. In the following passages, he has sought a confirmation from the believers whether they were loyal to him and also asserts his sincerity.

> Wherefore I beseech you that ye would confirm your love toward him.
>
> For to this end also did I write, that I might know the proof of you, whether ye be obedient in all things.
>
> (2 Corinthians 2:8–9)

> For we are not as many, which corrupt the word of God: but as of sincerity, but as of God, in the sight of God speak we in Christ.
>
> (2 Corinthians 2:17)

Along with stressing his sincerity, Paul has referred to 'many, which corrupt the word of God'. Though he has not clarified who these persons were, it appears to be a reference to the Apostles, as these 'many' have to be of a stature that their word carried enough weight to counter what Paul was preaching.

A further hint comes from Paul in the following passage that he had departed from what the Apostles were preaching.

> Who also hath made us able ministers of the new testament; not of the letter, but of the spirit: for the letter killeth, but the spirit giveth life.
>
> (2 Corinthians 3:6)

It is an admission that, at least in letter, what he was preaching was not the same as what the Apostles were preaching. His claim was that the spirit of what he preached was correct. The believers in Corinth appear to have wavered. At times they seem to have followed Paul, while at others their loyalty had switched over to the Apostles. Paul repeatedly stresses his sincerity and urges them to trust him, as can be seen in the following passages.

> But have renounced the hidden things of dishonesty, not walking in craftiness, nor handling the word of God deceitfully; but by manifestation of the truth commending

> ourselves to every man's conscience in the sight of God.
> But if our gospel be hid, it is hid to them that are lost:
> In whom the god of this world hath blinded the minds of them which believe not, lest the light of the glorious gospel of Christ, who is the image of God, should shine in them.
> But we preach not ourselves, but Christ Jesus the Lord; and ourselves your servants for Jesus' sake.
> (2 Corinthians 4:2–5)

> Receive us; we have wronged no man, we have corrupted no man, we have defrauded no man.
> (2 Corinthians 7:2)

After all the efforts the believers seem to have moved towards Paul, as is reflected in the following passage.

> And not by his coming only, but by the consolation wherewith he was comforted in you, when he told us your earnest desire, your mourning, your fervent mind toward me; so that I rejoiced the more.
> (2 Corinthians 7:7)

The rivalry with the Apostles comes out further in the following passages.

> For I am jealous over you with godly jealously: for I have espoused you to one husband, that I may present you as a chaste virgin to Christ.
> But I fear, lest by any means, as the serpent beguiled Eve through his subtilty, so your minds should be corrupted from the simplicity that is in Christ.
> For if he that cometh preacheth another Jesus, whom we have not preached, or if ye receive another spirit, which ye have not received, or another gospel, which ye have not accepted, ye might well bear with him.

> For I suppose I was not a whit behind the very chiefest apostles.
>
> (2 Corinthians 11:2–5)
>
> As the truth of Christ is in me, no man shall stop me of this boasting in the regions of Achaia.
>
> (2 Corinthians 11:10)
>
> For such are false apostles, deceitful workers, transforming themselves into the apostles of Christ.
>
> (2 Corinthians 11:13)
>
> Are they Hebrews? so am I. Are they Israelites? so am I. Are they the seed of Abraham? so am I.
> Are they ministers of Christ? (I speak as a fool) I am more; in labours more abundant, in stripes above measure, in prison more frequent in deaths oft.
>
> (2 Corinthians 11:22–23)
>
> I am become a fool in glorying; ye have compelled me: for I ought to have been commended of you: for in nothing am I behind the very chiefest apostles, though I be nothing.
> Truly the signs of an apostle were wrought among you in all patience, in signs, and wonders, and mighty deeds.
> For what is it wherein ye were inferior to other churches, except it be that I myself was not burdensome to you? forgive me this wrong.
>
> (2 Corinthians 12:11–13)

Here Paul has mentioned other preachers who preached Jesus in a different way and a different gospel. These other preachers were the Apostles, and to establish his authenticity against them he has claimed that he was not inferior to them being 'not a whit behind the very chiefest apostles'. He has proceeded to call them false apostles and deceitful workers. To strengthen his claim, he says that if they were Jews, so was he, and if they were ministers of Christ, he was more, as he had laboured more and suffered more. He further claims that he had shown them miracles to prove that he was an apostle. Finally, he asks the Corinthians in which way they thought they were inferior to the other Churches, evidently the Churches of the Apostles, and adds that except that no financial burden was caused to them because of him. A schism is evident.

The Epistle to the Galatians unfolds the same story, except that here the believers returning to him is not indicated. The tussle emerges from the following passage.

> I marvel that ye are so soon removed from him that called you into the grace of Christ unto another gospel:
>
> Which is not another; but there be some that trouble you, and would pervert the gospel of Christ.
>
> But though we, or an angel from heaven, preach any other gospel unto you than that which we have preached unto you, let him be accursed.
>
> As we said before, so say I now again, If any man preach any other gospel unto you than that ye have received, let him be accursed.
>
> (Galatians 1:6–9)

The opening lines reveal that the believers here were converted to Christianity by Paul, but they have left him and have become followers of some other preachers of Christ who had a different gospel. This, he claims, is not 'another gospel' but a perversion of the truth which would cause trouble to the believers. The level of tolerance, as was visible in the Epistle to the Romans, has faded away now, as he repeatedly curses anyone preaching a gospel different from what he had preached. These other preachers of a different gospel have to be the Apostles. This emerges from the fact that Paul proceeds to insist that he had received his gospel directly by revelations from Christ and not from the Apostles. This would have become necessary for him to claim, as the believers would have felt that the Apostles had accompanied Jesus in his life and would have known his teachings first-hand, while Paul would have come to know of them from the Apostles. As the two were preaching different things, they would have trusted the Apostles and rejected Paul. His assertion that he had not received his gospel from the Apostles but directly from Christ has been mentioned earlier (Galatians 1:11–12). He has proceeded to recall his interactions with the Apostles and to show that he received nothing from them. In trying to do so, he has introduced a contradiction with what has been stated in the Acts of the Apostles, which describe his first interaction with them. In the Acts, after Paul had been converted to Christianity because Jesus had appeared to him at Damascus, he is reported to have come in contact with the Apostles, as recorded in the following passage.

> But Saul increased the more in strength, and confounded the Jews which dwelt at Damascus, proving that this is very Christ.
> And after that many days were fulfilled, the Jews took counsel to kill him:
> But their laying await was known of Saul. And they watched the gates day and night to kill him.
> Then the disciples took him by night, and let him down by the wall in a basket.
> And when Saul was come to Jerusalem, he assayed to join himself to the disciples: but they were all afraid of him, and believed not that he was a disciple.
> But Barnabas took him, and brought him to the apostles, and declared unto them how he had seen the Lord in the way, and that he had spoken to him, and how he had preached boldly at Damascus in the name of Jesus.
> And he was with them coming in and going out at Jerusalem.
> (The Acts 9:22–28)

The Acts of the Apostles has recorded the natural reaction of a person who had been converted. From Damascus, he went to Jerusalem to confer and to be with the Apostles, who were the chief disciples of Jesus. In the Galatians, Paul had the necessity of asserting his authority independent of the Apostles. Therefore, after stating that he received the gospel directly from Christ, this is what he has said:

> But when it pleased God, who separated me from my mother's womb, and called me by his grace,
> To reveal his Son in me, that I might preach him among the heathen; immediately I conferred not with flesh and blood:
> Neither went I up to Jerusalem to them which were apostles before me; but I went into Arabia, and returned again unto Damascus.
> Then after three years I went up to Jerusalem to see Peter, and abode with him fifteen days.
> But other of the apostles saw I none, save James the Lord's brother.
> (Galatians 1:15–19)

Paul's contempt for the Apostles is apparent in these passages. He has asserted that after the Son of God was revealed to him, he conferred with no human being and did not go to Jerusalem to the Apostles. It was only after three years that he went there and was with Peter for 15 days and saw none of the others except James. This is in clear contradiction to what his disciple Luke has recorded in the Acts of the Apostles and is not a natural reaction of a person just converted, who would wish to confer with the leaders of his new faith immediately. The necessity of proving that his gospel and his teachings, though different, had an authority directly from Christ and so were not dependent on the approval of the Apostles, compelled him to take this stand. He has proceeded to mention his further interactions with the Apostles when he went to Jerusalem 14 years later, after which Peter had came to Antioch when Paul had split from them. He has mentioned that they were for following the Law of Moses and all Jewish practices but accepted his gospel to be preached amongst the Gentiles (Galatians 2:1–14).

His claim that the Apostles accepted his gospel is proved to be false by the fact that the Apostles preached the observance of Law because this is what the Galatians continued to believe, as emerges from the following passages.

> O foolish Galatians, who hath bewitched you, that ye should not obey the truth, before whose eyes Jesus Christ hath been evidently set forth, crucified among you?
>
> This only would I learn of you, Received ye the Spirit by the works of the law, or by the hearing of faith?
>
> (Galatians 3:1–2)

> But now, after that ye have known God, or rather are known of God, how turn ye again to the weak and beggarly elements, whereunto ye desire again to be in bondage?
>
> Ye observe days, and months, and times, and years.
>
> (Galatians 4:9–10)

> Tell me, ye that desire to be under the law, do ye not hear the law?
>
> (Galatians 4:21)

> Stand fast therefore in the liberty wherewith Christ hath made us free, and be not entangled again with the yoke of bondage.
>
> Behold, I Paul say unto you, that if ye be circumcised, Christ shall profit you nothing.
>
> For I testify again to every man that is circumcised, that he is debtor to do the whole law.
>
> (Galatians 5:1–3)

It is evident from this that the Christians in Galatia had moved away from Paul's teachings and were obeying the Law of Moses, as per the teachings of their new preachers, the Apostles. Some commentators have tried to explain these passages by stating that these people were Jews to begin with, and after being converted to Christianity, had reverted back to Jewish practices for which Paul was making this exhortation. This is not the correct position, as noted in the following passage.

> For neither they themselves who are circumcised keep the law; but desire to have you circumcised, that they may glory in your flesh.
>
> (Galatians 6:13)

It is evident that these Christians were not Jews as the new preachers were now requiring them to be circumcised. Having been with Paul for some time, these believers seem to have moved over to the Apostles and did not return, as is suggested in the following passage.

> Ye did run well; who did hinder you that ye should not obey the truth.
>
> (Galatians 5:7)

In this epistle, Paul has imputed cowardice on the Apostles and has claimed that they require the believers to follow Jewish practices only to save themselves from persecution. The following passage notes:

> As many as desire to make a fair shew in the flesh, they constrain you to be circumcised; only lest they should suffer persecution for the cross of Christ.
>
> (Galatians 6:12)

In the Epistle to the Philippians, evidence of a split between Paul and the Apostles comes from this passage,

> Now ye Philippians know also, that in the beginning of the gospel, when I departed from Macedonia, no Church communicated with me as concerning giving and receiving, but ye only.
>
> (Philippians 4:15)

Evidently, there must have been a schism in the Church, in which only the Church of the Philippians sided with Paul. All other Churches ceased to communicate with him. For almost all Churches to reject Paul, he would have had to be excommunicated by a very high religious authority. This could not have been any other than the Apostles. The Philippians had remained loyal to him, yet we find Paul cautioning them against his rivals in the following passages.

> Beware of dogs, beware of evil workers, beware of concision.
> For we are the circumcision, which worship God in the spirit, and rejoice in Christ Jesus, and have no confidence in the flesh.
>
> (Philippians 3:2–3)

> (For many walk, of whom I have told you often, and now tell you even weeping, that they are the enemies of the cross of Christ:
> Whose end is destruction, whose God is their belly, whose glory is in their shame, who mind earthly things.)
>
> (Philippians 3:18–19)

Paul is intemperate in his language. The statement that 'we' are of circumcision of the spirit and not of the flesh refers to the Apostles and is against circumcision. Though in this epistle Paul has repeatedly suggested that the believers in Philippi always remained loyal to him, even when all other Churches had ceased to communicate with him, a different picture emerges from the following passage of a different epistle.

> But even after that we had suffered before, and were shamefully entreated, as ye know, at Philippi, we were bold in our God to speak unto you the gospel of God with much contention.
>
> (1 Thessalonians 2:2)

Apparently, the claim that the Church at Philippi had sided with Paul is doubtful. It seems likely that all Churches ceased to communicate with Paul, once the Apostles removed him from their company. At that stage, Christianity had been preached only in the East and we have Paul stating in the following passage that the whole of Asia had left him.

> This thou knowest, that all they which are in Asia be turned away from me; of whom are Phygellus and Hermogenes.
>
> (2 Timothy 1:15)

The tussle between Paul and the Apostles, and the subsequent pressure on the believers from either side, can be seen in the following passages from the Epistle to the Colossians.

> And you, that were sometime alienated and enemies in your mind by wicked works, yet now hath he reconciled.
>
> (Colossians 1:21)

> If ye continue in the faith grounded and settled, and be not moved away from the hope of the gospel, which ye have heard, and which was preached to every creature which is under heaven, whereof I Paul am made a minister.
>
> (Colossians 1:23)

> And this I say, lest any man should beguile you with enticing words.
>
> (Colossians 2:4)

> Beware lest any man spoil you through philosophy and vain deceit, after the tradition of men, after the rudiments

of the world, and not after Christ.

> (Colossians 2:8)

> In whom also ye are circumcised with the circumcision made without hands, in putting off the body of the sins of the flesh by the circumcision of Christ.
>
> (Colossians 2:11)

> Let no man therefore judge you in meat, or in drink, or in respect of an holy day, or of the new moon, or of the sabbath days.
>
> (Colossians 2:16)

> Wherefore if ye be dead with Christ from the rudiments of the world, why, as though living in the world, are ye subject to ordinances.
>
> (Colossians 2:20)

The believers here appear to have left Paul in the past but were later reconciled. He cautions them to be wary of other preachers who would want them to follow the Law of Moses.

The First Epistle to the Thessalonians also outlines the tussle between the two sides to win over the believers. This is reflected in the following passage.

> For this cause, when I could no longer forbear, I sent to know your faith, lest by some means the tempter have tempted you, and our labour be in vain.
>
> But now when Timotheus came from you unto us, and brought us good tidings of your faith and charity, and that ye have good remembrance of us always, desiring greatly to see us, as we also to see you.
>
> (1 Thessalonians 3:5–6)

Paul appears to have earlier preached amongst the believers here, but was staying away as he was unsure of their allegiance to him. Timothy had gone to enquire of it and had reported of their faith in Paul, which was a cause of a great relief to him. What the other preachers were preaching has been detailed in the following passage of the second epistle.

> That ye be not soon shaken in mind, or be troubled, neither by spirit, nor by word, nor by letter as from us, as that the day of Christ is at hand.
>
> Let no man deceive you by any means: for that day shall not come, except there come a falling away first, and that man of sin be revealed, the son of perdition.
>
> (2 Thessalonians 2:2–3)

Paul has hinted that forged letters could be presented in his name. He preached that the Day of Judgement was very near, as near as to be within his lifetime. He cautions against someone who would preach otherwise. This suggests that the Apostles did not believe in the Day of Judgement. Paul's differences with these other preachers emerges also from the following passage of his Epistle to Timothy.

> As I besought thee to abide still at Ephesus, when I went into Macedonia, that thou mightiest charge some that they teach no other doctrine.
>
> Neither give heed to fables and endless genealogies, which minister questions, rather than godly edifying which is in faith: so do.
>
> Now the end of the commandment is charity out of a pure heart, and of a good conscience and of faith unfeigned:
>
> From which some have swerved having turned aside into vain jangling;
>
> Desiring to be teachers of the law; understanding neither what they say, nor whereof they affirm.
>
> (1 Timothy 1:3–7)

Paul, here, is not referring to Jews that were not Christian. He is referring Christian preachers as he asks Timothy to 'charge some that they teach no other doctrine.' These other teachers, he says, are desiring to be teachers of the law, an evident reference to the Apostles. His own view on the subject he expresses in the following passage.

> But we know that the law is good, if a man use it lawfully;
> Knowing this, that the law is not made for a righteous man, but for the lawless and disobedient, for the ungodly and for sinners, for unholy and profane, for murderers of fathers and murderers of mothers, for manslayers.
> For whoremongers, for them that defile themselves with mankind, for menstealers, for liars, for perjured persons, and if there be any other thing that is contrary to sound doctrine;
> According to the glorious gospel of the blessed God, which was committed to my trust.
> (1 Timothy 1:8–11)

The stress is that the Law was meant for evil people and not for followers of Christ who are prevented from evil by the very faith that they have in Christ. He further stresses that this was according to the gospel that was committed by God to him. The stress on the gospel committed to him is very significant, as it shows that this was not a part of the gospel that was being preached by the Apostles, whose views on the subject he had already mentioned.

Paul's epistle to Titus is confusing. In it, he has stated that he had left Titus at Crete to settle the affairs of the Church there and advices him on the conduct of a bishop. However, an earlier reference states that many followers had left Paul and that Titus was one of them.

> For Demas hath forsaken me, having loved this present world, and is departed unto Thessalonica; Crescens to Galatia, Titus unto Dalmatia.

Only Luke is with me. Take Mark and bring him with thee: for he is profitable to me for the ministry.

(2 Timothy 4:10–11)

At my first answer no man stood with me, but all men forsook me: I pray God that it may not be laid to their charge.

(2 Timothy 4:16)

Paul has painted a very bleak picture wherein he had been forsaken by all his followers except Luke, who had remained with him. It seems doubtful that Titus would leave Paul after having been appointed the Bishop of Crete. An answer to this question may never be found, but the conflict with the Apostles over the question of the Law is brought up in this epistle again in the following passages.

For there are many unruly and vain talkers and deceivers, specially they of the circumcision.

Whose mouths must be stopped, who subvert whole houses, teaching things which they ought not, for filthy lucre's sake.

(Titus 1:10–11)

Not giving heed to Jewish fables, and commandments of men, that turn from the truth.

Unto the pure all things are pure: but unto them that are defiled and unbelieving is nothing pure; but even their mind and conscience is defiled.

(Titus 1:14–15)

But avoid foolish questions, and genealogies, and contentions, and strivings about the law; for they are unprofitable and vain.

(Titus 3:9)

This reference here is to 'they of the circumcision'. This again is not to Jews who were not Christian because their 'mouths must be stopped'. It is a reference to the Apostles, who have been blamed for teaching things 'for filthy lucre's sake'.

The Epistle to the Hebrews is crucial for understanding this conflict between Paul and the Apostles. Commentators have long been confused with this epistle as Paul was the declared apostle of the Gentiles, while Peter was said to be for the Jews. Given this, it is unclear what necessitated Paul to write to the Jews and who these Jews were that have been addressed. A close examination of this epistle shows that it has been addressed to the Apostles themselves and was a call to them to adhere to Paul and his teachings. Several passages in it provide an insight on the points of dispute. First, the following passages.

> Wherefore, holy brethren, partakers of the heavenly calling, consider the Apostle and High Priest of our profession, Christ Jesus.
> (Hebrews 3:1)

> For we are made partakers of Christ, if we hold the beginning of our confidence steadfast unto the end.
> (Hebrews 3:14)

> Seeing then that we have a great high priest, that is passed into the heavens, Jesus the son of God, let us hold fast our profession.
> (Hebrews 4:14)

These passages show that those being addressed, who had been understood to be Jews, were, in fact, Christians. He has addressed them as 'holy brethren, partakers of the heavenly calling', which he could not have called the non-Christian Jews. He has further referred to Christ as 'the Apostle and High Priest' of the profession of both sides, which shows that the profession of the persons being addressed, like him, was the preaching of Christ. The third passage, too, refers to Jesus as the high priest of 'our profession', confirming the addressees to be the preachers of Christ. In the second passage, he includes them to be partakers of Christ, if the confidence with which they had begun was held steadfast unto the end. He is, thus, admitting that they had begun with the right faith, but that it had to be maintained till the end, giving an indication that he believed that they were not on the right path. Evidence for him questioning the correctness of their faith and the need for their being further instructed emerges from the following passage.

> For when for the time ye ought to be teachers, ye have need that one teach you again which be the first principles of the oracles of God; and are become such as have need of milk, and not of strong meat.
> (Hebrews 5:12)

Paul tells the Apostles that they need to be taught the basic principles of God again, for they have become like children, unable to see right and wrong.

The following passage is particularly significant because it not only shows that the Apostles were being addressed but also gives an indication of their doctrinal differences.

> Therefore leaving the principles of the doctrine of Christ, let us go on unto perfection; not laying again the foundation of repentance from dead works, and of faith towards God,
> Of the doctrine of baptisms, and of laying on of hands, and of resurrection of the dead, and of eternal judgement.
> And this will we do, if God permit.
> (Hebrews 6:1–3)

Paul has suggested to those addressed that the discussion on their differences regarding the 'principles of the doctrine of Christ' may be left out for the time being, which may be taken up in the future. For the present only the religious practices may be corrected, as he has stated ahead. The doctrinal differences, he has mentioned, are repentance for past deeds, faith in God, the doctrine of baptisms, laying of hands, the resurrection of the dead and eternal judgement. These points are fundamental in the belief system of Christians of all Churches today. Sins that have been committed can be pardoned if a person repents for them in the manner prescribed by the Church. Faith in Jesus Christ is sufficient for salvation, nothing more is required. Baptism automatically removes all sins of a person, because of which people like the Emperor Constantine waited till they were very close to death to be baptized. By the laying of the hand by the priest at the time of baptism, the Holy Spirit descends onto the person. At the end of the world, all the dead shall rise again with their bodies to receive judgement. The rewards and punishments, as per this judgement would be eternal. The evil would receive the punishment of suffering in hell eternally, while the good would enjoy the pleasures of heaven also eternally. These doctrinal differences could not have been with the non-Christian Jews, as they were internal issues within Christianity. In fact, one of the sects of Judaism, the Pharisees, believed in resurrection of the dead and eternal punishment. The differences could not have been with ordinary Christian believers either, as Paul could have used his authority as an apostle, that he claimed himself to be, or could have left them alone, deeming himself to be an apostle of the Gentiles only. These doctrinal differences could have been only with the Apostles, with whom he could not assert his authority as an apostle but could only argue his point. What follows confirms them to be Apostles, as is given in the passage below.

> For it is impossible for those who were once enlightened, and have tasted of the heavenly gift, and were made partakers of the Holy Ghost,

> And have tasted the good word of God, and the powers of the world to come,
> If they shall fall away, to renew them again unto repentance; seeing they crucify to themselves the Son of God afresh, and put him to open shame.
> (Hebrews 6:4–6)

This shows that the addressees were once enlightened, had tasted the heavenly gift and were partakers of the Holy Ghost, but now, in Paul's opinion, had fallen. They had also heard the word of God, an obvious reference to their having been the companions of Jesus in his lifetime. Their past good works are mentioned in the following passages.

> But, beloved, we are persuaded better things of you, and things that accompany salvation, though we thus speak.
> For God is not unrighteous to forget your work and labour of love, which ye have shewed toward his name, in that ye have ministered to the saints, and do minister.
> And we desire that every one of you do shew the same diligence to the full assurance of hope unto the end:
> That ye be not slothful, but followers of them who through faith and patience inherit the promises.
> (Hebrews 6:9–12)

Paul has acknowledged that they have shown their love towards God and 'have ministered to the saints, and do minister'. He calls upon them to be his followers and to have the same diligence that they had in the past.

Having called upon these 'Hebrews' to follow him, Paul dwells on the religious practices and beliefs that he wants them to change, while leaving the doctrinal difference out of the discussion for the moment, as evident in the following passages.

> If therefore perfection were by the Levitical priesthood, (for under it the people received the law,) what further need

was there that another priest should rise after the order of Melchisedec, and not be called after the order of Aaron?

For the priesthood being changed, there is made of necessity a change also of the law.

(Hebrews 7:11–12)

For it is evident that our Lord sprang out of Juda; of which tribe Moses spoke nothing concerning priesthood.

And it is yet far more evident: for that after the similitude of Melchisedec there ariseth another priest,

Who is made, not after the law of a carnal commandment, but after the power of an endless life.

For he testifieth, Thou art a priest for ever after the order of Melchisedec.

For there is verily a disannulling of the commandment going before for the weakness and unprofitableness thereof.

For the law made nothing perfect, but the bringing in of a better hope did; by the which we draw nigh unto God.

(Hebrews 7:14–19)

Paul asks the Apostles to give up their adherence to the Law of Moses, arguing that with Christ a new priesthood had emerged and with which the old Law stood annulled. The Law was inadequate to bring perfection, because of which something new and better had to be followed. He concludes his argument on the Law having become obsolete in the following manner.

In that he saith, A new covenant, he hath made the first old. Now that which decayeth and waxeth old is ready to vanish away.

(Hebrews 8:13)

Having spoken of the Law becoming obsolete, Paul proceeds to ask the Apostles to desist from the ritualistic practices, as laid down by the Law. This emerges from the following passages.

Then verify the first covenant had also ordinances of divine service, and a worldly sanctuary.

(Hebrews 9:1)

Which was a figure for the time then present, in which were offered both gifts and sacrifices, that could not make him that did the service perfect, as pertaining to the conscience;

Which stood only in meats and drinks, and divers washings, and carnal ordinances, imposed on them until the time of reformation.

But Christ being come an high priest of good things to come, by a greater and more perfect tabernacle, not made with hands, that is to say, not of this building;

Neither by the blood of goats and calves, but by his own blood he entered in once into the holy place, having obtained eternal redemption for us.

For if the blood of bulls and of goats, and the ashes of an heifer sprinkling the unclean, sanctifieth to the purifying of the flesh:

How much more shall the blood of Christ, who through the eternal Spirit offered himself without spot to God, purge your conscience from dead works to serve the living God?

(Hebrews 9:9–14)

But in those sacrifices there is a remembrance again made of sins every year.

For it is not possible that the blood of bulls and of goats should take away sins.

(Hebrews 10:3–4)

And every priest standeth daily ministering and offering oftentimes the same sacrifices, which can never take away sins:

But this man, after he had offered one sacrifice for sins for ever, sat down on the right hand of God.

(Hebrews 10:11–12)

> For by one offering he hath perfected for ever them that are sanctified.
>
> (Hebrews 10:14)

> Now where remission of these is, there is no more offering for sin.
>
> Having therefore, brethren, boldness to enter into the holiest by the blood of Jesus,
>
> By a new and living way, which he hath consecrated for us, through the veil, that is to say, his flesh;
>
> And having an high priest over the house of God;
>
> Let us draw near with a true heart in full assurance of faith, having our hearts sprinkled from an evil conscience, and our bodies washed with pure water.
>
> (Hebrews 10:18–22)

Paul has stated that the old covenant that Moses laid down had certain ordinances for the service of God. These involved the sacrifice of animals to be conducted on a regular basis, till Christ reformed them. As the blood of animals was not able to remove the sins of the believers, he offered a sacrifice of his own self, by which he has sanctified them forever. Once we have received remission for our sins and have been perfected by him by this one sacrifice, there is no further need for any more sacrifices. While addressing the Apostles, he says that as we have had the 'boldness to enter, into the holiest by the blood of Jesus', let us have a true faith. He affirms the requirement of faith and it being sufficient for salvation.

Towards the end of the epistle, while exhorting the Apostles for several things, Paul makes a significant statement:

> But I beseech you the rather to do this, that I may be restored to you the sooner.
>
> (Hebrews 13:19)

Paul, separated from the Apostles over their differences, now requests that he be restored as he was prepared to leave the doctrinal differences unresolved for the time and was asking them only to change their ritualistic practices. Though it is Paul who is writing to be restored to their communion, yet he seems to be laying down conditions for the same.

Paul's opposition to the Law of Moses and his belief that faith was sufficient for salvation has come up at several places. Here, a new element—his advising the Apostles to give up animal sacrifices—has been introduced. It may come as a surprise to many, but Christians did offer animal sacrifices in the Churches in the early centuries. The passage below illustrates the same.

> We must believe, then, that God has no need, not only of cattle, or any other earthly and material thing, but even of man's righteousness, and that whatever right worship is paid to God profits not Him, but men. For no man would say he did a benefit to a fountain by drinking, or to the light by seeing. And the fact that the ancient church offered animal sacrifices, which the people of God now-a-days read of without imitating, proves nothing else than this, that those sacrifices signified the things which we do for the purpose of drawing near to God, and inducing our neighbour to do the same. A sacrifice, therefore, is the visible sacrament or sacred sign of an invisible sacrifice
> (*The Writings of Early Church Fathers*, Vol. 2, Augustine, City of God, Book X, Chapter 5)

There is no ambiguity in Augustine's statement that the ancient church offered animal sacrifices, which we find Paul advising the Apostles to give up. There are further references to such sacrifices by the Arians, a Christian group that was declared heretical by the Catholic Church—a point significant also for linking this practice to the Apostles, as Arianism was essentially the belief of the Eastern Church wherein apostolic traditions had survived longer. The following passages point to this fact.

> Did not the Arians and the Gentiles offer those sacrifices in the great Church in the Caesareum, and utter their blasphemies against Christ as by His command?
> (*The Writings of the Early Church Fathers*, Vol. 13, Athanasius, Historia Arianorum, Part VIII, Para 74)

> These are the doctrines for which they are contending; for these they assail the ancient Council, because its members did not propound the like, but anathematized the Arian heresy instead, which they were so eager to recommend. This was why they put forward, as an advocate of their irreligion, Asterius who sacrificed, a sophist too, that he might not spare to speak against the Lord, or by a show of reason to mislead the simple. And they were ignorant, the shallow men, that they were doing harm to their own cause. For the ill savour of their advocate's idolatrous sacrifice betrayed still more plainly that the heresy is Christ's foe.
> (*The Writings of the Early Church Fathers*, Vol. 13, Athanasius, Councils of Ariminum and Seleucia, Part II, Para 20)

Apart from what the Bible sheds light upon, the belief system of the Apostles is also reflected in the beliefs of the Ebionites, an early sect of Jewish Christians. After the death of Christ, his brother James became the Bishop of Jerusalem. This remained the principal seat of Christian leadership for quite some time and all Apostles owed allegiance to it even when they were stationed elsewhere and had established their episcopates. Most of the followers of the Church of James were Jews and got dispersed when the Romans sacked Jerusalem. These Christians have been called Ebionites and have often been referred to as heretics. Their beliefs emerge from the following passages.

Those who are called Ebionites agree that the world was made by God; but their opinions with respect to the Lord are similar to those of Cerinthus and Carpocrates. They use the Gospel according to Matthew only, and repudiate the Apostle Paul, maintaining that he was an apostate from the law. As to the prophetic writings, they endeavour to expound them in a somewhat singular manner: they practice circumcision, persevere in the observance of those customs which are enjoined by the law, and are so Judaic in their style of life, that they even adore Jerusalem as if it were the house of God.

(*The Writings of the Early Church Fathers*, Vol. 1, Irenaeus, Adversus Haeresus, Book I, Chapter 24)

This statement of Irenaeus outlines the schism between Paul and the Apostles. The Ebionites, who were of the Church of James and had the Apostles on their side, accepted only the Gospel of Matthew as their scripture and repudiated Paul for rejecting their beliefs. Their practices were of Judaism, which we find Paul trying to restrain the Apostles from preaching. Origen, while responding to Celsus, gives a similar account of the Ebionites, as may be seen in the following passages.

Here he has not observed that the Jewish converts have not deserted the law of their fathers, in as much as they live, according to its prescriptions, receiving their very name from the poverty of the law, according to the literal acceptation of the word; for Ebion signifies 'poor' among the Jews and those Jews who have received Jesus as Christ are called by the name of Ebionites.

(*The Writings of the Early Church Fathers*, Vol. 4, Origen, Book II, Chapter 1)

Let it be admitted, moreover, that there are some who accept Jesus, and who boast on that account of being

Christians, and yet would regulate their lives, like the Jewish multitude, in accordance with the Jewish law, and these are the two fold sect of Ebionites.

> (*The Writings of the Early Church Fathers*, Vol. 4, Origen, Book V, Chapter 61)

For there are certain heretical sects which do not receive the Epistles of Apostle Paul, as the two sects of Ebionites, and those who are termed Encratites. Those then, who do not regard the apostle as a holy and wise man, will not adopt his language.

> (*The Writings of the Early Church Fathers*, Vol. 4, Origen, Book V, Chapter 65)

These passages from Origen confirm the statement of Irenaeus about the Ebionites. They did not consider Paul to be an apostle or even a holy and wise man. It is, however, of interest here that Origen considered the Ebionites to be a heretical sect. Evidently, the Church of Paul was terming the Church of the Apostles as heretical by his time. The Ebionites were, however, the people following the customs laid down by the Apostle James.

There are other writers, too, who have made similar statements, such as:

> The Ebionaeans, however, acknowledge that the world was made by Him who is in reality God, but they propound legends concerning the Christ similarly with Cerinthus and Carpocrates. They live conformably to the customs of the Jews, alleging that they are justified according to the law, and saying that Jesus was justified by fulfilling the law.
>
> (*The Writings of the Early Church Fathers*, Vol. 5, Hippolytus, Refutation of All Heresies, Book VIII, Chapter 22)

The ancients quite properly called these men Ebionites, because they held poor and mean opinions concerning Christ. In their opinion the observance of the ceremonial law was altogether necessary, on the ground that they could not be saved by faith in Christ alone and by a corresponding life.

These men, moreover, thought that it was necessary to reject all the epistles of the apostle, whom they called an apostate from the law: and they used only the so-called Gospel according to the Hebrews and made small account of the rest.

The Sabbath and the rest of the discipline of the Jews they observed just like them, but at the same time, like us, they celebrated the Lord's days as a memorial of the resurrection of the saviour.

(*The Writings of the Early Church Fathers*, Vol. 24, Eusebius Pamphilus, Prolegomena, Book III, Chapter 27)

Those who are called Encratites. They indeed use the Law and Prophets and Gospels, but interpret in their own way the utterances of the sacred scriptures. And they abuse Paul and reject his epistles, and do not accept even the Acts of the Apostles.

(*The Writings of the Early Church Fathers*, Vol. 24, Eusebius Pamphilus, Prolegomena, Book IV, Chapter 29)

This shows that the Encratites was a Christian sect closely related to the Ebionites. Both rejected Paul and his works and acknowledged only the Gospel of Matthew, which was also the gospel according to the Hebrews, as their scripture. They followed all Jewish customs and observed the Law completely.

The Apostles were preaching adherence to the Law and, at least initially, were preaching to the Jews alone. The conflict between the two sides can also be seen in the statements of these ancient writers. The following passages are of interest in this regard.

> Wherefore also Marcion and his followers have betaken themselves to mutilating the Scriptures, not acknowledging some books at all; and curtailing the Gospel according to Luke and the Epistles of Paul, they assert that these are alone authentic, which they have themselves thus shortened.
> (*The Writings of the Early Church Fathers*, Vol. 1, Irenaeus, Adversus Haeresus, Book III, Chapter 12)

> But again, we allege the same against them who do not recognize Paul as an apostle: that they should either reject the other words of the Gospel which we have come to know through Luke alone, and not make use of them.
> (*The Writings of the Early Church Fathers*, Vol. 1, Irenaeus, Adversus Haeresus, Book III, Chapter 15)

> Now this heresy of yours does not receive certain scriptures; and whichever of them it does receive, it perverts by means of additions and diminutions, for the accomplishment of its own purpose; and such as it does receive, it receives not in their entirety; but even when it does receive any up to a certain point as entire, it never the less perverts even these by contrivance of diverse interpretations.
> (*The Writings of the Early Church Fathers*, Vol. 3, Tertullian, Prescriptions Against Heretics, Chapter 17)

> One man perverts the Scriptures with his hand, another their meaning by his exposition. For although Velentinus seems to use the entire volume, he has none the less laid violent hands on the truth only with a more cunning mind and skill than Marcion. Marcion expressly and openly used the knife, not the pen, since he made such an expression

of the scriptures as suited his own subject matter.
(*The Writings of the Early Church Fathers*,
Vol. 3, Tertullian, Prescriptions
Against Heretics, Chapter 38)

Nevertheless these persons argue still to the effect that this demolition of temples, this condemnation of sacrifices, and this shattering of all images, are brought about, not in virtue of the doctrine of Christ Himself, but only by the hand of His apostles, who, as they contend, taught something different from what he taught.
(*The Writings of the Early Church Fathers*,
Vol. 15, Augustine, Harmony of Gospels,
Book I, Chapter 16)

It appears, from the above passages, that in the early centuries, there were several Christian sects that did not acknowledge Paul as an apostle and rejected his epistles and the gospel linked to him. These Christians, evidently, were the followers of the Apostles. The last passage is of interest, as in it Augustine has stated that there were people who argued that what the Christians were doing was not according to the doctrine of Christ, but as per that of his Apostles. They had further stated that the Apostles taught something different from what Christ taught. Augustine has mentioned all Apostles here because, much before his time, the Pauline Church had linked Peter to itself, which, as would emerge ahead, was not true. Because the Pauline Church claimed that it had received its teachings and traditions from Peter and Paul and gave the impression that both were of one mind and taught the same thing, it claimed its practices to have come from all the Apostles. As this is not true, the statement that the Apostles taught something different from what Christ preached has to be understood to be referring to Paul alone.

That the Apostles were preaching to the Jews alone and

were Judaizing the Gentiles on conversion to Christianity finds mention in the following passages.

> But those who believed clove to the disciples, and departed not from them, because they saw that whatsoever they taught the multitude, they themselves carried into practice before all men; and when affliction and persecution arose against the disciples, they rejoiced to be afflicted with them, and received with gladness stripes and imprisonment for confession of their faith in Christ; and all the days of their life they preached Christ before the Jews and the Samaritans.
>
> (*The Writings of the Early Church Fathers*,
> Vol. 8, Ancient Syriac Documents,
> The Teachings of the Apostles)

> Peter, however, by his making as though salvation consisted in Judaism, was compelling the Gentiles to Judaize.
>
> (*The Writings of the Early Church Fathers*, Vol. 12,
> Augustine, On Lying, Para 8)

> What shall we say of what is also wonderful, that he who carefully observes may find that it is possible that certain persons, without violating Christian charity, may yet teach what is useless, as Peter wished to compel the Gentiles to observe Jewish customs.
>
> (*The Writings of the Early Church Fathers*,
> Vol. 13, Augustine, Anti-Donatist Writings,
> Book IV, Chapter 2)

The Apostles have been called the disciples at numerous places. The Syriac documents quoted above state that they taught only the Jews and the Samaritans. The other references confirm that the Apostles focused on the Jews, while the Gentiles, on being converted, were Judaized.

The views of Christ on this issue are quite clearly mentioned in the Bible. He wished to preach among the Jews alone and had no interest in any other race, as can be gleaned from the following passages.

> But he answered and said, I am not sent but unto the lost sheep of the house of Israel.
> Then came she and worshipped him, saying, Lord, help me.
> But he answered and said, It is not meet to take the children's bread, and to cast it to dogs.
> (Matthew 15:24–26)

> These twelve Jesus sent forth, and commanded them, saying, Go not into the way of Gentiles, and into any city of the Samaritans enter yet not:
> But go rather to the lost sheep of the house of Israel.
> (Matthew 10:5–6)

The first passage tells of an incident wherein a Canaanite woman wished to be healed by Jesus. He refused to do so, saying that he had come only for 'the lost sheep of the house of Israel'. In the next passage, Jesus sends the 12 Apostles to preach and with a clear direction that they preach only to 'the lost sheep of Israel', avoiding the Gentiles and the Samaritans. Though a contrary statement from Jesus has been recorded in the Acts of the Apostles and elsewhere after his resurrection (discussed later in this book), excluding even the Samaritans shows how limited the scope of preaching was as laid down by Jesus. The Samaritans were descendants of Jacob and should have been counted within the house of Israel. They had been separated about a thousand years before Christ. The Jewish kingdom was united in the times of David and Solomon. After Solomon, it was split into Judah and Samaria. The Jews of Samaria were called the Samaritans. Though it was only a political division, it made an impact on their religion also because Solomon had built the Temple at Jerusalem, and the people of Judah prayed there. The Samaritans did not believe that this Temple was the house of God and had a place on a mountain in Samaria identified for the purpose. As they separated after Solomon, they acknowledged all the early parts of the Bible, including the Law of Moses, but did not acknowledge the prophets who came later. The passages noted below reveal some more information.

> The ten tribes, indeed, which Jeroboam the servant of Solomon received, being appointed the king in Samaria, were distinctively called Israel, although this had been the name of that whole people; but the two tribes, namely, of Judah and Benjamin, which for David's sake, lest the kingdom should be wholly wrenched from his race, remained subject to the city of Jerusalem, were called Judah, because that was the tribe when David sprang.
>
> On the division of the people, therefore, Rehoboam, son of Solomon, reigned in Jerusalem as the first king of Judah, and Jeroboam servant of Solomon, in Samaria as king of Israel.
>
> (*The Writings of the Early Church Fathers*, Vol. 2, Augustine, City of God, Book XVII, Chapter 21)

> For the Samaritans made use of these books, and were under the same law: for it was from it they had circumcision.
>
> For there was a contention between the Samaritans and the Jews, because the Jews worshipped God in the temple built by Solomon; but the Samaritans, being situated at a distance from it, did not worship there. For this reason the Jews, because they worshipped God in the temple, boasted themselves to be better than the Samaritans.
>
> (*The Writings of the Early Church Fathers*, Vol. 16, Augustine, On John, Tractate XV, Para 23)

Another schism is that of the Samaritans; for they deny the resurrection of the dead, and assert that God is not to be worshipped in Jerusalem but on Mount Gerizim.
(*The Writings of the Early Church Fathers*, Vol. 8, Pseudo-Clementine Literature Book I Chapter 54)

Turn now to the Samaritans, who, receiving the law only, allow not the prophets.
(*The Writings of the Early Church Fathers*, Vol. 30, Cyril, Lecture XVIII, Para II)

Our fathers worshipped in this mountain; and ye say, that in Jerusalem is the place where men ought to worship.
(John 4: 20)

These passages show how closely the Samaritans were related to the Jews. Ten tribes had gone to the kingdom of Samaria and two to Judah. Augustine has called those going to Samaria as Israel and the remaining as Judah. These were, however, called Samaritans by Jesus as well as by the Apostles. The separation of the kingdom and the Temple coming up at Jerusalem had led to this split.

There was a conflict between Paul and the Apostles, thus emerges from all these writings. Though the differences ran far deeper, but as Paul and the subsequent writers have stressed on the continued adherence to Judaism and the focus on preaching only amongst the Jews, their difference on these points emerge more prominently in these writings. The views of Jesus are clearly on the side of the Apostles. Even for the Law of Moses, there is a statement from Him, 'I came not to destroy the law, but to fulfill'.

2

THE MYTHS CREATED

Paul and the Pauline Church, in their struggle against the Apostles and the Apostolic Church, produced scriptures and created several myths in them to establish their theology. As the Pauline Church, in the course of time, wiped out its rival, whatever scriptures have survived, have come down to us through their traditions alone. This makes the task of knowing what the Apostles taught difficult, as even the parts of the scriptures that have come from them have the possibility of interpolations and distortions. In the New Testament, the Gospel of Luke, the Acts of the Apostles and the 14 epistles of Paul are all admittedly Pauline. What is left are the three Gospels—of Matthew, Mark and of John, the seven short epistles—one of James, two of Peter, three of John and one of Jude, and the book of Revelation. Of these, the Gospel of Matthew alone was accepted by the Ebionites, the Christians of the Church of James, and has already come up in a passage quoted earlier. That the gospel was recorded for the Jews is mentioned in the following passage.

> Of Matthew again it is said, that when those who from amongst the Jews had believed came to him, and besought him to leave to them in writing those same things, which he had spoken to them by word, he also composed his Gospel in the language of the Hebrews.
> (*The Writings of the Early Church Fathers*, Vol. 19, John Chrysostom, Homilies on Matthew, Homily 1)

This gospel is certainly from the Apostles, but unfortunately the original Hebrew version is not available, and what has survived has come through the Pauline Church. It has to be accepted as carrying the message of the Apostles, but great care has to be taken to spot the interpolations. There are a couple of very interesting comments of Augustine that provide some help in this regard:

> For Matthew is understood to have taken it in hand to construct the record of the incarnation of the Lord according to the royal lineage, and to give an account of most part of His deeds and words as they stood in relation to this present life of man. Mark follows him closely, and looks like his attendant and epitomizer. For in his narrative he gives nothing in concert with John apart from the others: by himself separately, he has little to record; in conjunction with Luke, as distinguished from the rest, he has still less; but in concord with Matthew, he has a very large number of passages. Much, too, he narrates in words almost numerically and identically the same as those used by Matthew, where the agreement is either with the evangelist alone, or with him in connection with the rest.
> (*The Writings of the Early Church Fathers*, Vol. 15, Augustine, Harmony of the Gospels, Book I, Chapter 2)

> Luke, on the other hand, had no one connected with him to act as his summarist in the way that Mark was attached to Matthew.
> (*The Writings of the Early Church Fathers*, Vol. 15, Augustine, Harmony of the Gospels, Book I, Chapter 3)

These remarks of Augustine depict the close connection between the Gospels of Matthew and Mark. He has stated that

THE MYTHS CREATED • 53

Mark was an epitomizer of Matthew. As the Gospel of Mark was originally written in Greek and not in Hebrew, it appears that once the followers of the Apostles increased amongst the Gentiles, the Hebrew gospel had to be translated into Greek, which is what was done by Mark. What is now treated as a separate gospel was perhaps only a Greek version of the Hebrew gospel in which Mark had taken the liberty of only presenting the facts instead of translating the text word by word. As this appears to be the position, the Gospel of Mark, too, has to be considered to have originated in the apostolic traditions. The Ebionites not considering it as a part of their scriptures would have been because of their taking it to be only a summary in Greek of their Gospel. The two gospels, having been the same originally, are of immense help in trying to find the interpolations in them, since whatever is missing in either, except if it was omitted in the summarized translation, would be in the category of suspected text.

The Gospel of John, although treated as a distinct category with spiritual leanings, cannot be from the Apostle. Had it been from the Apostle John, it would have been a part of the scriptures accepted by the Ebionites. Moreover, like Peter, John was illiterate, as has been mentioned in the Acts of the Apostles (The Acts 4:13). This has been further stated in the following passage about John.

> As for worldly instruction, we may learn from these facts that he had none at all of it. Besides, Luke testifies this when he writes not only that he was ignorant, but that he was absolutely unlettered.
> (*The Writings of the Early Church Fathers*, Vol. 23, John Chrysostom, Homilies on John, Homily 2)

The Gospel of John not originating from the Apostle is further established by the fact that it was written to counter the beliefs of the Christians of the Apostolic Church, which is evident in the following passage.

> John, the apostle whom Jesus most loved, the son of Zebedee and brother of James, the apostle whom Herod, after our Lord's passion, beheaded, most recently of all the evangelists wrote a Gospel, at the request of the bishops of Asia, against Cerinthus and other heretics and especially against the then growing dogma of the Ebionites, who assert that Christ did not exist before Mary.
>
> (*The Writings of the Early Church Fathers*, Vol. 26, Jerome, Lives of Illustrious Men, Chapter 9)

Jerome has recorded that the Gospel of John had been written to counter the Ebionites who believed that Jesus did not exist before his mother. It is clear that John, the Apostle, could not have written it as he was a part of the Apostolic Church headed by James. The Ebionites believed what James and the other Apostles preached. This Gospel has to be treated as a forgery in the name of the Apostle.

Of the seven epistles, only the Epistle of James appears to be genuine. The remaining six—two of Peter, three of John and one of Jude—are Pauline in their contents. They are forged documents that have been created to suggest that the Apostles and Paul taught the same things and that there was no difference of opinion amongst them. The time when these epistles were created also varies because even some early Church Fathers, while commenting on which parts of the New Testament are genuine, have stated that only one epistle of Peter and one of John are genuine, while the remaining of their epistles have been considered to be forged by them as they did not find mention in earlier records.

The Book of Revelation, which is the last book of the New Testament, has been doubted by several people from the very beginning. Several Church Fathers have listed the books that should be treated to be a part of the New Testament. A larger number has not included the Revelation in them. This book is ascribed to John. Of those who have accepted it to be a part of the New Testament, many have stated that this is John the Apostle, while a few have stated that it was a different John. The following passage from Dionysius is of interest in this regard.

> Now some before our time have set aside this book, and repudiated it entirely, criticizing it chapter by chapter, and endeavouring to show it to be without either sense or reason. They have alleged also that its title is false; for they deny that John is the author. Nay, further, they hold that it can be no sort of revelation, because it is covered with so gross and dense a veil of ignorance. They affirm, therefore, that none of the apostles, nor indeed any of the saints, nor any person belonging to the Church, could be its author, but that Cerinthus, and the heretical sect founded by him and named after him the Cerinthian sect, being desirous of attaching the authority of a great name to the fiction propounded by him, prefixed that title to the book
> (*The Writings of the Early Church Fathers*, Vol. 6, Dionysius, From the Two Books on the Promises)

This shows that from a very early stage there was a view in the Church that no saint or even ordinary Christian could be an author of this work, leave aside the Apostle. A plain reading of the Revelation brings out that this is a pre-Christian Jewish work in which certain changes have been incorporated to bring in the name of Jesus Christ to make it a part of Christian Scriptures. In its beginning, three chapters have been added, which are clearly out of place. This can be said because the main body of the book speaks of John being taken to heaven to be shown how things were to come, whereas in the first three chapters, he is told to inform the seven Churches of Asia that their practices are disapproved by God. The Churches named are of Ephesus, Smyrna, Pergamos, Thyatira, Sardis,

Philadelphia and Laodicea. Of these, John the Apostle himself was of Ephesus. Apart from the general ideas mentioned, disapproval of a specific sect and a person has also been mentioned, as may be seen in the passages below.

> But this thou hast, that thou hatest the deeds of the Nicolaitans, which I also hate.
>
> (Revelations 2:6)
>
> So hast thou also them that hold the doctrine of the Nicolaitans, which thing I hate.
>
> (Revelations 2:15)
>
> Notwithstanding I have a few things against thee, because thou sufferest that woman Jezebel, which calleth herself a prophetess, to teach and to seduce my servants to commit fornication, and to eat things sacrificed unto idols.
>
> (Revelations 2:20)

These are evidently statements of a sectarian strife, which someone has added at the beginning of the main Apocalypse. In the centuries preceding Christ, the Jews produced a lot of similar literature, all of which is categorized as apocalyptic literature. As the name suggests, the common theme in them is that the world is coming to an end, and when it does, God will judge all persons, whether dead or alive, and give them eternal rewards or punishments for their deeds. Quite often there is a vivid description of people suffering the worst possible tortures, especially if such persons were the Chaldeans or their kings. The normal laws of nature were often reversed in them to ensure the continuation of the torture till eternity, for instance, the person is described to be burning in the hottest possible fire, but his body does not get reduced to ashes to end the sufferings, and though the sinner is in the midst of fire, he is shown to be suffering in complete darkness.

It all started with Nebuchadnezzar, the Babylonian Emperor

invading Judea and defeating the Jews. He proceeded to destroy the Temple of God built by Solomon and took the Jews away to Babylon as captives. The Jews had a firm belief that God lived in the inner chamber of the temple, and except the chief priest, who also went in only after performing certain rituals, nobody ever entered that chamber. It was believed that anyone who did so would be burnt immediately. Paul gives us an idea of this belief in the Bible in the following passage.

> Then verily the first covenant had also ordinances of divine service, and a worldly sanctuary.
>
> For there was a tabernacle made; the first, wherein was the candlestick, and the table, and the shewbread; which is called the sanctuary.
>
> And after the second veil, the tabernacle which is called the Holiest of all;
>
> Which had the golden censer, and the ark of the covenant overlaid round about with gold, wherein was the golden pot that had manna, and Aaron's rod that budded, and the tables of the covenant;
>
> And over it the cherubims of glory shadowing the mercy seat; of which we cannot now speak particularly.
>
> Now when these things were thus ordained, the priests went always into the first tabernacle, accomplishing the service of God.
>
> But into the second went the high priest alone once every year, not without blood, which he offered for himself, and for the errors of the people.
>
> (Hebrews 9:1–7)

The description of the layout of the temple above shows that it had an outer chamber that the priests entered to perform the rituals and an inner chamber that nobody entered except the high priest, once a year, and that too after offering a sacrifice for atonement of sins. Nebuchadnezzar had not only violated all these rules, he had destroyed the temple and had pillaged all costly articles that the Jews considered holy. God had burnt him neither immediately nor thereafter, as he lived to be an old man and died peacefully. This had a devastating effect on the belief system of the Jews and answers had to be sought for this unexpected response on the part of God and what he intended to do for the injuries inflicted on His abode. Against this backdrop, several persons who prophesied and claimed that they could see the future emerged. They are the people who have written these apocalyptic works. They explained that God had allowed Nebuchadnezzar to destroy the temple as a punishment to the Jews for their sins. He would, however, not let Nebuchadnezzar and the Babylonians go unpunished, though no punishment from Him could be seen being inflicted on him during his lifetime. The punishment that Nebuchadnezzar deserved was far greater than what they had believed were given to people for their sins because the sins of others were against fellow human beings, while Nebuchadnezzar's crime was against God Himself. The punishment had to be in proportion to the offence and so the suffering had to be till eternity. The Revelation being a part of this apocalyptic literature of the Jews emerges from the following passages.

> And I saw another angel ascending from the east, having the seal of the living God: and he cried with a loud voice to the four angels, to whom it was given to hurt the earth and the sea,
>
> Saying, Hurt not the earth, neither the sea, nor the trees, till we have sealed the servants of our God in their foreheads.
>
> And I heard the number of them which were sealed: and there were sealed an hundred and forty and four thousand of all the tribes of the children of Israel.
>
> (Revelations 7:2–4)

The angel marks out the Jews so that they could be spared before the other angels start the work of destruction. It is the same idea which, in the times of Moses, was used to mark the houses of the Jews in Egypt so that God could spare them from his wrath. Further ahead in the Book where the doors for entry to the new order have been made, they were also only for the Jews, as may be seen in the following passages.

> And I saw a new heaven and a new earth: for the first heaven and the first earth were passed away; and there was no more sea.
> And I John saw the holy city, new Jerusalem, coming down from God out of heaven, prepared as a bride adorned for her husband.
>
> (Revelations 21:1–2)

> And had a wall great and high, and had twelve gates, and at the gates twelve angels, and names written thereon, which are the names of the twelve tribes of the children of Israel.
>
> (Revelations 21:12)

The people who were to be saved while the rest of the world was to be destroyed were to be only Jews, and people for whom the New Jerusalem had descended from heaven were also to be only Jews. With this as its prophecy, the Revelations is a part of the scriptures of the Christians only because at several places alterations and additions have been made to give it a Christian slant. It was written with immense hatred for the Babylonians, as evident in the followings passages.

> And there followed another angel, saying, Babylon is fallen, is fallen, that great city, because she made all nations drink of the wine of the wrath of her fornication.
>
> (Revelations 14:8)

And the sixth angel poured out his vial upon the great river Euphrates; and the water thereof was dried up, that the way of the kings of the east might be prepared.

(Revelations 16:12)

And the great city was divided into three parts, and the cities of the nations fell: and great Babylon came in remembrance before God, to give unto her the cup of the wine of the fierceness of his wrath.

(Revelations 16:19)

And there came one of the seven angels which had the seven vials, and talked to me, saying unto me, Come hither; I will shew unto thee the judgement of the great whore that sitteth upon many waters.

(Revelations 17:1)

And upon her forehead was a name written, MYSTERY, BABYLON THE GREAT, THE MOTHER OF HARLOTS AND ABOMINATIONS OF THE EARTH.

(Revelations 17:5)

Standing afar off for the fear of her torment, saying, Alas, alas, that great city Babylon, that mighty city! for in one hour is thy judgement come.

(Revelations 18:10)

And a mighty angel took up a stone like a great millstone, and cast it into the sea, saying, Thus with violence shall that great city Babylon be thrown down, and shall be found no more at all.

(Revelations 18:21)

The Book of Revelations has devoted six chapters to describe the torments of Babylon that would accompany its destruction in the future. Though the name is clear and even the river Euphrates is mentioned, Christian commentators have argued that the name Babylon has been used figuratively for Rome. This became necessary as the Christians had no reason to have a grudge against the Babylonian Empire, which had ended several centuries before Christ. To claim that Babylon has been used for Rome is an unnatural explanation to an obvious text. Nebuchadnezzar destroyed the temple of Jerusalem in 587 BC and the Persian Emperor defeated the Babylonians and brought an end to the Babylonian Empire in 539 BC. The Revelations, claimed to be an Apocalypse of John, is an Apocalypse written between 587 BC and 539 BC by a Jew who is still expecting the fall of Babylon in the near future. Its inclusion in the Christian scriptures itself is open to question and the possibility of it being linked to the Apostles, in any way, can certainly be ruled out.

The portions of the Bible that are Pauline cannot be rejected completely but have to be viewed with a lot of care. Despite their slant to establish a particular theology, they continue to be records of the times of Jesus and a little thereafter. In such a situation, they do contain many episodes that are recorded correctly.

With the scriptures so created, Paul and the Pauline Church built up myths to create faith in their system, for which they raised Jesus to the level of God. For raising his status to that of God, the Church created myths of supernatural conditions associated with his birth, of miracles performed by him in his lifetime and of his rising from the dead. In doing so, the claims prophesied by different prophets in the Old Testament that were to be associated with the Messiah when he was to come were linked to Jesus to show that he had fulfilled those prophecies, so he was the Christ who had been expected for so long.

The birth of Jesus is described in only two gospels, those of Matthew and Luke. Its absence from the Gospel of Mark, a summary of the Gospel of Matthew in Greek gives an indication that in Matthew this is an interpolation and was not there originally. There are major contradictions also in the story related by the two evangelists. Luke has stated that when Mary was espoused to Joseph, the angel Gabriel came to her and informed her that she shall conceive the son of God by the Holy Ghost. The reporting in Matthew does not mention Gabriel informing Mary. Therein it is stated that when Mary was espoused to Joseph, before they came together, she was found with the child of the Holy Ghost. Joseph had wanted to leave her quietly, when an angel appeared to him in a dream and informed that she had conceived of the Holy Ghost and asked him to take her as his wife. Augustine, in trying to harmonize the gospels, has stated that both things had happened and each of the two evangelists has reported one.

Luke has informed next that when Mary was 'great with child', Joseph took her to Bethlehem. The reason given for this is that a census was being conducted under the orders of Caesar Augustus for taxing people, so Joseph had to be recorded at Bethlehem, as that was the city of David and 'he was of the house and lineage of David'. After the child was born, an angel appeared to some shepherds who were tending to their flock at night and told them that the saviour had been born in the city of David and they would find him wrapped in swaddling clothes, lying in a manger. These shepherds came and saw Jesus and went to spread word of what had happened. Luke has further stated that after the days of purification were over, the parents brought Jesus to Jerusalem to offer the customary sacrifices. At the temple, two enlightened persons, Simeon and the prophetess Anna, recognized Jesus as the saviour. After performing all the customary rituals, Joseph and Mary returned to their home in Nazareth in the province of Galilee.

Matthew mentions that Jesus was born in Bethlehem but does not explain why his parents went there. After that, a completely different story has been recorded. Three wise men from the east reach Jerusalem and enquire, 'Where is he that is born king of the Jews?' They claim to have seen a star and followed it to come to worship him. Herod, the king of the Jews, is troubled by this and asks these men to inform him when they find the baby so that he, too, may worship him. The wise men followed the star and reached Bethlehem, where the star stood over where the child was. The men find Jesus and worship him with the gifts they had brought. On being warned by God in a dream not to return to Herod, they went away to their country. Thereafter, the angel appeared to Joseph in a dream and asked him to take away the mother and the child to Egypt, as Herod would try to kill the child, and to remain there until it was safe. Joseph took Mary and Jesus to Egypt and remained there till the death of Herod, who on discovering that the wise men had left without informing him, killed all children below two years of age in Bethlehem and in the coasts nearby. On Herod's death, the angel informed Joseph of the same and asked him to go to Israel. Joseph, however, decided to go to Nazareth instead.

The main supernatural occurrence associated with the birth of Jesus is that of his mother having conceived while remaining a virgin, Immaculate Conception, as it is called. If this could be so, only God could make it happen and that conception would have to be from God, making the child the son of God. Before coming to this issue, some other events with their contradictions may be seen, as all of them have been stated in the Bible to have occurred to fulfil certain prophecies of the Old Testament. The birth of Jesus has been shown at Bethlehem because Micah had prophesied that Christ would come 'from the seed of David from Bethlehem'. The reason given by Luke for Joseph and Mary to go Bethlehem when Mary was expecting a child is not convincing. If a census is being conducted, it records the persons at the place where they happen to be at the time of such enumeration. It cannot require a person to have himself recorded at a place where his forefathers were about 1,100 years earlier. If Luke's account is to be believed, the Romans were conducting the census for the purpose of taxing all people. If Joseph got himself recorded at Bethlehem because David, his supposed forefather, lived there 1,100 years ago, Joseph would have been required to pay tax at Bethlehem. He, however, returned to Nazareth in the province of Galilee, which is 157 km away from Bethlehem. The timing of the Roman census also does not match with this account. Jesus is reported to have been born in the concluding years of the reign of Herod, who died in 4 BC. Jesus would, thus, have been born between 6 BC and 4 BC. Roman records show that the census was conducted in Judea in AD 6, which would be too late for the birth of Jesus. It is obvious that the element of birth in Bethlehem, to show that Micah's prophecy stood fulfilled, has been added several decades later when it was hazily remembered that a Roman census had taken place, but the exact date of the same had been lost. Herod ordering the killing of all infants below two years of age stands contradicted by the fact that the area was under Roman control and the king of each ethnic group in the area had jurisdictions over its people only in respect of their internal disputes. Therefore, Herod had no authority to order the execution of anyone, as emerges in the case of Jesus, who had to be taken to the Roman authorities to obtain orders for his crucifixions. The other events like the star having been seen by the wise men of the east and angel appearing to shepherds are matters of faith and can be left at that. The sequence of events after the birth of Jesus, as reported by the two gospels, do not match even remotely as Matthew has reported the departure of Joseph, Mary and Jesus to Egypt, while Luke does not even mention it.

The other issue of the Immaculate Conception, apart from being beyond the course of nature, has major difficulties if it is examined on available facts. The first is that many Christians, especially the Ebionites, did not believe in it and believed that Jesus was the son of Joseph and was born in the manner all other human beings are born. A large number of Church Fathers have mentioned this. Some of the passages are given below.

> Carpocrates, again, and his followers maintain that the world and the things which are therein were created by angels greatly inferior to the unbegotten Father. They also hold that Jesus was the son of Joseph, and was just like other men, with the exception that he differed from them in this respect, that in as much his soul was steadfast and pure.
> (*The Writings of the Early Church Fathers*, Vol. 1, Irenaeus, Against Heresies, Book I, Chapter 25)

> Cerinthus, again, a man who was educated in the wisdom of the Egyptians. He represented Jesus as having not been born of a virgin, but as being the son of Joseph and Mary according to the ordinary course of human generation.
> (*The Writings of the Early Church Fathers*, Vol. 1, Irenaeus, Against Heresies, Book I, Chapter 26)

> The Ebionites following these, assert that He was begotton by Joseph, thus destroying, as far as in them lies, such a marvelous dispensation of God, and setting aside the testimony of the prophets which proceeded from God.
> (*The Writings of the Early Church Fathers*, Vol. 1, Irenaeus, Against Heresies, Book III, Chapter 21)

> This opinion will be very suitable for Ebion, who holds Jesus to be a mere man, and nothing more than a descendant of David.
> (*The Writings of the Early Church Fathers*, Vol. 3, Tertullian, On the Flesh of Christ, Chapter 14)

> The Ebionites, who will have the Son of God to be a mere

man, begotten by human pleasure, and the conjunction of Joseph and Mary.
(*The Writings of the Early Church Fathers*, Vol. 7, Apostolic Teaching and Constitution, Book VI, Chapter 6)

The matter of the Ebionites believing that Jesus was the son of Mary and Joseph, and was born the way all human beings are born, is a particularly serious one. As mentioned earlier, they were the Jews who had become Christians and were the followers of the Church of Jerusalem, which had James as its first bishop. It was, thus, the Church of the Apostles. James was the brother of Jesus and the only gospel these people acknowledged to be scriptures was that of Matthew. One can argue that not only is their testimony on the birth of Jesus more credible than the rest, but their disbelief in his virgin birth would mean that this part of the Gospel of Matthew is an interpolation. It has been recorded by Augustine that the Manicheans denied that Matthew recorded this, which can be seen in the following passage.

Yet, when I begin to quote the Gospel of His Apostle Matthew, where we have the whole narrative of Christ's birth, you forthwith deny that Matthew wrote the narrative.
(*The Writings of the Early Church Fathers*, Vol. 13, Augustine, Contra Faustum, Book 38)

This seems to be the correct position as the first two chapters of Matthew deal with the genealogy of Joseph and the birth of Christ. If they are treated as interpolations and the said gospel is taken to start from the third chapter, it will match with the Gospel of Mark, which is reported to be its summary, as both would then begin with John the Baptist heralding the way of the Lord. The genealogy of Joseph, too, does not fit in and appears to have been introduced in Matthew only to fulfil the prophecy that Christ would come from the seed of David.

Apart from inconsistencies in the list with that given by Luke, Jesus would not be from the seed of David by linking Joseph to him, if the virgin birth is to be believed, because in that case the human element involved would be of Mary alone and she was in no way a descendent of David, not being even from his tribe of Judah but from that of Levi.

The Church, in defence of the virgin birth, has all along argued that it had been prophesied. This is mentioned in the Bible also in the following passage.

> Now all this was done, that it might be fulfilled which was spoken of the Lord by the prophet, saying,
> Behold, a virgin shall be with child, and shall bring forth a son, and they shall call his name Emmanuel, which being interpreted is, God with us.
> (Matthew 1:22–23)

This was Isaiah's prophecy. The full statement is, 'Therefore the Lord himself shall give you a sign; Behold, a virgin shall conceive, and bear a son, and shall call his name Emmanuel' (Isaiah 7:14). The Jews pointed out that there was no such prophecy from Isaiah or any other prophet. They stated that Isaiah had stated a young woman shall be with child and shall bring forth a son. He had not stated that a virgin shall be with child. This was an error on the part of the translators that the word for young woman had been translated as virgin. Several Church Fathers have written about it, but Jerome has used the Hebrew words that were in question. The passage from him is given below.

> I know that the Jews are accustomed to meet us with objection that in Hebrew the word Almahdq does not mean a virgin, but a young woman. And, to speak truth a virgin is properly called Bethulah.
> (*The Writings of the Early Church Fathers*, Vol. 29, Jerome, The Writings of Jerome, Book I, Para 32)

Jerome has proceeded to argue that 'Almah' would mean not just a virgin but a hidden virgin, as the word was used for Rebecca in the Genesis when she approached the well to draw water and she was a virgin. In effect, the argument is that if a girl is a virgin and she has been called a girl, the word girl would mean a hidden virgin. John Chrysostom, while dwelling on this point, has stated that the translators, by some divine inspiration, used the right word because this is what was to happen. This would make it a prophecy of the translators and not of the Prophet Isaiah. Tertullian, on this point, has insisted that it has to mean virgin and not a young woman as the statement has to be seen from the beginning, which say 'Therefore the lord himself shall give you a sign'. Tertullian has concluded that as it had to be sign from God to show that Christ had been born, it had to be a virgin conceiving because a young woman conceiving is a normal occurrence and cannot be a sign from God for the birth of the Christ. This is an argument against the obvious.

The mistake occurred in the translation from Hebrew to Greek. It was Ptolemy, the Pharaoh of Egypt, who, while collecting all notable works for his library at Alexandria, had got the Jewish scriptures translated into Greek. To ensure that the translation was done honestly, he had commissioned 70 Jews who were well-versed in Hebrew, as well as Greek, to translate the Tanakh. They were kept in isolation from each other to ensure that they could not have mutual consultations and deliberately produce a wrong translation to hide certain aspects of their religion. When they had completed the translation, all of them were matched and were found to be agreeing with each other. A final Greek version of the Tanakh was presented based on those translations, which is known as the Septuagint Version. In the Bible, the Tanakh of the Jews is the Old Testament. The error of translating the word 'almahdq' to virgin and not young woman has occurred in the Septuagint

Version. This is significant, as it shows that the person who interpolated the story of a virgin conceiving and also mentioned that this was to fulfil the prophecy of Isaiah, was unacquainted with Hebrew and his access to the Tanakh was limited to its Greek translation, the Septuagint Version. This will not only confirm that Matthew did not record this in his gospel but will exclude even Paul from having been the source for it, which would mean that this is an interpolation not only in the Gospel of Matthew but in that of Luke as well. Paul's writings also show that the concept of birth from a virgin for Jesus had not emerged in his time. In all his writings, while stressing on the divinity of Jesus, Paul has repeatedly referred to his rising from the dead but has nowhere mentioned that he was born of a virgin. Even in the Epistle to the Hebrews, while telling of the doctrinal differences, which he asked to be left for a future discussion, he does not speak of the birth from a virgin as one such difference, though the Apostles did not believe in it, as is evident from the beliefs of the Ebionites. In fact, but for the two gospels mentioning it, there is no mention of it again anywhere in the Bible, which gives an impression that it is a late interpolation. It seems that neither Paul nor the Pauline Church had such a concept in his time and the same emerged later. On the contrary, Paul refers to Jesus in a way that would show that he believed Joseph to be his father, as may be seen in the passage below.

> Concerning his son Jesus Christ our Lord, which was made of the seed of David according the flesh;
> And declared to be the son of God with power, according to the spirit of holiness, by the resurrection from the dead.
> (Romans 1:3–4)

Paul has declared Jesus to be of the seed of David according to the flesh and has made a distinction in his being declared the son of God. He became the son of God by the resurrection from the dead and not from his birth. This would mean that Jesus in his physical body was the son of Joseph, who has been shown as a descendent of David. He became the son of God by his holiness, which became manifest in his resurrection from the dead. As the genealogy of Joseph and the birth of Christ of a virgin create a contradictory situation, it is evident that the genealogy in Luke was a part of the original view of Paul, and the story of the birth from a virgin was interpolated in it by someone later. In Matthew, both are interpolations. There is a long discourse from Augustine on the issue of Jesus being the son of David. Some excerpts from it are given below.

> The Catholic, which is also the apostolic doctrine is, that our Lord and Saviour Jesus Christ is both the Son of God in His divine nature, and the Son of David after the flesh.
>
> He is called the son of David on account of His taking form of a servant from Virgin Mary, the wife of Joseph.
>
> It might also be the case that some of David's blood flowed in Mary herself, so that the flesh of Christ, although produced from a virgin, still owed its origin to David's seed.
>
> Those who prefer the authority of the sacred Gospel to that heretical fiction must conclude that Mary was not unconnected with the family of David.
>
> We believe that Mary, as well as Joseph, were of the family of David, because we believe the scriptures, which assert both that Christ was of the seed of David after the flesh, and that His mother was the Virgin Mary, He having no human father. Therefore, whoever denies the relationship of Mary to David, evidently opposes the pre-eminent authority of those passages of the scripture.
>
> (*The Writings of the Early Church Fathers*, Vol. 13, Augustine, Contra Faustum, Book XXIII)

As is evident, a new element had to be brought in by Augustine to claim that Mary, too, was a descendant of David, something the Bible has not stated anywhere. In fact, Luke, while recording the reasons for Joseph and Mary going to Bethlehem at the time of Christ's birth, records 'because he was of the house and lineage of David'. He does not say that both of them were of his lineage. Moreover, it would have been futile to record the genealogy of Joseph in the two gospels, if Jesus was to be of the seed of David, since Mary was his descendant. In such a case, the genealogy of Mary would have been relevant. Augustine finally appeals to the authority of the scriptures and asserts that as both things have been recorded therein, this has to be believed. He and other Church Fathers faced such difficulties at many places in explaining the Bible, as they had to uphold every word of it to be true, even if there were mutual contradictions. This led Augustine to propound the view, 'First have faith, then you will understand.' In doing so, he overturned the concept of understanding, which is based on seeing the correctness of the reasons in a given statement, while faith leads to belief, which may or may not be based on reason.

Chrysostom has also struggled with this question, as may be seen in the following passages.

> And this because the questions are many and frequent. See, for instance, at once in the beginning of his Gospel, how many difficulties might be raised one after the other. At first, wherefore the genealogy of Joseph is traced, who was not the father of Christ. Secondly, whence may it be manifest that he derives His origin from David, while the forefathers of Mary, who bore Him, are not known, for the Virgin's genealogy is not traced. Thirdly, on what account Joseph's genealogy is traced, when he had nothing to do with the birth; while with regard to the Virgin, who was the

> very mother, it is not shown of what fathers or grandfathers, or ancestors she is sprung.
> (*The Writings of the Early Church Fathers*, Vol. 19, John Chrysostom, Homilies on Matthew, Homily 1)
>
> Of which then is it necessary to speak first? How the Virgin is of David. How then shall we know that she is of David? Hearken unto God telling Gabriel to go unto 'a virgin betrothed to a man (whose name was Joseph), of the house and lineage of David.' What now wouldest thou have plainer than this, when thou hast heard that the Virgin was of the house and lineage of David?
> (*The Writings of the Early Church Fathers*, Vol. 19, John Chrysostom, Homilies on Matthew, Homily 2)

Unlike Augustine, who argued that Mary, too, was of the lineage of David, Chrysostom has propounded that she became of the lineage of David by her marriage to Joseph. This may be acceptable to explain the beginning of the gospel, which states, 'The book of generation of Jesus Christ, the son of David, the son of Abraham' but it will fall short in explaining Paul calling him 'of the seed of David'.

The non-Christian writers have been nasty over this claim of the Church, as can be seen in the following passages that give the views of Porphyry and Celsus.

> Porphyry writes 'Jewish tradition and later pagan critics knew Jesus as the son of a woman named Miriam or Miriamne, who had been violated and became pregnant by a Roman soldier whose name often appears as Panthera in Talmudic and Midrashic sources. The single parent tradition, if not the story of Jesus' illegitimacy is still apparent in Mark, as is an early attempt to show Jesus' freedom from the blemish of his background.
>
> To counter the reports of Jesus' illegitimacy, more than

to secure his divine stature, his mother was declared the recipient of a singular divine honour: Jesus was the son of Mary—a virgin—'through the holy spirit.'
(Joseph Hoffman, Porphyry's 'Against the Christian,'
The Literary Remains)

But let us now return to where the Jew is introduced, speaking of the mother of Jesus, and saying that 'when she was pregnant she was turned out of doors by the carpenter to whom she had been betrothed, as having been guilty of adultery, and that she bore a child to a certain soldier named Panthera.'
(*The Writings of the Early Church Fathers*, Vol. 4, Origen, Against Celsus, Book I, Chapter 32)

Then Celsus says, 'The body of God would not have been so generated as you, O Jesus, were.' He disbelieves the account of His conception by the Holy Ghost, and believes that He was begotten by one Panthera, who corrupted the Virgin.
(*The Writings of the Early Church Fathers*, Vol. 4, Origen, Against Celsus, Book I, Chapter 59)

The Church had made a claim that it exposed Mary to such ugly insinuations, which were apparently untrue because the Ebionites believed that Joseph was the father of Jesus. It is odd to find Porphyry making such remarks, as Augustine held him in very high esteem, as can be seen in the following passage.

For it is the same God who promised both, and predicted that both would come to pass, the God whom the pagan deities tremble before, as even Porphyry, the noblest of pagan philosophers, testifies.
(*The Writings of the Early Church Fathers*, Vol. 2, Augustine, City of God, Book XXII, Chapter 3)

Despite Augustine's views about Porphyry, the Church destroyed all of Porphyry's books in AD 448, leaving only what has been quoted of him by other authors to survive. He was from Tyre and had written extensively.

The biggest difficulty in admitting the birth of Christ from a virgin stems from the fact that both his parents, Mary and Joseph, were not his followers. Matthew has reported that when Joseph wanted to leave Mary quietly as she was found with a child, an angel appeared to him in a dream and informed him that she had conceived of the Holy Ghost. Luke has reported that the angel Gabriel appeared to Mary and told her that she would conceive of the Holy Ghost and give birth to the Son of God. Both of them had the testimony from an angel that the Son of God was to be born of Mary. Moreover, nobody could have known better than Mary herself that she was a virgin and had conceived to give birth to a child in the same state. In such a situation, Joseph and Mary should have been the first and foremost believers in the divinity of Christ. The Bible makes no mention of Joseph after the childhood of Jesus, while the references to Mary show that she was not a believer. This can be seen in the following passages.

> While he yet talked to the people, behold, his mother and his brethren stood without, desiring to speak with him.
>
> Then one said unto him, Behold, thy mother and thy brethren stand without, desiring to speak with thee.
>
> But he answered and said unto him that told him, Who is my mother? and who are my brethren?
>
> And he stretched forth his hand toward his disciples, and said, Behold my mother and my brethren!
>
> For whosoever shall do the will of my Father which is in heaven, the same is my brother, and sister, and mother.
> (Matthew 12:46–50)

> There came then his brethren and his mother, and, standing without, sent unto him, calling him.

> And the multitude sat about him, and they said unto him, Behold, thy mother and thy brethren without seek for thee.
>
> And he answered them, saying, Who is my mother, or my brethren?
>
> And he looked round about on them which sat about him, and said, Behold my mother and my brethren!
>
> For whosoever shall do the will of God, the same is my brother, and my sister, and mother.
>
> (Mark 3:31–35)

> Then came to him his mother and his brethren, and could not come at him for the press.
>
> And it was told him by certain which said, Thy mother and thy brethren stand without, desiring to see thee.
>
> And he answered and said unto them, My mother and my brethren are these which hear the word of God, and do it.
>
> (Luke 8:19–21)

This reporting by the three evangelists is of an incident that had occurred when Jesus had gone to his hometown Nazareth. John has made no mention of it. The mother and brothers of Jesus came to see him. It is noteworthy that his father Joseph did not even come to see him. This is the only mention of Mary in Mark and the only mention in Matthew and Luke after the childhood of Jesus, and shows that Mary and the brothers of Jesus were not his followers. His brother James is later reported to be his disciple and was one of the Apostles, but the brothers that came with Mary were not. The followers were seated inside, whom he pointed out and recognized to be his brothers, sisters and mother. Tertullian has dwelt on this in the following passage.

> But there is some ground for thinking that Christ's answer denies his mother and brethren for the present, as even

> Apelles might learn. 'The Lord's brethren had not yet believed in Him.' So it is contained in the Gospel which was published before Marcion's time. Whilst there is at the same time a want of evidence of His mother's adherence to Him, although the Marthas and the other Marys were in constant attendance on Him, in this very passage their unbelief is evident. Jesus was teaching the way of life, preaching the kingdom of God and actively engaged in healing infirmities of body and soul, but all the while, whilst strangers were intent on him, His very nearest relatives were absent.
> (*The Writings of the Early Church Fathers*, Vol. 3, Tertullian, On the Flesh of Christ, Chapter 7)

Tertullian is candid in his statement. If this passage of the Bible is left out, then there is a lack of evidence of Mary being an adherent of Jesus, just as there is a lack of evidence for Joseph being his adherent, as nothing is mentioned. However, in this passage, the unbelief on Mary's part is evident.

Chrysostom has also stated the same thing while speaking of this incident, which may be seen in the passage below.

> For in fact that which she had essayed to do, was of superfluous vanity; in that she wanted to show the people that she hath power and authority over her Son, imagining not as yet anything great concerning Him, whence also her unreasonable approach.
> (*The Writings of the Early Church Fathers*, Vol. 19, John Chrysostom, Homilies on Matthew, Homily 44)

John has mentioned a different interaction of Jesus with his mother, noted in the passage below.

> And the third day there was a marriage in Cana of Galilee; and the mother of Jesus was there:
> And both Jesus was called, and his disciples, to the marriage.

> And when they wanted wine, the mother of Jesus saith unto him, They have no wine.
> Jesus saith unto her, Woman, what have I to do with thee? mine hour is not yet come.
>
> (John 2:1–4)

This is the incident in which Jesus made wine of water. He did proceed to make it when it had fallen short, but when his mother mentioned to him, his reaction was, 'Woman, what have I to do with thee?' Though a question of faith is not indicated in the interaction, his response does not appear to be very polite. This annoyance on his part could be due to Mary's absence of faith, while strangers were becoming his disciples.

It is, thus, a situation wherein the Church has asked the people to believe that Jesus was the Son of God because his mother conceived Him from the Holy Ghost while she was a virgin and gave birth to him while still a virgin, but the mother who gave birth to this child, did not believe that he was so.

A lone remark comes from the Nag Hammadi Library, which says that Jesus had a twin. This is in the following passage.

> The secret words that the Saviour spoke to Judas Thomas which I, even I, Mathaias, wrote down, while I was walking, listening to them speak with one another.
>
> The Saviour said, 'Brother Thomas while you have time in the world, listen to me, and I will reveal to you the things you have pondered in your mind.
>
> 'Now, since it has been said that you are my twin and true companion, examine yourself, and learn who you are, in what way you exist, and how you will come to be. Since you will be called my brother, it is not fitting that you be ignorant yourself'.
>
> (The Nag Hammadi Library,
> The Book of Thomas the Contender)

Jesus has called Judas Thomas his twin in this passage. This is the only place where such a claim could be found. The Nag Hammadi Library is a collection of a large number of Gnostic works, which were accidently found buried near Nag Hammadi in Egypt, neatly packed in skin and placed in properly sealed pitchers. Their sheer number led historians to call it a library. Apparently they belonged to a monastery nearby and the monks, to save them from being destroyed when the Church was destroying all heretical works, packed them properly and buried them. They were accidently discovered in 1945 and are amongst the best sources available to know about Gnostic Christianity. They alone have mentioned that Jesus had a twin brother. None of the Church Fathers has written anything, which could be even by way of refutation of any such claim. It is difficult to say how credible this one single statement could be, but if it is true, it would have to be believed that twins were born of the Holy Ghost of whom only one was believed to be the Son of God.

After showing the extraordinary conditions involved in his birth to establish the divinity of Christ, the next element that has been brought in for the same purpose is the miracles that have been attributed to him. Whether such things are possible or not can be left to faith, but things incidental to them are of interest on this point. The Jews had a belief that a Christ would come in the future. Since Jesus had emerged as a religious leader, they were prepared to accept him to be the Christ, provided he performed some miracles for them and showed some signs by which his divinity could be manifest. This is evident in the following passages.

> Then certain of the scribes and of the Pharisees answered, saying, Master, we would see a sign from thee.
> But he answered and said unto them, An evil and adulterous generation seeketh after a sign; and there shall

no sign be given to it, but the sign of the prophet Jonas:

For as Jonas was three days and three nights in the whale's belly; so shall the Son of man be three days and three nights in the heart of the earth.
(Matthew 12:38–40)

The Pharisees also with the Sadducees came, and tempting desired him that he would shew them a sign from heaven.

He answered and said unto them, When it is evening, ye say, It will be fair weather: for the sky is red.

And in the morning, It will be foul weather to day: for the sky is red and lowring. O ye hypocrites, ye can discern the face of the sky; but can ye not discern the signs of the times?

A wicked and adulterous generation seeketh after a sign; and there shall no sign be given unto it, but the sign of the prophet Jonas. And he left them and departed.
(Matthew 16:1–4)

And the Pharisees came forth, and began to question with him, seeking of him a sign from heaven, tempting him.

And he sighed deeply in his spirit and saith, Why doth this generation seek after a sign? verily I say unto you, There shall no sign be given unto this generation.
(Mark 8:11–12)

And when the people were gathered thick together, he began to say, This is an evil generation: they seek a sign; and there shall no sign be given it, but the sign of Jonas the prophet.

For as Jonas was a sign unto the Ninevites, so shall also the Son of man be to this generation.
(Luke 11:29–30)

The three gospels have reported that the Jews were seeking a sign from Jesus, evidently to know whether he was the Christ that they had been expecting for so long. Jesus refused to give them a sign. In Matthew and Luke, it has been mentioned 'except the sign of Jonas', which hints at his resurrection. This is an evident interpolation in Matthew not only because it is not a part of the Gospel of Mark but also because the Apostles did not believe in the resurrection of Christ, as would emerge ahead. On being asked, Jesus has, thus, refused to perform a miracle for the Jews. This refusal on the part of Jesus has been reported in the gospels amidst so many miracles that they have reported he was already performing. From this evidence, one can conclude that the stories of the miracles in these gospels are a later interpolation and were not in them originally, otherwise such a request from the Jews would have been redundant, and Christ's statement, 'there shall no sign be given,' would also be in contradiction to the facts. The Gospel of Luke represents the views of Paul. In it, the words 'but the sign of Jonas the prophet' match with the views of Paul, as he propounded the myth of the resurrection of Jesus, but here, too, the emphasis that this would be the only sign that would be given shows that even in Luke all the stories of miracles attributed to Jesus are a later interpolation.

The picture that emerges from John is totally different, as may be seen in the following passage.

> Then came the Jews round about him, and said unto him, How long dost thou make us to doubt? If thou be the Christ, tell us plainly.
>
> Jesus answered them, I told you, and ye believed not: the works that I do in my Father's name, they bear witness of me.
>
> But ye believe not, because ye are not of my sheep, as I said unto you.
>
> My sheep hear my voice, and I know them, and they follow me.
>
> (John 10:24–27)

John has contradicted many things with the rest of the Bible in this statement. The first is that Jesus was prepared to publicly acknowledge that he was the Christ. Next, he has said that he had performed so many miracles, but despite them, they did not believe in his divinity. The third is that they, the Jews, were not his sheep. The last, that his sheep, meaning the Gentiles, hear him and follow him. Even where stories of miracles have been reported, Jesus is found to be telling the people not to reveal what he had done. Evidently, he was not prepared to make a public statement of his divinity. John, however, tells us that he told the Jews that he had already said so. He proceeds to say that they were not convinced despite his many miracles, while in the other three gospels he had refused to give a sign. Evidently, the Gospel of John was written much later and by then miracles had been interpolated in the other gospels to which John has referred to. The last two points are significant, as Jesus has been reported to have parted from the Jews, declaring them to be 'not of my sheep' and to have accepted the Gentiles to be his sheep and his followers. This goes completely against the picture of Jesus as it emerges from the rest of the Bible where he says, 'I am not sent but unto the lost sheep of the house of Israel'. Jesus is not reported to be preaching amongst the Gentiles in his life, neither were his Apostles doing so initially after his death. John's statement, however, shows that Jesus had repudiated the Jews and already had a large number of Gentiles as his followers, amongst whom he had obviously preached. This was Paul's approach in the preaching of Christianity. It is evident that the Gospel of John is the creation of a Gentile Church and of a time when a sufficiently large number of non-Jews had become its followers.

Apart from the response of Jesus to the requests made by the Jews to perform miracles, the reactions of the people who were witness to the reported miracles are of interest.

In one instance, he is reported to have cast out devils from two persons who were possessed of them and these went into a herd of swine that ran violently and perished in the sea. The reaction of the people is reported in the following passage.

> And they that kept them fled, and went their ways into the city, and told every thing, and what was befallen to the possessed of the devils.
> And behold, the whole city came out to meet Jesus: and when they saw him, they besought him that he would depart out their coasts.
>
> (Matthew 8:33–34)

Jews have been reported to be rearing swine in this passage, which could not have come from Matthew, who was himself a Jew and so was well-acquainted with their customs and beliefs. People have been reported to have asked Jesus to leave the place after coming to know that he had cast out devils from two persons possessed of them. The reaction of the people to a good deed performed is shown to be negative. The same is reported in the following passages for other miracles.

> And when the devil was cast out, the dumb spake: and the multitudes marveled, saying, It was never so seen in Israel.
> But the Pharisees said, He casteth out devils through the prince of the devils.
>
> (Matthew 9:33–34)

> Then saith he to the man, Stretch forth thine hand. And he stretched it forth; and it was restored whole, like as the other.
> Then the Pharisees went out, and held a council against him, how they might destroy him.
>
> (Matthew 12:13–14)

> But when the Pharisees heard it, they said, This fellow doth not cast out devils, but by Beelzebub the prince of the devils.
>
> (Matthew 12:24)

In several other instances, the reaction of the people who were witness to the miracles has been reported to be very awkward and contrary to normal human behaviour. It is not just the non-believing Jews who have been reported to have reacted in an unnatural manner, but even the disciples of Christ have been shown to have been unaffected by the stated miracles. Though Matthew and Mark have not reported any other disciple appointed by Jesus except the 12 Apostles, Luke has reported the appointment of 70 more who were sent out in twos by him to preach. Their reaction on return to Jesus is reported in the following passage.

> And the seventy returned again with joy, saying, Lord even the devils are subject unto us through thy name.
>
> And he said unto them, I beheld Satan as lightening fall from heaven.
>
> Behold, I give unto you power to tread on serpents and scorpions, and over all the power of the enemy: and nothing shall by any means hurt you.
>
> (Luke 10:17–19)

The 70 disciples have been reported by Luke to be overjoyed on their return, as they found that they had the power over devil. Jesus had given them further power to step on serpents and scorpions. Their enemies were made subject to them and nothing could hurt them. Such disciples, on seeing the miracles that have been reported, should have believed that he was the Son of God and should have been the most ardent believers. Their faith could not have been shaken by anything. Yet, John reports something else in the following passage.

> From that time many of his disciples went back, and walked no more with him.
> Then said Jesus unto the twelve, Will ye also go away?
> Then Simon Peter answered him, Lord, to whom shall we go? thou hast the words of eternal life.
>
> (John 6:66–67)

The disciples who had been reported by Luke to be overjoyed for having the power over devils by the name of Jesus and who would have been witness to all the miracles that he did as they accompanied him, have been reported by John to have gone away. Only the 12 Apostles were left. It is again a situation wherein the Church has asked the followers to believe that Jesus was the Son of God because of all the miracles that he has been reported to have performed, but his followers, who lived with him and who would have witnessed all the reported miracles, did not develop any such faith and left him after some time. Amongst the 12 chief disciples, the Apostles, one did not have the required level of faith in him, as he betrayed him to the priests for 30 pieces of silver. This may be explained to the faithful by the Church by saying that the Devil entered into him, as has been reported by the Bible, or that this happened because there was a prophesy to this effect, but to reason, there is no Devil, no prophesy that can cause a man to do something. It is his free will that has been exercised. Judas Iscariot betraying Jesus to the priests for 30 pieces of silver is an act of an Apostle, duly chosen and appointed as such by Jesus. He would have spent all his time in his company, listening to what he said and watching what he did. No miracle, whether it was turning water into wine or a making alive a man who had been dead and buried for four days, could make him see in Jesus anything that could retain his faith.

Apart from the reactions of people who are reported to be witnesses to the miracles not being in tune with what they reportedly saw, at times what is reported is not historically correct and is in contradiction to what had been said earlier. The passages below are of the occasion when Jesus made alive Lazarus, the brother of Mary Magdalene, who had been dead and buried for four days.

> Then many of the Jews which came to Mary, and had seen the things which Jesus did, believed on him.
> But some of them went their ways to the Pharisees, and told them what things Jesus had done.
> Then gathered the chief priests and the Pharisees a council, and said, What do we? For this man doeth many miracles.
> If we let him thus alone, all men will believe on him: and the Romans shall come and take away both our place and nation.
> (John 11:45–48)

> Nor consider that it is expedient for us, that one man should die for the people, and that the whole nation perish not.
> (John 11:50)

> Then from that day forth they took counsel together for to put him to death.
> (John 11:53)

After witnessing such a miracle, a man dead and buried for four days is made alive and he walks out of his grave, the report is that many of the Jews believed in him but all did not. Some went away and reported to the Pharisees, as if by way of a complaint. These Pharisees, too, who had earlier sought from him a sign so that they could believe that he was the expected Christ, now feel that he was dangerous for the nation because his miracles would draw the people to believe in him and that would cause the Romans to take away their land and people. This not only shows an abnormal reaction on the part of the witnesses to the miracle and the Pharisees but also reflects that the person who wrote it was not acquainted with the political conditions of Judea of the time, as it was already a Roman territory with a Roman governor before the birth of Jesus. Even in their past, the Jews had sovereign authority for a very limited period. Most of the time, Judea was under the imperial control of the Egyptians, Babylonians, Persians or Macedonians. Even if they had been an independent nation, how the people believing in Jesus could cause the Romans to come and subdue them has not been stated by John. The Pharisees, however, concluded that one man should die rather than the entire nation. If John is to be believed, the Jews decided to kill Jesus because he was performing miracles, though just a little while ago, he had stated that the Jews asked Jesus whether he was the expected Christ, and the other three evangelists have stated that the Jews asked him to give a sign so that they may believe that he was the Christ. On one hand, the miracles were sought to clear the doubt that he was the Christ and, on the other, the decision was taken to kill him because he was performing them and because if that was not done, the Jewish nation would be taken over by the Romans.

That the miracles attributed to Christ and his Apostles were not believed to be true by many people is evident in the following passage.

> But if this record of events is false, as you say, how comes it that in so short a time the whole world has been filled with such a religion? or how could nations dwelling widely apart, and separated by climate and by the convexities of heaven, unite in one conclusion? They have been prevailed upon, say my opponents, by mere assertions been led into vain hopes.
>
> Nay, because they saw all these things to be done by Christ Himself and by His Apostles.
>
> But our writers, we shall be told, have put forth these

statements with false effrontery; they have extolled small matters to an inordinate degree, and have magnified trivial affairs with most pretentious boastfulness. And would that all things could have been reduced to writing, both those which were done by Himself, and those which were accomplished by His Apostles with equal authority and power.
> (*The Writings of the Early Church Fathers*, Vol. 6, Arnobius, Adversus Gentes, Book I)

It appears that a large number of miracles performed by Christ in his childhood were also in circulation in the early centuries. These did not finally find a place in the gospels and were lost. This is evident in the following passage.

> Hence it remains clear to us, that the miracles which they say belong to Christ's childhood, are false, and the inventions of certain who bring them into notice. For if He had begun from His early age to work wonders, neither could John have been ignorant of Him, nor would the multitude have needed a teacher to make Him known.
> (*The Writings of the Early Church Fathers*, Vol. 23, John Chrysostom, Homilies on John, Homily 17)

Chrysostom tells of John the Baptist testifying that he saw the spirit descending from heaven like a dove and settling on Jesus when he baptized him. He has stated that this shows that the miracles attributed to Jesus as a child are false, because if they had been true, John would have known him from before and the people, too, would have known him and would not have had the requirement of a teacher to inform them of his divinity. All other miracles attributed to Jesus of his childhood have no mention in the Bible, but one has crept into it. This is of Jesus at the age of 12, seated in the Temple with the doctors of religion and talking to them on points of religion and their astonishment at his understanding and answers (Luke 2:43–49). As per the reasoning of Chrysostom, this miracle would evidently be false.

The next element introduced by Paul and the Pauline Church to establish the divinity of Jesus was the myth of his having risen from his grave on the third day after he had died and had been buried. The resurrection of Jesus has been used by Paul for two purposes, one, to establish that Jesus was the Son of God, and, two, to establish the theory amongst the Christians of the resurrection of the dead on the Day of Judgement to receive judgement from God for their deeds. What happens after death is a question that has baffled man for long. Several views have emerged to answer this question, which have led to beliefs that have been adopted by different religions. One is that of the resurrection of the dead at the end of the world on the Day of Judgement to receive eternal rewards and punishments for the deeds done. The second is, of the transmigration of soul. The third view denies the existence of soul and holds that existence comes to an end with death and there is nothing left of the person thereafter to be rewarded or punished. In the last view, there are two opinions—one denies the existence of God also, while the other acknowledges His existence. In the belief of resurrection also, there are two views. In one only the soul is resurrected, while in the other the soul rises along with the same body that it had. It is believed that after death the soul waits for the end of the world, when the Day of Judgement would finally arrive, and it would then rise with the body, as per the Christian belief, to receive judgement from God. As per this judgement, the reward or punishment would last till eternity. The reward promised was a stay in heaven with all possible comforts and pleasures, while the punishment was to burn in the fires of hell, both continuing till eternity. The body would only suffer in the fire of hell but would not be destroyed by it to end the suffering. The objective fixed for a person in such a situation was to do good deeds, especially those declared to be good by the religion so that the reward of going to heaven may be obtained. In the view of the transmigration of the soul, it is believed that after the death of a living being, the soul is born again as another living being with a new body. There is no heaven or hell as the places designated for reward or punishment, but according to the deeds done, the soul is born again in this world only, in a good form or otherwise. This cycle of births and deaths continues till eternity, but it is possible for a soul to come out of this cycle and to be one with God, which is called salvation. The objective fixed for a person in such a situation is to achieve salvation. In a belief wherein the existence of soul is denied but God is acknowledged, the punishments and rewards for the deeds are believed to be in this life itself or on the generations that follow, and for those denying the existence of both soul and God, the world is an open playfield with no judge or controller. Whatever may happen in life remains due to worldly reasons with nobody to reward or punish in this life or anytime thereafter.

Though these beliefs have major contradictions in them, the Jews of the time appear to be holding all the three beliefs. It is strange for groups following the same religion to have such contradictory beliefs on this fundamental issue for a religion, but that is what Judaism had at the time when Christ was born. This emerges from the following passage.

> For the Sadducees say that there is no resurrection, neither angel, nor spirit: but the Pharisees confess both.
> (The Acts 23:8)

Two groups have been named the Sadducees and the Pharisees. The Sadducees are reported to be neither believing in resurrection nor in the soul. They did believe in God as they are reported to be sacrificing to Him, but they did not believe in the angels. Evidently, this was a group that believed that existence ended with death and there was no scope for reward or punishment for the person after he had died. Since they believed in God, the role left for Him to reward and punish, was during their lifetime or to extend it to their children after them. The second group named as the Pharisees are reported to be believing in both, the resurrection and the soul. Paul has stated in the Acts of the Apostles and elsewhere that he was a Pharisee. Thus, his belief from his childhood is clear. No third sect amongst the Jews has been mentioned in the Bible, but the same has been mentioned by other writers, as may be seen from the passages below.

> Josephus in the second book of the history of the Jewish captivity, and in the eighteenth book of the Antiquities, and the two treatises against Apion, describes three sects of the Jews, the Pharisees, Sadducees and Essenes. On the last of these he bestows wondrous praise because they practiced perpetual abstinence from wives, wine and flesh, and made a second nature of their daily fast.
> (*The Writings of the Early Church Fathers*, Vol. 29 Jerome, Writings of Jerome, Book II)

> For there is a division amongst them into three sorts; and the adherents of the first are the Pharisees but of the second the Sadducees, while the rest are the Essenes. These practice a more devotional life, being filled with mutual love, and being temperate. And they turn away from every act of inordinate desire, being averse even to hearing of things of the sort. And they renounce matrimony, but they take the boys of others, and thus have an offspring begotten for them. And they lead these adopted children into an observance of their own peculiar customs, and in this way bring them up and impel them to learn the sciences.
> (*The Writings of the Early Church Fathers*, Vol. 5, Hippolytus, Refutation of all Heresies, Book II, Chapter 13)

The third sect mentioned is of the Essenes. They were, evidently, monks, as they did not marry and led a life of devotion, abstaining from worldly things. Their belief system emerges from the Dead Sea Scrolls, which shows that they had a belief in the transmigration of soul. The prevalence of this view amongst the Jews can be seen in the following passage of the Bible.

> And his disciples asked him, saying, Why then say the scribes that Elias must first come?
> And Jesus answered and said unto them, Elias truly shall first come, and restore all things.
> But I say unto you, That Elias is come already, and they knew him not, but have done unto him whatsoever they listed. Likewise shall also the Son of man suffer of them.
> Then the disciples understood that he spake unto them of John the Baptist.
> (Matthew 17:10–13)

The Jews had a belief that when the Christ shall come, Elias will come before him and make things ready. He was also to introduce him to the people. This shows that at least from the time of Elias, if not earlier, the Jews also had a belief in the existence of the soul and it being born again. Unlike the two names, the Sadducees and the Pharisees, no name is found in the Bible for the group having this belief unless the word 'scribe' is deemed to be so. The word, however, seems to have been used just for the learned and not for any specific group amongst the Jews. Evidently, this was the view of the Essenes. The discussion in this passage is between the Apostles and Jesus. Jesus replies to their query by saying that Elias had already come and the Apostles understood that he was referring to John the Baptist. It is evident that Jesus and his Apostles believed in the transmigration of the soul and not in the other two beliefs that were prevalent amongst the Jews, which the Sadducees and the Pharisees held. This is significant as the Apostolic

Church, as would later be discovered, is found to be having this same belief.

It is against this backdrop that Paul built up the myth of Jesus rising from his grave on the third day after his death and burial. A gradual development in the idea is visible in the Bible, as perhaps the earlier belief of the Pharisees in the resurrection was limited to the resurrection of the soul only. Paul has propounded the resurrection of the body also along with the soul. This is a very difficult concept to defend, as the body is seen to have been destroyed after the death of a person. Paul had to bring in the myth of Jesus rising with his body and showing the same to his disciples, to prove his concept that the body shall also rise to receive the rewards and punishments on resurrection, just as Jesus, too, rose not as a spirit but with his body also. The growth of the myth can be seen by comparing how it has been reported at different places in the Bible. Nowhere has the actual rising of Jesus from the grave been described. What has been stated is what happened after he had supposedly risen, as the sepulchre in which he had been buried was found open and empty. In Matthew, the description can be found in the following passages.

> In the end of the sabbath, as it began to dawn towards the first day of the week, came Mary Magdalene and the other Mary to see the sepulchre.
> And, behold, there was a great earthquake: for the angel of the Lord descended from heaven, and came and rolled back the stone from the door, and sat upon it.
> (Matthew 28:1–2)

> And the angel answered and said unto the women, Fear not ye: for I know that ye seek Jesus, which was crucified.
> He is not here: for he is risen, as he said. Come, see the place where the Lord lay.
> And go quickly, and tell his disciples that he is risen

from the dead; and, behold, he goeth before you into Galilee; there shall ye see him: lo, I have told you.

And they departed quickly from the sepulchre with fear and great joy; and did run to bring his disciples word.

And as they went to tell his disciples, behold, Jesus met them, saying, All hail. And they came and held him by the feet, and worshipped him.

Then said Jesus unto them, Be not afraid: go tell my brethren that they go into Galilee, and there shall they see me.

(Matthew 28:5–10)

Then the 11 disciples went away into Galilee, into a mountain where Jesus had appointed them.

And when they saw him, they worshipped him: but some doubted.

And Jesus came and spoke unto them, saying, All power is given unto me in heaven and in earth.

Go ye therefore, and teach all nations, baptising them in the name of the Father, and of the Son, and of the Holy Ghost.

Teaching them to observe all things whatsoever I have commanded you: and, lo, I am with you always, even unto the end of the world. Amen.

(Matthew 28:16–20)

This account in the Gospel of Matthew is significant, as this was the only gospel that was acknowledged as true by the Ebonites, the followers of the Church of James, which, without dispute, was the Church of the Apostles. The Apostles did not believe in the story of resurrection of Jesus as is clear from Paul's Epistle to the Hebrews wherein this has been stated as a point of doctrine on which they had differences. It also emerges from the First Epistle to the Corinthians, when Paul is found arguing how some have believed that there would be no resurrection. Paul has repeatedly stated in his epistles that Jesus rose from the dead, 'according to my gospel'. His stress that it was according to his gospel shows that the other gospel that he has often referred to, which was the Gospel of the Apostles, did not say so. The interpolations here are evident. The way they have been done reveals the manner in which the original Gospel of Matthew was tampered with. No word appears to have been deleted or amended, even if it left inconsistencies in the account. This would have been important when the believers with the original copies would have questioned those with the interpolated copies. They would have been able to show that their copies contained each word that was there in the copies of those who had the original, only that their copies had more. With this they would have been able to say that the original copies were incomplete and they had the complete text. There is a major inconsistency in the response of the Apostles, as reported in this account. The women have seen the sepulchre empty and have been told that Jesus has risen from the dead. They were further asked to inform the disciples that they should go to Galilee, where they would find him. The natural reaction of anyone on getting the information that the sepulchre, where the body had been laid, is empty would have been to go there to confirm the information. This could not be interpolated in the account, as, evidently, Matthew had recorded that the 11 disciples had gone away to Galilee to the mountain where Jesus used to meet them earlier. The interpolators had no option to leave this inconsistency, as they could not delete or modify what was already there.

Matthew appears to have given an account of an absolutely normal situation. The day after the burial was a Sabbath, so nobody could go to the grave, but as soon as the Sabbath was over, the women went to mourn. The Apostles had a threat to their life, as is evident from the description of the arrest of

Jesus, where he asks the soldiers to let them go. None of them was present at his burial and during the crucifixion; only John has claimed in his gospel that he was there. This claim seems to be dubious not only because the said gospel does not appear to have been written by the Apostle but also because of his absence during the burial. If he had been present during the crucifixion, he should have taken a leading role in his burial, which was done by Joseph, a stranger who shared his name with Christ's father. Once they had fled Jerusalem, they returned to their native place Galilee and went to the place that they used to visit with Christ. There they worshipped him as their teacher. Some felt his presence, while others doubted the same. It is the Apostles that Matthew refers to when he talks of the doubting followers. It is an absolutely normal situation in which interpolations have been brought in, which, too, seems to have been incorporated in stages to cover each point of doubt or confusion that may have cropped up because of an incomplete statement. In the first part of interpolation, the angel has told the women that Jesus has risen from the dead and has asked them to rush to the disciples and inform them that he is going to Galilee, where they would see him. The women, accordingly, are reported to have run to inform the disciples, though even this was not necessary, as Jesus has been reported to have himself told earlier that he would go to Galilee after he has risen from the dead. The account so far brings in the concept of resurrection but still falls short of the resurrection of the body, for which a further interpolation was brought in, perhaps at a later date. In this, the women meet Jesus on the way to the disciples. They hold his feet and worship him, while he asks them to go to the disciples to tell them to go to Galilee. With this, Jesus in his physical body has been established, and to confirm the same, his feet have been held. But the women had already been told by the angel to tell the disciples that Jesus had gone to Galilee and they would see him there. Since no new reason could be invented, as Matthew had already recorded that the 11 disciples had gone away to Galilee, Jesus has been shown to have told them the same thing. The purpose was to establish that Jesus rose from the dead, not as a spirit, but with his body.

At Galilee, too, Matthew appears to have ended with the statement that when the Apostles saw him, they worshipped him, but some doubted. On the point of this doubt by the Apostles, an incident of Thomas has been recorded in another gospel to show that doubt could have remained even after bearing witness to the incidents. However, as some of the Apostles doubted his presence, it is evident that he did not appear as a physical entity. It was only a feeling amongst some of them that he was present in spirit. To this, an interpolation has been added that he came and spoke to them. Again, the element of his physical presence has been brought in. This is in contradiction to what was stated in the previous line, where he was in such a state that some doubted that he was there at all. The account proceeds to say that Jesus asked them to teach all nations. Jesus, after resurrection, has, thus, contradicted the living Jesus. While alive, he sent out his disciples to preach only amongst the Jews, asking them to stay away not only from the Gentiles but even from the Samaritans, who were from the children of Jacob. Asking them to teach all nations is an interpolation and is untrue, because if Jesus had even at this stage asked the Apostles to teach all nations, they would have preached amongst the Gentiles from the very beginning. There is plenty of evidence to show that in the beginning they were preaching only amongst the Jews and it was only after some time, perhaps due to the influence of Paul, that they started preaching amongst others also. If this command of Jesus to the Apostles is deemed to be true, it will also negate the claim of Paul that he was the Apostle of Gentiles, while Peter was that of the circumcision, because then there would be no such division, and Peter, as he was considered as the chief amongst the Apostles, would have been the Apostle of all, whether Gentiles or Jews. It is evident that the persons who were interpolating were focused on a single point and wished to establish it, for which they did not take care to ensure that something else may not get contradicted by the introduction of a new statement.

Mark seems to have found the disciples' journey to Galilee and their worshipping Jesus on the mountain to be unimportant for inclusion in the Greek summary of the Gospel of Matthew. He seems to have ended his narrative with the burial where Mary Magdalene and Mary the mother of Joses were present. This provided scope for adding the account of the resurrection without being impeded by the conclusion already recorded by the evangelist. The account given in the said gospel is in the passage below.

> And when the sabbath was past, Mary Magdalene, and Mary the mother of James, and Salome, had brought sweet spices, that they might come and anoint him.
>
> And very early in the morning the first day of the week, they came unto the sepulchre at the rising of the sun.
>
> And they said among themselves, Who shall roll us away the stone from the door of the sepulchre?
>
> And when they looked, they saw that the stone was rolled away: for it was very great.
>
> And entering into the sepulchre, they saw a young man sitting on the right side, clothed in a long white garment; and they were affrighted.
>
> And he saith unto them, Be not affrighted: Ye seek Jesus of Nazareth, which was crucified: he is risen; he is not here: behold the place where they laid him.
>
> But go your way, tell his disciples and Peter that he goeth before you into Galilee: there shall ye see him, as he said unto you.

And they went out quickly, and fled from the sepulchre; for they trembled and were amazed: neither said they any thing to any man; for they were afraid.

Now when Jesus was risen early the first day of the week, he appeared first to Mary Magdalene, out of whom he had cast seven devils.

And she went and told them that had been with him, as they mourned and wept.

And they, when they had heard that he was alive, and had been seen of her, believed not.

After that he appeared in another form unto two of them, as they walked, and went into the country.

And they went and told it unto the residue: neither believed they them.

Afterward he appeared unto the eleven as they sat at meat, and upbraided them with their unbelief and hardness of heart, because they believed not them which had seen him after he was risen.

And he said unto them, Go ye into all the world, and preach the gospel to every creature.

He that believeth and is baptized shall be saved; but he that believeth not shall be damned.

And these signs shall follow them that believe; In my name shall they cast out devils; they shall speak with new tongues;

They shall take up serpents; and if they drink any deadly thing, it shall not hurt them; they shall lay hands on the sick, and they shall recover.

So then after the Lord had spoken unto them, he was received up into heaven, and sat on the right hand of God.

And they went forth, and preached everywhere, the Lord working with them, and confirming the word with signs following. Amen.

(Mark 16:1–20)

A plain reading of this account shows that it has been recorded by more than one person and at different times. The recording is such that it describes something already mentioned elsewhere in the Bible but does not take the narrative to its logical conclusion, leaving contradictions within what is being stated as well as with what has been stated elsewhere. Like Matthew, here also two Marys are reported to have gone to the sepulchre. Mark has reported only these two to have been present at the crucifixion also. Matthew's report for those present at the crucifixion are 'Mary Magdalene, and the Mary the mother of James and Joses, and the mother of Zebedee's children'. This gives an impression that there were three Marys, but while stating the names of the persons who went to the sepulchre, he says 'Mary Magdalene and the other Mary', which makes it evident that Mary the mother of James and Joses, and the mother of Zebedee's children is one and the same person. There would, thus, be only two Marys and not three. Mary, the mother of Jesus, is not reported in these two gospels to have been present at the time of the crucifixion or to have gone to the sepulchre when Jesus is reported to have risen from the dead. In the zeal to write something new, the interpolator has added that the two Marys went to the sepulchre with sweet spices so that they may anoint him. Matthew had simply recorded that they went to the sepulchre without giving a reason, which can be deemed to have been to mourn at the grave. By adding that their intention was to anoint the body, a very odd reason has been recorded. Jesus had died and had been buried for two days. In all communities wherein the body is anointed, the same is done before it is buried. A body cannot be brought out of the grave after two days to be anointed. The account proceeds to claim that the two women found the sepulchre open and on entering, found a young man sitting in a long white garment, who told them that Jesus had risen and asked them to tell the disciples that he has gone to Galilee and that they would see him there. The woman were afraid and ran away from there and in their fear told nobody about it, not even the Apostles to whom they were supposed to deliver this message.

The narrative of the first interpolator seems to end at this point. With this, though it seems unnatural for the two Marys to have not gone to the Apostles to tell them of what had happened, it removes the inconsistency in the reporting found in Matthew, where it is stated that the Apostles, on coming to know of the body of Jesus not being in the sepulchre, did not go there themselves to see what had happened but had gone away to Galilee. Here they were not informed by the witnesses and were already on their way to Galilee, so there was no reason for them to come back to check the sepulchre from where the body of Christ had disappeared. They already knew that Jesus would meet them at Galilee, as he had said so while he was alive and there was no need for the angel or the young man clothed in a long white garment to send this information to them through the two women who went to the sepulchre as soon as Sabbath was over. It appears that this narrative was added in the Gospel of Mark after people questioned the logic of the narrative of Matthew wherein the Apostles were unaffected by the report of Jesus's body being missing from the sepulchre and proceeded to Galilee.

With the narrative by the first interpolator ending with the statement that the two women ran out of the sepulchre and, though asked to inform the Apostles, did not say anything to anyone because of their fear, a fresh narrative starts thereafter by the second interpolator. He begins the story afresh by recounting the people to whom Jesus had appeared after his resurrection. This part is aimed at showing that the Apostles did not believe that Christ had risen even after they had been told by people who had seen him, till he appeared to them also and rebuked them for their disbelief. It was Paul who had been propounding amongst the Christians the theory of resurrection as believed by the Pharisees, and to support that, it was he who needed to create evidence in the form of the resurrection of Christ. The Apostles, evidently, did not believe in this till the end, so the narrative in Mark is to show how they had refused to believe even when witnesses told them of it. Contradictions have cropped up in doing so. It is reported that after Jesus had risen, he first appeared to Mary Magdalene, and she went and told this to 'them that had been with him', but they did not believe it. The first narrative shows Mary Magdalene and Mary the mother of James, and Salome had gone to the sepulchre, where a young man clothed in white garments told them that Jesus had risen from the dead and would be seen in Galilee. There were two Marys, and they remained together, while Jesus did not appear to them in this narrative. Matthew has recorded that he appeared to them on the way, and they worshipped him, holding his feet. Here, too, both women were together and Jesus appeared to both of them. Mary Magdalene has not been described as being alone at any stage in these two gospels, and there is no mention of Jesus to have appeared to her, yet while recounting the people to whom he appeared, she alone is named. The account proceeds to state that she went and told this to 'them that had been with him', an obvious reference to the Apostles, and they did not believe her. Here, it has not been stated that she had found the sepulchre empty but only that Jesus had appeared to her, because of which it cannot be said that the Apostles did not go to see the sepulchre for themselves.

Next, after Mary Magdalene, the account states that Jesus appeared in another form to two of the Apostles as they walked in the countryside, but when they went back and informed the rest, they did not believe them. The stress again is on the Apostles refusing to believe that Jesus had risen from the dead, though in this instance, he had not appeared in his own body but in a different form. This recording appears to be of a stage when Paul had not crystallized his idea of resurrection. The idea of the resurrection of the body also, on the Day of Judgement, seems to have developed in him gradually. It seems that initially it was only resurrection, which would have remained only of the soul, but on repeated questioning, it became of the body also. The appearance of Christ in any different forms would not support the resurrection of the body. The account does not shed light on how the two Apostles were able to recognize him when he had appeared in a different form.

The narration reaches the last of the people to whom Jesus had appeared on rising from the dead. It is the 11 Apostles who remained after Judas, the twelfth, had left the company and was reported to have committed suicide. The place where he appeared has not been reported, as it has just been stated 'as they sat at meat.' He is reported to have upbraided them for their refusal to believe that he had risen, even when those who had seen him had reported it to them. These 11 include the two who had seen Jesus and had reported of it to the rest but were not believed. He further commanded them to preach the gospel to every creature. This is the same as has been recorded by Matthew that he commanded that they preach to all nations, contradicting the command of the living Jesus. The account further provides the signs of a true believer, which, fortunately, no Christian would have tried to test their faith, and concludes with a report that after speaking to the Apostles in this manner, Jesus was received into the heaven and sat on the right hand of God.

This final interpolation in Mark, thus, gives a complete account of all the occasions on which Jesus was believed to have appeared up to the time when it was recorded, as it was intended to be a recapitulation of all such instances. All stories of his appearance, other than these three occasions, would have to be believed to have been developed after this account had been recorded. Compared with Matthew, this has one additional occasion where Jesus is reported to have appeared in a different form to two of his disciples. The place where he appeared to the Apostles is also different—in Matthew they were praying on the mountain in Galilee when he appeared, while here 'they sat at meat'. How he appeared to Mary Magdalene has not been reported in Mark, while in Matthew he appeared to the two Marys on the way. While noticing these contradictions, it has to be appreciated that these writers did not have the luxury of having the complete Bible before them, duly bound into a volume wherein the pages could be flipped to go to Matthew or Mark or anywhere else. They had individual gospels before them, in which they were incorporating stories to establish a particular concept, and were not in position to compare it with the rest. Truth and truth alone could have withstood the test in such diverse recordings, which apparently was an unfortunate casualty in Paul's struggle to establish concepts that were contradictory to what the Apostles were preaching.

Luke was a disciple of Paul. His gospel is the Gospel of Paul, which he has mentioned in his epistles. As the entire gospel has been recorded independently, there was no necessity in it to maintain unchanged what had already been recorded by the original writer and to synchronize the new statements with it. His account is recorded in the passage below.

> Now upon the first day of the week, very early in the morning, they came unto the sepulchre bringing the spices which they had prepared, and certain others with them.
> And they found the stone rolled away from the sepulchre.
> And they entered in, and found not the body of the Lord Jesus.
> And it came to pass, as they were much perplexed thereabout, behold two men stood by them in shining garments:
> And as they were afraid, and bowed down their faces

to the earth, they said unto them, Why seek ye the living among the dead?

He is not here, but is risen: remember how he spake unto you when he was yet in Galilee,

Saying, the Son of man must be delivered into the hands of sinful men, and be crucified, and the third day rise again.

And they remembered his words,

And returned from the sepulchre, and told all these things unto the eleven, and to all the rest.

It was Mary Magdalene, and Joanna, and Mary the mother of James, and other women that were with them, which told these things unto the apostles.

And their words seemed to them idle tales, and they believed them not.

Then arose Peter, and ran unto the sepulchre; and stooping down, he beheld the linen clothes laid by themselves, and departed, wondering in himself at that which was come to pass.

And, behold, two of them went that same day to a village called Emmaus, which was from Jerusalem about three score furlongs.

And they talked together of all these things which had happened.

And it came to pass, that, while they communed together and reasoned, Jesus himself drew near, and went with them.

But their eyes were holden that they should not know him.

And he said unto them, What manner of communications are these that ye have one to another, as ye walk, and are sad?

And one of them, whose name was Cleopas, answering said unto him, Art thou only a stranger in Jerusalem, and hast not known the things which are come to pass therein these days?

And he said unto them, what things? And they said unto him, Concerning Jesus of Nazareth, which was a prophet mighty in deed and word before God and all the people:

And how the chief priests and our rulers delivered him to be condemned to death, and have crucified him.

But we trusted that it had been he which should have redeemed Israel: and beside all this, to day is the third day since these things were done.

Yea, and certain women also of our company made us astonished, which were early at the sepulchre;

And when they found not his body, they came, saying, that they had also seen a vision of angels, which said that he was alive.

And certain of them which were with us went to the sepulchre, and found it even so as the women had said: but him they saw not.

Then he said unto them, O fools, and slow of heart to believe all that the prophets have spoken:

Ought not Christ to have suffered these things, and to enter into his glory?

And beginning at Moses and all the prophets, he expounded unto them in all the scriptures the things concerning himself.

And they drew nigh unto the village, whither they went: and he made as though he would have gone further.

But they constrained him, saying, Abide with us: for it is toward evening, and day is far spent. And he went in to tarry with them.

And it came to pass, as he sat at meat with them, he took bread, and blessed it, and brake, and gave to them.

And their eyes were opened, and they knew him; and

he vanished out of their sight.

And they said one to another; Did not our heart burn within us, while he talked with us by the way, and while he opened to us the scriptures?

And they rose up the same hour, and returned to Jerusalem, and found the eleven gathered together, and them that were with them.

Saying, the Lord is risen indeed, and hath appeared to Simon.

And they told what things were done in the way, and how he was known of them in breaking of bread.

And as they thus spake, Jesus himself stood in the midst of them, and saith unto them, Peace be unto you.

But they were terrified and affrighted, and supposed that they had seen a spirit.

And he said unto them, Why are ye troubled? and why do thoughts arise in your hearts?

Behold my hands and my feet, that it is I myself: handle me, and see; for a spirit hath not flesh and bones, as ye see me have.

And when he had thus spoken, he shewed them his hands and his feet.

And while they yet believed not for joy, and wondered, he said unto them, Have ye here any meat?

And they gave him a piece of a broiled fish, and of an honeycomb.

And he took it, and did eat before them.

And he said unto them, These are the words which I spake unto you, while I was yet with you, that all things must be fulfilled, which were written in the law of Moses, and in the prophets, and in the psalms, concerning me.

Then opened he their understanding, that they might understand the scriptures,

And said unto them, Thus it is written, and thus it

behoved Christ to suffer, and to rise from the dead the third day:

And that repentance and remission of sins should be preached in his name among all nations, beginning at Jerusalem.

And ye are witnesses of these things.

And, behold, I send the promise of my Father upon you: but tarry ye in the city of Jerusalem, until ye be endued with power from on high.

And he led them out as far as to Bethany, and he lifted up his hands, and blessed them.

And it came to pass, while he blessed them, he was parted from them, and carried up into heaven.

And they worshipped him, and returned to Jerusalem with great joy:

And were continually in temple, praising and blessing God. Amen.

(Luke 24:1–53)

Luke has reported that the women who had followed Jesus from Galilee were present at the time of crucifixion. Matthew and Mark bear no mention of anyone who followed Jesus and his 12 disciples from Galilee. Even Luke, in his narrative of the events as they unfolded from their arrival in the vicinity of Jerusalem, does not mention these women till they are said to be present at the crucifixion. These women are reported to have gone to the sepulchre with spices on the first day of the week. The purpose of carrying spices has not been mentioned. Amongst these women are named Mary Magdalene, Joanna and Mary, the mother of James. Even Luke has not mentioned that Mary, the mother of Jesus, was present on this occasion. Matthew, in his recording of the gospel, had stated that the Apostles had gone away to Galilee and worshipped Jesus on a mountain and while some believed he was there, some doubted.

As this could not be changed, the interaction of Christ with his disciples has been shown at Galilee only. Although for them to go to Galilee was the most obvious decision, to escape the danger to their own lives in Jerusalem, Luke has not mentioned Galilee at all, and all events are reported to have happened in and around Jerusalem. As per his account, they stayed back at Jerusalem, though they were not present at the crucifixion or the burial of Jesus.

The women are reported to have gone to the sepulchre, which they found open. They entered and found that the body of Jesus was not there. Instead, they find two men standing in shining garments, who tell them that Jesus had risen as he had said earlier. Christ does not appear to these women, only two men in shining garments do. Unlike in Matthew and Mark wherein the women were told to inform the Apostles that Jesus would see them in Galilee, these men only inform the women that he had risen. They inform the Apostles of what had happened but are not believed. The writer was so focused on the point of Jesus rising from the dead that the disappearance of the body from the sepulchre was lost to him. The open sepulchre and the missing body are physical events that can happen even for reasons other than the dead coming alive and walking out of the grave. There could not have been any reason for someone to disbelieve such a report outright, but because Luke was so focused on establishing the Apostles' disbelief in the resurrection of Christ that even when they were told about the missing body, this has been reported to have been rejected by them. Finally, only Peter is reported to have gone to the sepulchre to see for himself what had been reported. On seeing the sepulchre empty, he is reported to have departed wondering what had happened. This is an unnatural reaction on the part of Peter because even if a person does not believe that the dead has risen, the absence of the body has to be a matter of concern.

Having reported Peter's examination of the sepulchre and having found it empty, the narration moves to the two disciples encountering Jesus while walking in the countryside. In this, Jesus is not recognized by them, which shows that he was not in his own body. He tells them that whatever had happened had happened to fulfil the prophecies that had been made by the prophets since the times of Moses. The disciples recognize him only when he broke the bread and gave it to them. Once he was recognized, Jesus vanished from their sight. This appearance of Jesus would not support the theory of resurrection of the body along with the soul, as he did not appear in his own body. For this, the next appearance follows immediately thereafter. It is reported that as the two disciples were narrating their encounter with Jesus to the remaining Apostles and others, Jesus appeared in their midst and asked them to see his hands and feet to be sure that he had a body because a spirit does not have hands and feet. To establish the presence of his body further, he asks for food and eats a piece of broiled fish and honeycomb that is given to him. He tells them that the prophecies about him had to be fulfilled, for which he went through all that he had suffered. He commands them to preach amongst all nations and then walks over to Bethany, from where he is carried into heaven.

If the accounts given in these three gospels are compared, the summary given in Mark of all the appearances of Jesus seems to be the summary of Luke's account, with the exception that Mary Magdalene is also reported to have seen him. This may have been an error on the part of the person summarising what Luke had written, and the two men in the sepulchre may have been mistakenly reported as the appearance of Jesus. The women have been reported in Mark also to have gone to the sepulchre with spices, though there the purpose is clearly stated, while Luke does not mention it. The account in Matthew places the Apostles on a mountain in Galilee when Jesus appeared to them, while Luke gives the place to be Jerusalem. Mark is silent on this point. Matthew does not say that after meeting and commanding the Apostles to preach amongst all nations, Jesus rose to heaven, while Mark and Luke say so. Mark, just as he is silent about the place where Jesus appeared to the Apostles, is also silent about the place from where Jesus ascended to heaven. Luke states that he walked over to Bethany and ascended to heaven from there. The command to preach amongst all nations is common in all three gospels, which is in contradiction to the commands of the living Jesus. In effect, Mark, who was the 'summarist' of Matthew in translating his gospel into Greek, has been made a 'summarist' of Luke when it came to reporting of the resurrection of Jesus.

The last gospel is attributed to John. It does not seem to be so and appears to be late composition in which several things have been added to support certain beliefs in the gospel that had developed amongst the Christians by then and to provide an explanation for statements that had been made earlier. Unlike the other gospels, John mentions that Mary, the mother of Jesus, was present at the crucifixion of Christ. He also claims that he himself was also present. None of the other evangelists have said this, and both assertions appear to be untrue. Mary would have been far away in Galilee and could not have been in Jerusalem. Though Luke says that some women followed Jesus from Galilee, even he does not mention that Mary was one of them. Till a day earlier, when Jesus is reported to be observing the Passover, he is reported to have been with only his disciples, and there is no mention of his mother being present even in the account of John. It seems likely that the cult of Mary had by then begun to emerge in the Pauline Church, for which Mary was introduced by John at the crucifixion of Jesus as an expression of her motherly love towards him. Jesus told John, 'Behold thy mother', thus making Mary a mother figure for the church. In describing the resurrection of Christ, John appears to be trying to remove the discrepancies that had been left in the records made by others till then. This may be seen in the passages below.

The first day of the week cometh Mary Magdalene early, when it was yet dark, unto the sepulchre, and seeth the stone taken away from the sepulchre.

Then she runneth, and cometh to Simon Peter, and to the other disciple, whom Jesus loved, and saith unto them, They have taken away the Lord out of the sepulchre and we know not where they have laid him.

Peter therefore went forth, and that other disciple, and came to the sepulchre.

So they ran both together: and the other disciple did outrun Peter, and came first to the sepulchre.

And he stooping down, and looking in, saw the linen clothes lying; yet went he not in.

Then came Simon Peter following him, and went into the sepulchre, and seeth the linen clothes lie,

And the napkin, that was about his head, not lying with the linen clothes, but wrapped together in a place by itself.

Then went in also the other disciple, which came first to the sepulchre, and he saw, and believed.

For as yet they knew not the scripture, that he must rise again from the dead.

Then the disciples went away again unto their own home.

But Mary stood without at the sepulchre weeping: and as she wept, she stooped down, and looked into the sepulchre,

And seeth two angels in white sitting, the one at the head, and the other at the feet, where the body of Jesus had lain.

And they say unto her, Woman why weepest thou? She

saith unto them, Because they have taken away my Lord, and I know not where they have laid him.

And when she had thus said, she turned herself back, and saw Jesus standing, and knew not it was Jesus.

Jesus saith unto her, Woman, why weepest thou? whom seekest thou? She, supposing him to be the gardener, saith unto him, Sir, if thou have borne him hence, tell we where thou hast laid him, and I will take him away.

Jesus saith unto her, Mary. She turned herself, and saith unto him, Rabboni; which is to say, Master.

Jesus saith unto her, Touch me not; for I am not yet ascended to my Father: but go to my brethren, and say unto them, I ascend unto my Father, and your Father; and to my God, and your God.

Mary Magdalene came and told the disciples that she had seen the Lord, and that he had spoken these things unto her.

Then the same day at evening, being the first day of the week, when the doors were shut where the disciples were assembled for fear of the Jews, came Jesus and stood in the midst, and saith unto them, Peace be unto you.

And when he had so said, he shewed unto them his hands and his side. Then were the disciples glad, when they saw the Lord.

Then said Jesus to them again, Peace be unto you: as my Father hath sent me, even so send I you.

And when he had said this, he breathed on them, and saith unto them, receive ye the Holy Ghost:

Whose soever sins ye remit, they are remitted unto them; and whose soever sins ye retain, they are retained.

But Thomas, one of the twelve, called Didymus, was not with them when Jesus came.

The other disciples therefore said unto him, We have seen the Lord. But he said unto them, Except I shall see in his hands the print of the nails, and put my finger into the print of the nails, and thrust my hand into his side, I will not believe.

And after eight days again his disciples were within, and Thomas with them: then came Jesus, the doors being shut, and stood in the midst, and said, Peace be unto you.

Then saith he to Thomas, reach hither thy finger, and behold my hands; and reach hither thy hand, and thrust it into my side: and be not faithless, but believing

And Thomas answered and said unto him, My Lord and my God.

Jesus saith unto him, Thomas, because thou hast seen me, thou hast believed: blessed are they that have not seen, and yet have believed.

And many other signs truly did Jesus in the presence of his disciples, which are not written in this book:

But these are written, that ye might believe that Jesus is the Christ, the Son of God; and that believing ye might have life through his name.

(John 20:1–31)

After these things Jesus shewed himself again to the disciples at the sea of Tiberias; and on this wise shewed he himself.

These were together Simon Peter, and Thomas called Didymus, and Nathanael of Cana in Galilee, and the sons of Zebedee, and two other of his disciples.

Simon Peter saith unto them, I go a fishing. They say unto him, We also go with thee. They went forth, and entered into a ship immediately; and that night they caught nothing.

But when the morning was now come, Jesus stood on the shore: but the disciples knew not that it was Jesus.

Then Jesus saith unto them, Children, have ye any meat? They answered him, No.

And he said unto them, Cast the net on the right side of the ship, and ye shall find. They cast therefore, and now they were not able to draw it for the multitude of fishes.

Therefore that disciple whom Jesus loved saith unto Peter, It is the Lord. Now when Simon Peter heard that it was the Lord, he girt his fisher's coat unto him, (for he was naked,) and did cast himself into the sea.

And the other disciples came in a little ship; (for they were not far from land, but as it were two hundred cubits,) dragging the net with fishes.

As soon then as they were come to land, they saw a fire of coals there, and fish laid thereon, and bread.

Jesus saith unto them, Bring of the fish which ye have now caught.

Simon Peter went up, and drew the net to land full of great fishes, an hundred and fifty and three: and for all there were so many, yet was not the net broken.

Jesus saith unto them, Come and dine. And none of the disciples durst ask him, Who art thou? Knowing that it was the Lord.

Jesus then cometh, and taketh bread, and giveth them, fish likewise.

This is now the third time that Jesus shewed himself to his disciples, after that he was risen from the dead.

(John 21:1–14)

In this account, it is Mary Magdalene alone who has been reported to have gone to the sepulchre. The other Mary who had accompanied her, according to the accounts of Matthew and Mark, and who, according to Luke, had accompanied Mary along with Joanna, is not mentioned by John. Even Mary, the mother of Jesus, who had been reported in this gospel to have been present at the crucifixion, is not seen going to the sepulchre. In fact, after the crucifixion, she does not find mention in the gospel. As this is not a natural behaviour for a mother, it seems likely that the mention of Mary, the mother of Jesus's, presence at the crucifixion of Christ is a later interpolation.

Mary Magdalene finds the sepulchre open and runs back to inform Peter and John of the same, who run to the place and find the body missing from it. The writer is so focused on trying to establish the belief in resurrection that when he mentions that John went into the sepulchre, it has been stated, 'he saw, and believed'. There was nothing to believe as yet because only the body was missing. Jesus had not appeared to anyone after his death till then nor had an angel informed of his rising, as per his account. It is stated further that Peter and John returned home after finding the sepulchre empty. This is an unexpected behaviour, given the circumstance. There was no effort on their part to enquire of the same, and they left quietly, which gives the impression as if they were aware of the story ahead that the dead would rise and would be coming to see them. Mary Magdalene alone is left behind to search for the body, and Jesus appears before her. One can glean that he has not appeared in his own form because Mary Magdalene is unable to recognize him. She identifies him only when he calls out her name. This appearance of Jesus to Mary Magdalene alone clears the position that had been created by Mark in his reporting of the appearances of Jesus after his death. He had stated that first he appeared to Mary Magdalene, next to the two disciples walking in the countryside and, last, to the Apostles. It was only in Matthew that it had been reported that Jesus appeared to Mary Magdalene, but there, the other Mary was also present. This discrepancy seems to have been a point of debate in the early years of Christian belief. John seems to have built up a story of Mary Magdalene going to the sepulchre alone to clear this very issue.

As noted previously, Peter and John have been reported

to have returned home. They were from Galilee and did not have a home in Jerusalem, where Jesus had been crucified and buried. They were poor people and could not afford to even hire a place for themselves, which is evident from the fact that after the feast of the Passover, Jesus, with his disciples, had gone out of the town to a garden. They were not found by the soldiers sleeping in an inn, but in a garden, under the open sky, when Jesus was arrested. Moreover, as disciples of Jesus, there was a threat to their lives too. Given this context, it is odd that the Gospel of John has stated that they went back home to Jerusalem. In the earlier gospels, a house has not been mentioned for the Apostles in Jerusalem. It should be noted though that such an impression has been given by Mark and Luke, who claimed that Jesus appeared behind closed doors. John makes it explicit.

Jesus, after Mary Magdalene recognizes him, tells her 'touch me not; for I am not yet ascended to my Father: but go to my brethren, and say unto them, I ascend to my Father, and your Father; and to my God, and your God.' Here, Jesus has restrained Mary Magdalene from touching him. The reason given is that he had not yet ascended to his Father. The writer has given an impression that Jesus would have allowed her to touch him only after he had ascended to his Father. How could Mary Magdalene have reached there? He has further asked her to tell his disciples that he ascends to his Father and their Father. Jesus has not asked her to tell them that he would be seeing them, whether at Galilee or elsewhere, but only that he 'ascends'. By saying 'my Father and your Father', he has also removed the distinction between himself and the disciples. This is not exactly in line with the Pauline theology, which treats Christ to be the Son of God, so at par with God, while there is an unbridgeable chasm between the Creator and the creation.

The account proceeds to say that Jesus appeared to the

Apostles that same evening when they were assembled and the doors were shut. It confirms that they were living in a house. There he breathed on them and said 'Receive ye the Holy Ghost'. He further said that whose sins they remitted, their sins would be remitted and of those they retained, they would be retained. The Church developed a concept that it had the power to remit sins. This concept, however, had not emerged so early to have been a part of the gospel. It is evident that this was incorporated much later to provide a sanction for it straight from Christ.

After this appearance, which was in the evening on the day when his sepulchre was found empty, Jesus appeared to the disciples a second time after eight days. The sole reason for this was that Thomas was not there on the first occasion, and when he was informed of his appearance, he declared that he would not believe unless he sees in his hands the print of the nails and thrusts his hand into his side. Jesus appeared again when the doors were shut and asked Thomas to see his hands and to thrust his hand into his side. This is, evidently, an effort to establish the theory of the resurrection of the body beyond any doubt and also to efface the effect of the Apostles not believing, as was reported by Matthew. In the other gospels, the Apostles were able to only see Jesus after he had risen from the dead. In this, one of them had been given the opportunity to even touch him to be sure that it was a physical body. Jesus here has asked Thomas to touch him, while a little while ago he had refrained Mary Magdalene from doing so because he had not yet ascended to his Father. He had not ascended even now, but no reason has been given for this change of heart. Chrysostom has struggled in his Homily to explain this. Jesus has proceeded to tell Thomas that he believed because he saw, but blessed are they who have not seen and yet believe. It is an exhortation to people to believe in the resurrection of Christ and in the theory of resurrection instead of being a doubting

Thomas, and with this the doubts of some of the Apostles, as mentioned by Matthew, have also been taken care of.

The Gospel of John, when it was originally written, appears to have ended with the twentieth chapter, as the last two paragraphs of the said chapter, as quoted above, give a conclusion. It is stated therein that Jesus did give many other signs in the presence of the Apostles, which have not been recorded, and those that have been recorded have been written so that people may believe that Jesus is the Christ, the Son of God, and by believing in Him, they may attain an eternal life on the Day of Judgement. These are the parting statements of the writer. However, after the said conclusion, there is one more chapter in the gospel. In this, another appearance of Jesus has been recorded, this time on the sea of Tiberias in Galilee. Only seven Apostles are reported to have been present there. It has not been mentioned where the remaining four were or how these seven reached Galilee, because they were in Jerusalem on the earlier occasion and Jesus had reportedly asked them to stay in Jerusalem.

The incident reported at the sea of Tiberius does not have Jesus in his own body, as he is not recognized by the disciples. The seven disciples had gone out fishing at night and had not been able to catch any fish. In the morning, Jesus was seen standing on the shore. He asks them to cast the net on the right side of the ship, and when they did so, a lot of fishes were caught. By this, John is reported to have recognized the man on the shore to be Jesus. When all seven disciples reach the shore, they find a fire of coal with fish and bread laid on it. Though fish was already there on the fire, Jesus asks for more fish and calls them to dine with him. The narrative continues with Jesus asking Peter to feed his sheep, telling him how he would die by being crucified and light-heartedly refusing to say how John would meet his death. The chapter ends with the writer testifying that he is John and concludes by stating that Jesus did many more things, which, if written, could not be contained in the books.

As the story mentions that Jesus told Peter that he would die by being crucified, this is evidently an interpolation made after the myth of Peter having being crucified in Rome had been developed. Peter was not crucified, neither in Rome nor anywhere else, as would be discovered later. It is difficult to understand why this appearance of Jesus has been added in the gospel, because by doing so, the seven Apostles are shown to have disobeyed Jesus, who has been reported to have asked them to continue to stay in Jerusalem. This has been maintained in the Acts of the Apostles also, where it is reported that all the Apostles continued to stay in Jerusalem, along with the women, who included Mary, the mother of Jesus. It is possible that someone included this to synthesize all the reports of his appearance after the resurrection. In the Gospel of Matthew, it had been reported that Jesus appeared to his disciples in Galilee. It must have been in circulation amongst the believers that apart from appearing in Jerusalem, he had also appeared to the Apostles in Galilee. As the Gospel of Matthew, with this story in it, would not have been available, a story was built up. There would not have been a way to know that in Matthew he had been reported to have appeared on a mountain. As the sea is that most prominent feature of Galilee, the location was given there. The manner in which Jesus has been shown to have appeared is also odd. On all other occasions, he has just appeared or, at best, on one occasion, has asked for food and eaten broiled fish and honeycomb. In this case, he has been shown to have come only to give the seven Apostles a sumptuous breakfast after a fruitless night of hard labour. He is shown to be ready with a fire of coal, with bread and fish laid on it. As Matthew had reported that some of the Apostles doubted that Jesus was present at the place, Jesus here is not shown as his own person but as someone else.

Apart from the gospels, the resurrection of Jesus has been described elsewhere, too, in the Bible—in the Acts of the Apostles and in one of the epistles of Paul. The following passages are from the Acts of the Apostles.

Until the day in which he was taken up, after that he through the Holy Ghost had given commandments unto the apostles whom he had chosen:

To whom also he shewed himself alive after his passion by many infallible proofs, being seen of them forty days, and speaking of the things pertaining to the kingdom of God:

And, being assembled together with them, commanded them that they should not depart from Jerusalem, but wait for the promise of the Father, which, saith he, ye have heard of me.

For John truly baptized with water; but ye shall be baptized with the Holy Ghost not many days hence.

(The Acts 1:2–5)

But ye shall receive power, after that the Holy Ghost is come upon you: and ye shall be witnesses unto me both in Jerusalem, and in all Judea, and in Samaria, and unto the uttermost part of the earth.

And when he had spoken these things, while they beheld, he was taken up; and a cloud received him out of their sight.

And while they looked steadfastly toward heaven as he went up, behold, two men stood by them in white apparel;

Which also said, Ye men of Galilee, why stand ye gazing up into heaven? This same Jesus, which is taken up from you into heaven, shall so come in like manner as ye have seen him go into heaven.

Then returned they unto Jerusalem from the mount

called Olivet, which is from Jerusalem a sabbath day's journey.

(The Acts 1:8–12)

Here it has been reported that Jesus kept appearing to the Apostles for 40 days, though the number of such appearances have not been mentioned. The figure of 40 days cannot be found in the gospels. In Matthew, it has only been reported that when the Apostles returned to Galilee, they prayed to him on the mountain, and Jesus spoke to them. The account ends there and does not speak of his ascension to heaven, though it is implied that this must have happened immediately thereafter. In Mark, the appearances are given as if they were by way of recapitulation. He is reported to have ascended to heaven after his last meeting with all the Apostles, after having appeared earlier to Mary Magdalene and the two disciples. Though Mark does not note the time and place of these three appearances, he gives an impression that all three occurred on the same day—the day on which the sepulchre was found empty. Luke is specific on this point. He has not mentioned that Jesus appeared to Mary Magdalene, but has stated that on the same day on which the sepulchre was found empty, he was seen by the two disciples and then again by all the Apostles together, after which he walked with them to Bethany and was carried up into heaven. Bethany and Mount Olivet may be taken to be the same since Bethany is on the slopes of Mount Olivet. As per this account, he rose from the dead and, on the same day, ascended to heaven. The Acts of the Apostles is also attributed to Luke. It is impossible for Luke to have written two contradictory things, one in the gospel and the other in the Acts. It is evident that the first few chapters in the Acts are a later interpolation and will come up for discussion later in the book. John has not spoken of Jesus's ascension to heaven. His narrative of the appearances also leaves the time indeterminate. After appearing to Mary Magdalene and all the Apostles except Thomas, on the day on which he had risen from the dead, Jesus reappears eight days later to all the Apostles. This time, to convince Thomas that he had really risen from the dead with his body, for which he may touch him to be sure. After this, he is reported to have appeared to seven Apostles on the sea of Tiberius. The time of the occurrence has not been stated, but this appearance is an apparent later incorporation into the gospel, which had already recorded its concluding remarks before this. But even if this is taken to be correct, it is suggested that he ascended to heaven from the sea of Tiberius. This has also been stated by Tatian while harmonising the four gospels.

After mentioning that Jesus appeared to his Apostles for 40 days, the Acts of the Apostles specifically notes only one such appearance which was to be the last. This has been reported to have been at Mount Olivet because the disciples returned from there after Jesus had been taken into heaven. Luke had reported that Jesus had appeared to the Apostles in their house in Jerusalem and, after that, had walked over to Bethany from where he ascended to heaven. The Acts of the Apostles has stated the appearance to be at the Mount Olivet itself, from where he ascended after interacting with disciples. Here, again, while he asks them to stay in Jerusalem, the purpose that has been stated for it is to receive the Holy Ghost that would come upon them. The Acts has gone on to describe the coming of the Holy Ghost upon the Apostles. But this was not required as Jesus had already given the Holy Ghost to the Apostles, as has been recorded by John in the following passage.

> And when he said this, he breathed on them, and saith unto them, Receive ye the Holy Ghost.
>
> (John 20:22)

The Holy Ghost was thus breathed onto the Apostles by Jesus himself when he had appeared to them. There was no reason for them to stay on in Jerusalem to receive it. The reasons why Luke, John and the Acts have insisted on the presence of the Apostles in Jerusalem are not clear, when it is evident that there was danger to them in the city and they have been reported to have fled when Jesus was arrested. They are not reported to have been present at the crucifixion of Christ except for John, who is claimed to have been present only in the gospel ascribed to him. At his burial, none of them have been stated to have been there, as a stranger is said to have taken his body and to have buried it. Despite their absence from such major events till Friday evening, they are all said to be in Jerusalem and staying in a house on Sunday morning. The outer limit between the burial of Jesus on Friday evening and the women finding the sepulchre open and the body missing is 36 hours, if Sunday morning is taken to be the time. Some Church Fathers have speculated that it could be Saturday evening, as Matthew has written, 'In the end of the sabbath, as it began to dawn toward the first day of the week.' They have stated that the day for the Jews was from sunset to sunset. The Sabbath would, thus, end at sunset on Saturday, and the first day of the week would begin to dawn with the same sunset. It has not been stated 'when it began to dawn', but 'when it began to dawn towards the first day of the week'. This, they have said, should mean when the day starts, which would be Saturday evening. This would make the time between the burial and the discovery of the empty sepulchre only 24 hours. Should the duration be estimated to be 36 hours, it is too short a period for such a major change in the scenario. Jesus with his disciples did not have a place to stay, as, after the feast of the Passover, he has been reported to have gone to a garden with the Apostles, where all of them spent the night. Towards dawn on Friday, he was arrested and the Apostles are reported to have fled except two who have been said to have gone up to the house of the priests, after which even they went missing. On Friday, Jesus is tried, convicted, crucified and buried. None of the Apostles were there, but on Sunday morning, they are reported to be staying in a house in Jerusalem and remain there. Despite there being such a mismatch, this is the picture the evangelists have painted.

There is an interesting mention of the resurrection in the first epistle of Paul to the Corinthians. This is in the following passage.

> For I delivered unto you first of all that which I also received, how that Christ died for our sins according to the scriptures;
> And that he was buried, and that he rose again the third day according to the scriptures:
> After that he was seen of Cephas, then of the twelve:
> After that, he was seen of above five hundred brethren at once; of whom the greater part remain unto this present, but some are fallen asleep.
> After that, he was seen of James; then of all the apostles.
> And last of all he was seen of me also, as of one born out of due time.
>
> (1 Corinthians 15:3–8)

This statement of Paul turns topsy-turvy the entire account of the resurrection that had been given by the gospels despite their contradictions. He has stated that Jesus was first seen by Peter, followed by 500 brethren at once. After this, he was seen by James and all the Apostles and, finally, by Paul himself. The gospels have not stated at any place that Jesus was seen after his resurrection by anyone except the 11 Apostles and the two Marys. Paul has brought in 500 believers to whom he has been reported to have appeared at once. After that, he is reported to have been seen by James alone and then by all the 12 Apostles.

THE MYTHS CREATED • 125

Finally, Paul claims, he appeared to him also. It seems that the Gospel of Luke was not recorded in the beginning, as that is the gospel representing the views of Paul. It seems that for a very long time the utterances of Paul remained verbal, in which, while spreading the propaganda of the resurrection of Jesus, he said whatever came to his mind, because of which what he has stated in this epistle in not in tune with what finally got recorded in the Gospel of Luke. As nothing had yet been written down, there was no way in which anyone could point out that he was contradicting his own statements. This epistle appears to have been of this stage. He has made a statement of who saw first, who next and who last, just as it came to his mind. As no such thing had happened and fiction was being turned into belief by continuous propaganda, there was no original story with which it had to be matched. Over a period of time, when, after several repetitions, the stories finally settled with Paul, Luke appears to have recorded his gospel wherein he has mentioned the two appearances on the same day, first to two Apostles walking in the countryside and then to all of them in their abode, after which Jesus is reported to have walked over to Bethany and ascended to heaven. Further, the claim that he, too, saw Jesus, if it is to mean that he saw him like the rest before he ascended to heaven, would be absurd, because he was not a believer by then and has been reported to be persecuting Christians much after this.

It would, thus, be seen that the myth of Jesus rising from the dead was created by Paul and was later expanded by the Pauline Church, because of which what they produced has so many stark contradictions that nobody can reconcile them despite countless attempts that have been made without success over the centuries. In doing so, Paul established the concept of the resurrection of the body on the Day of Judgement in line with his belief as a Pharisee. This he did for Jesus, who was evidently an Essene and had the belief of transmigration of the soul. That the Apostles and the Apostolic Church did not believe in this emerges from the fact that in the early centuries there were Christians who did not believe in the resurrection. Today, this belief is fundamental to the Christian faith, but there was a time when some Christians did not believe in it, as suggested in the following passage.

> The following, then, are his words: 'It is folly on their part to suppose that when God, as if He were a cook, introduces the fire which is to consume the world, all the rest of the human race will be burnt up, while they alone will remain, not only such of them as are then alive, but also those who are long since dead, which latter will arise from the earth clothed with the self-same flesh (as during life); for such a hope is simply one which might be cherished by worms. For what sort of human soul is that which would still long for a body that had been subject to corruption? Whence, also, this opinion of yours is not shared by some of the Christians, and they pronounce it to be exceedingly vile, and loathsome, and impossible, for what kind of body is that which, after being completely corrupted, can return to its original nature, and to the self-same first condition out of which it fell into dissolution? Being unable to return any answer, they betake themselves to a most absurd refuge, viz., that all things are possible to God.'
> (*The Writings of the Early Church Fathers*, Vol. 4, Origen, Against Celsus, Book V, Chapter 14)

Origen is arguing against Celsus, who had raised certain issues against the Christian faith. He has quoted Celsus verbatim wherein it has been reported that some Christians did not believe in the theory of resurrection of the dead and openly denounced it to be 'exceedingly vile, and loathsome, and impossible'. Paul, in his Epistle to the Hebrews, had mentioned that the doctrinal issues on which they had differences may be left out for a discussion on a future date. Amongst the doctrinal issues listed by him, resurrection was one. It is evident that these Christians, who have been reported by Celsus to be not believing in resurrection, were the followers of the Apostles.

Celsus has raised some more points which are noted in the passage below.

> If Jesus desired to show that his power was really divine, he ought to have appeared to those who had ill-treated him, and to him who had condemned him, and to all men universally.
>
> For he had no longer occasion to fear any man after his death, being, as you say, a God; nor was he sent into the world at all for the purpose of being hid.
>
> (*The Writings of the Early Church Fathers*, Vol. 4, Origen, Against Celsus, Book II, Chapter 63)

It is, thus, evident that Paul built up a theology in which Christ was raised to the level of the Son of God, being equal to God and more relevant than Him to men, because it was declared that He would be coming on behalf of God on the Day of Judgement to judge people for their deeds. In such a situation, He would be kind to the people who believed in Him and, even where there were sins on their part, His grace would be extended, but for those who did not believe, the doors of heaven stood firmly closed and no amount of good deeds could get them an entry into heaven. There was also a necessity of establishing the theory of the resurrection of the body on the Day of Judgement, for which an example was created in the resurrection of Jesus with his body.

As attention has remained focused on the rising of Jesus, it has been missed out that the Bible has reported that several other persons also rose from the dead. This may be seen in the passage below.

> And the graves were opened; and many bodies of the saints which slept arose,
>
> And came out of the graves after his resurrection, and went into the holy city, and appeared unto many.
>
> (Matthew 27:52–53)

This report from Matthew is of the time when Jesus died on the cross. It has been stated that the graves were opened and many saints who had been dead came out of the graves and went into Jerusalem and appeared to many. This was a far stronger evidence in favour of the theory of the resurrection of the body as these saints would have been dead several centuries earlier, while Jesus had died just then. They had moved around freely in the city and would have been seen by all and sundry, while Jesus had been seen by only his disciples and the two Marys. Despite this, neither Paul nor anyone else has mentioned them in support of their arguments, which makes it obvious that even they did not believe in it and this is an insertion by an overenthusiastic interpolator. The account does not say what they did or what happened to them, whether they went back to their graves after taking to task the people who had crucified Jesus or lived a normal life to die again. In fact, they could not have possibly ascended to heaven with their bodies since this honour was only limited to the Son of God.

3

ACQUIRING APOSTOLIC AUTHORITY

The theology and the belief system that was built up by Paul needed to be linked with the teachings of Jesus because he had been projected as the Son of God. This could have been possible only if it could be shown that it came from the Apostles. Towards this end, Paul built an image for himself as an apostle and, later, the Pauline Church linked Peter to him and to itself. With these two steps, the Pauline teachings became the teachings of Jesus. Paul was a self-proclaimed apostle. He had never met Jesus in his lifetime and, after a stage, was compelled to declare that he had not received anything from the Apostles either, but whatever he was preaching he had received directly from Jesus. Thus, he declared himself to be an apostle in some of his epistles, but added that he had not been so appointed by any man but by the authority of God. A simple declaration was not enough. Paul needed to construct the aura of an apostle for himself. This effort on his part is evident in the Bible. The Acts of the Apostles appears to have been recorded for this purpose alone. As would emerge ahead, the first few chapters in it, which describe the Acts of Peter, seem to have been added to the Acts at a subsequent date. The original book seems to have been limited to building up the image of Paul alone as an apostle, with all supernatural powers associated in the minds of the believers that an exalted disciple of Jesus would be possessing.

Paul has proceeded to show extraordinary things associated with himself. The first, in this regard, were the extraordinary circumstances of his transformation from an ardent Jew who was persecuting the Christians into a Christian himself. The next were the miracles that he has claimed to have performed at different times, and the last was the sufferings and martyrdom that have been claimed. However, in recording them, so many contradictions have been left that it becomes apparent that the claims are false. The Acts of the Apostles tells us that Saul, who became Paul on conversion to Christianity, was very enthusiastic in killing the disciples of Jesus in Jerusalem. In his enthusiasm, he went to the high priest of the temple and obtained from him letters authorising him to bind and bring the Christians from the synagogues of Damascus to Jerusalem so that they could be punished. Several issues emerge here. It raises the question whether there were Christians at Damascus at all at such an early stage, as Jesus never went to Damascus and there is no report of the Apostles having gone there either.

Paul is reported to have become an apostle a year after the death of Jesus and to have preached for 35 years:

> And Paul entered into the apostleship a year after the ascension of Christ, and beginning at Jerusalem, he advanced as for as Illyricum and Italy, and Spain, preaching the Gospel for five and thirty years. And in the time of Nero he was beheaded at Rome, and was buried there.
> (*The Writings of the Early Church Fathers*, Vol. 5, Hippolytus, On the Twelve Apostles)

Though Hippolytus has stated that Paul became an apostle a year after that death of Christ, this would have been the time when he became a Christian. He does not seem to have claimed himself to be an apostle till he parted company from the Apostles. This statement from Hippolytus shows what the Church believed about him. For the purpose of examining the claim of the Acts of the Apostles that Saul wished to go and bring the Christians in Damascus to Jerusalem, this one year after the death of Jesus is relevant, as this would have been the time when Saul would be persecuting the Jews. It is a near impossibility for Christians to have been there in Damascus at that time in any significant number to constitute a separate identity amongst the Jews. The Apostles, when they started preaching outside Judea, began with Antioch and that too could not have been as early as within a year after the death of Jesus. The next issue is that even if there were Christians in Damascus and Saul wished to bind them to bring to Jerusalem, what was his capacity to be in a position to accomplish this task. He did not command a contingent of soldiers. He was not a brigand either. All that is reported of him is that he was a tent-maker from Tarsus. How does a tent-maker from Tarsus accomplish this task, which the Acts of the Apostles has claimed? The last issue is what authority does the letter from the high priest to the synagogues of Damascus bestow on Saul to do what has been claimed. The high priest of the temple could write to the synagogues on religious matters or some internal matters of the Jews. Binding people and taking them from one place to another was not something which the priests could do even themselves, leave aside authorising someone else to do it. They did not have the authority to do it even in Jerusalem, as in the case of Jesus, whom they had to take to the Roman governor. Even later, when Paul is described as having been arrested, he was taken into custody by the Roman governor. Damascus is in present-day Syria. That was a time when the Roman Empire and the Parthian Empire were engaged in a long-lasting struggle for supremacy in this area. The boundary between the two empires fluctuated several times during those centuries. In all likelihood, Damascus would have been a part of the Parthian Empire at the time when the Acts of the Apostles has claimed that Saul went there with the intention to capture and bring the Christians to Jerusalem. Even if the area did not happen to fall in a different empire, any attempt on the part of Saul to bind people and to take them away against their will would have been a crime in the eyes of law, and the government of the place would have taken Saul into custody for committing it. The story, thus, of how Saul got converted to Christianity begins with claims that seem to be untrue. It has been created only to add an element of drama.

The story further states that as Saul travelled to Damascus and was close to it, a light shone on him from heaven. He fell to the ground and heard a voice asking, 'Saul, Saul, why persecutest thou me?' Saul asked who it was that was speaking, and the reply came, 'I am Jesus whom thou persecutest.' Saul asked what he should do, to which the Lord replied, 'Arise, and go into the city, and it shall be told thee what thou must do.' Saul found that he had lost his eyesight and, with the help of his fellow travellers, moved on to reach Damascus in three days. In Damascus, a disciple named Ananias had a vision of Jesus, who told him to go to a street called 'Straight', into the house of Judas to find a man called Saul of Tarsus. He goes on to tell Ananias that Saul had received a vision that his sight would be restored when Ananias would put his hand on him. Ananias expressed his fear about Saul, as he had heard all the evil he had done to Christians in Jerusalem and had now come with the authority from the high priests to capture all of them. Jesus reassured Ananias that Saul was now a believer and was the 'chosen vessel' to bear his name to the Gentiles. Ananias went out and found Saul, placed his hand on Saul and said, 'Brother Saul, the Lord, even Jesus, that appeared unto thee in the way as thou comest, hath sent me, that thou mightiest receive thy sight, and be filled with the Holy Ghost.' Saul's sight was restored immediately and he arose and was baptized.

This is all that has been initially reported by the Acts of the Apostles as Paul's interaction with Jesus. As he approached Damascus, a light from heaven shone on him by which he became blind and fell to the ground. He saw nobody, but a voice was heard by him as well as those accompanying him, which said, 'Saul, why persecutest thou me.' After that, he was told it was Jesus who had come and had asked him to go ahead to Damascus where he would receive further instructions. Jesus is, thus, neither reported to have been seen by him nor has been shown to have imparted any teachings to him. It is only stated that he would be told what to do when he reached the city. The other people, who were with Saul and had heard the voice along with him and were witness to his loss of sight for three days, are not reported again in the Bible. Ananias, who is reported to have had a longer vision of Jesus than Saul's, is also not mentioned again. Paul has not included him even in the list of persons who saw Jesus after his death, though here he is mentioned as one of those. The same incident is repeated twice in the Acts of the Apostles after Paul has been reported to have been arrested in Jerusalem and he states this as a part of his defence on two different occasions. What Jesus is reported to have told him on the second occasion is given in the following passage.

> But rise, and stand upon thy feet: for I have appeared unto thee for this purpose, to make thee a minister and a witness both of these things which thou hast seen, and of those things in which I will appear unto thee;
> Delivering thee from the people, and from the Gentiles, unto whom now I send thee,
> To open their eyes, and to turn them from darkness to light, and from the power of Satan unto God, that they may receive forgiveness of sins, and inheritance among them which are sanctified by faith that is in me.
> (The Acts 26:16–18)

Jesus is shown to have spoken much more than he had earlier. He has declared Paul to be his apostle and has given the command of going to the Gentiles to preach amongst them. The location, however, where this interaction took place remains the same, the vicinity of Damascus. The reporting, however, changes in the second epistle to the Corinthians as reported in the passage below.

> It is not expedient for me doubtless to glory. I will come to visions and revelations of the Lord.
>
> I knew a man in Christ above fourteen years ago, (whether in the body, I cannot tell; or whether out of the body, I cannot tell: God knoweth;) such an one caught up to the third heaven.
>
> And I knew such a man, (whether in the body, or out of the body, I cannot tell: God knoweth;)
>
> How that he was caught up into paradise, and heard unspeakable words, which it is not lawful for a man to utter.
>
> Of such an one will I glory: yet of myself I will not glory, but in mine infirmities.
>
> For though I would desire to glory, I shall not be a fool; for I will say the truth: but now I forbear, lest any man should think of me above that which he seeth me to be, or that he heareth of me.
>
> And lest I should be exalted above measure through the abundance of the revelations, there was given to me a thorn in the flesh, the messenger of Satan to buffet me, lest I should be exalted above measure.
>
> For this thing I besought the Lord thrice, that it might depart from me.
>
> And he said unto me, My grace is sufficient for thee: for my strength is made perfect in weakness. Most gladly therefore will I rather glory in my infirmities that power of Christ may rest upon me.
>
> (2 Corinthians 12:1–9)

The incident reported in this epistle is the same as was reported in the Acts of the Apostles. This emerges from the fact that he is referring to something that had happened 'above fourteen years ago.' In the Epistle to the Galatians also, Paul has mentioned these 14 years. There he has described the incident of Damascus and then spoken of going to Jerusalem 14 years later with Barnabas to meet the Apostles to settle the issue of Judaizing the Gentiles on their conversion to Christianity. This visit was the beginning of his separation from the Apostles, which confirms that Paul was with the Apostles for 14 years and parted company thereafter.

In the reporting of this incident in the Acts of the Apostles, Jesus had said nothing in particular. He had only said, 'Saul, Saul, why persecutest thou me', and on being asked what should be done, Paul was told that he would receive further instructions on reaching Damascus. At Damascus, Jesus does not appear again to Paul. He had appeared to Ananias and had asked him to look for Paul at an address given by him and to place his hand on him. Ananias had done so, by which Saul's eyesight was restored. This can only be treated as a miracle that had occurred to instil faith in Paul, though he should not have been in need of any such miracle to develop faith because Jesus had personally spoken to him three days earlier. No further instructions were given by Ananias. He only said, 'Brother Saul, the Lord, even Jesus, that appeared unto thee in the way as thou camest, hath sent me, that thou mightiest receive thy sight, and be filled with the Holy Ghost.' In the Epistle to the Corinthians, Paul has claimed that he saw Jesus and was taken up into paradise, where he heard unspeakable words, which it is not lawful for a man to utter. He has further stated that he asked the Lord thrice to take away his weakness and all three times the Lord answered that his grace was sufficient for him. It is evident that during the 14 years that Paul was with the Apostles, he mentioned neither his visions of Jesus nor his interactions with him. After parting company from them, as he began to build up his image as an apostle, the story of the spectacular circumstances associated with his conversion to Christianity were created. As time passed, additions were made to it wherein he claimed that he had been taken to paradise by Jesus, where he saw what was there and heard the deepest possible mysteries, which were not lawful for him to disclose. It is evident that this was only an exercise on his part to gain credibility amongst the believers—to show them that he had received the secrets directly from Jesus and, if what he taught was different from what the Apostles were teaching, he was to be trusted more because he had received the truth from the divine Jesus, while the others had received the incomplete message from the human Jesus.

After being baptized, the Acts of the Apostles reports Paul to be in Damascus for some days, preaching in the synagogues, declaring that Jesus was the Christ. This angered the Jews and they conspired to kill him, keeping watch on the gates of the city day and night. Here it is only the Jews who have been reported as wanting to kill him and of keeping watch on the gates to prevent him from escaping. This, too has received an exaggerated expression in the epistles, as may be seen from the passage below.

> In Damascus the governor under Aretas the king kept the city of the Damascenes with a garrison, desirous to apprehend me:
> And through a window in a basket was I let down by the wall, and escaped his hands.
> (2 Corinthians 11:32–33)

Paul has raised his importance in his Epistle to the Corinthians. Instead of the Jews wanting to kill him, as was reported in the Acts of the Apostles, here it is the governor of Damascus who has been reported to be wanting to apprehend him. The reason for this has not been reported. It could not possibly have been of any interest to the governor of an alien city what the Jews were debating about in their synagogues. Two different accounts of what Paul did after leaving Damascus have already been mentioned earlier. In the Acts of the Apostles, it is stated that he went to Jerusalem to meet the Apostles and was with them for some time. In the Epistle to the Galatians, it is reported, 'I went into Arabia, and returned again unto Damascus.' Here he missed out that he had described his stealthy escape from Damascus when there was grave danger to his life. His return to Damascus would mean to go back to that danger. In the Acts of the Apostles, it was just the Jews who were wanting to kill him, but in his second Epistle to the Corinthians, he had claimed that it was the governor of the city who was wanting to apprehend him and had put the city under a garrison. His return to Damascus would have led to an immediate arrest at the hands of the governor, with all other consequences.

It is evident that the story that has been recorded of Paul's conversion to Christianity, with spectacular happenings, is untrue. It was intended to exalt his status so that he could be in a position to compete with the Apostles in his attempt to draw the Christians away to his faith. In doing so, whatever occurred to him at whatever time was recorded without taking care to see if something different or contradictory had been stated elsewhere. As truth was not a necessary precondition and a fiction was created with so many loose ends, the weaknesses of the story become apparent when the description of the events given at different places are put together and compared.

After narrating the supernatural events that are said to be associated with the conversion of Paul to Christianity, the Acts mentions several miracles that he is reported to have performed to convince the believers that he was an apostle. These range from healing people who were sick to restoring the lives of dead people. Even a touch of his apparel has been stated to be having the effect of curing people suffering from very serious diseases. These are matters of faith and can be left out of the examination to see whether it be at all possible for such things to occur. However, some related facts are of immense interest in this regard. The passage below is his advice to Timothy.

> Drink no longer water, but use a little wine for thy stomach's sake and thine often infirmities.
>
> (1 Timothy 5:23)

Timothy was one of the closest associates of Paul. He had been circumcised on being converted to Christianity after Paul and Barnabas had gone to Jerusalem from Antioch to obtain clarifications from the Apostles on the necessity of Judaizing the Gentiles on their conversion. Evidently, he had a very weak constitution and was frequently sick. He also seems to have had problems with his stomach. Paul, who was healing the sick with a touch of his hand and restoring to life people who had died, did not use his powers to end the 'often infirmities' of his dear disciple. He has prescribed the use of a little wine in place of water as the remedy for it. A similar situation emerges in another epistle, which may be seen in the passage below.

> Yet I supposed it necessary to send to you Epaphroditus, my brother, and companion in labour, and fellow soldier, but your messenger, and he that ministered to my wants.
> For he longed after you all, and was full of heaviness, because that ye had heard that he had been sick.
> For indeed he was sick nigh unto death: but God had mercy on him; and not on him only, but on me also, lest I should have sorrow upon sorrow.
>
> (Philippians 2:25–27)

Epaphroditus, a very close associate of Paul, is reported to be very sick. He was near death in his sickness, but Paul did nothing to relieve him of his disease by the use of his powers to perform miracles. All he has been stated to have done was to wait for God's mercy. Paul was himself close to death on one occasion, as is reported in the following passage.

> For we would not, brethren, have you ignorant of our trouble which came to us in Asia, that we were pressed out of measure, above strength, insomuch that we despaired even of life:
>
> But we had the sentence of death in ourselves, that we should not trust in ourselves, but in God which raiseth the dead:
>
> Who delivered us from so great a death, and doth deliver: in whom we trust that he will yet deliver us.
>
> (2 Corinthians 1:8–10)

These inconsistencies had been noticed in the past, and the Church Fathers had been compelled to explain them to whatever extent it was possible. This may be seen from the passages below.

> The sceptics propose yet a further enquiry, by asking for what reason Timothy neither healed himself, nor was healed by his instructor, when he was reduced to this state. Whilst the Apostle raised the dead, cast out devils and conquered death with abundant ease, they could not even restore the body of one sick man. Paul is not ashamed, and does not blush, after the many and great signs which he had displayed even by simple word, yet, in writing to Timothy, to bid him take refuge in the healing virtue of wine.
>
> (*The Writings of the Early Church Fathers*, Vol. 18, John Chrysostom, Homilies on the Statutes, Homily 1)

> For when thou seest the Apostles raising the dead, yet themselves sick, and unable to remove their own infirmities, thou mayest clearly perceive, that the resurrection of the dead man was not affected by the power of him who raised him, but by the energy of the spirit. For in proof that they were frequently sick, hear what Paul saith respecting Timothy, 'Use a little wine for thy stomach's sake, and

thine often infirmities.' And again, of another he saith, 'But Trophimus I have left at Miletus sick.' And writing to the Philippians, he said, 'Epaphroditus was sick nigh unto death.' For if, when this was the case, they accounted them to be gods, and prepared to do sacrifice unto them, had not such infirmities not existed, to what extent of impiety might not men have proceeded, when they beheld their miracles. As then in this case, he suffered their nature to remain in a state of infirmity and permitted those repeated trials, in order that they might not be thought to be gods.
(*The Writings of the Early Church Fathers*, Vol. 18, John Chrysostom, Homilies on the Statutes, Homily I0)

It was a difficult situation to explain in which Chrysostom has taken a stand that this was done by Paul on purpose so that the people may know that it was the spirit of God that did all the miracles and not the person. He has also referred to an incident that has been reported in the Acts of the Apostles regarding Paul and Barnabas, when they had fled to Lystra and Derbe, the cities of Lycaonia. On seeing Paul heal an invalid, the people thought they were Jupiter and Mercurius and have been reported to have made preparations to offer sacrifices to them. Chrysostom has explained that in a situation wherein the Apostles performed only those few miracles while remained sick themselves or left their close associates sick, the people were prepared to consider them to be gods, what would they have done had the Apostles removed their own infirmities as well as those of their disciples. It was only to ensure that the people did not treat them as gods that the Apostles used to suffer the infirmities and used to let their close associates also suffer them. This is evidently a forced explanation because Paul was building up an image of being something very close to divine for himself. He has often stated, 'Christ speaks in me.' In such a situation, even if he did not want to be thought of as a heathen god to whom sacrifices were to be offered, he did want to be looked upon as an apostle with the aura of divinity attached to it. Had this not been true, there would not have been any need to perform any of the miracles. The bare fact that emerges from this is that while at places stories of miracles have been incorporated, when it came to the usual business of life, Paul emerges as being bereft of any such power in his dealings.

After showing him to be performing miracles, an aura has been built around Paul by building up stories of his sufferings and martyrdom. In the Acts of the Apostles as well as in his epistles, a large number of incidents have been reported wherein he has been reported to have been brutally assaulted and an impression is given that he was kept as a prisoner and finally executed for preaching Christianity. Though the later stories tell us that Peter and he were executed on the same day under the orders of the Emperor Nero, the Bible does not give an account of how he or Peter were killed. It gives a detailed report of events that should be understood to have led to Paul's death, but ends on a totally different note. In the Acts of the Apostles, the last eight chapters are devoted to the description of how Paul was arrested in Jerusalem and kept in custody for a long time before being sent to Rome. It states that some Jews from Asia saw him in the Temple and called out the people to apprehend him, telling them that he had been teaching people to give up the Law of Moses and other Jewish beliefs. While being led away in chains, Paul sought to speak to the people and revealed the manner in which he had been converted to Christianity after seeing a vision of Jesus. As the people became violent on listening to him, the chief captain brought him into the castle and ordered that he be interrogated by scourging. Paul claimed that he was a Roman citizen and asked whether it was lawful to scourge a citizen who was not condemned. The chief captain was scared on knowing that he was a Roman citizen and removed his chains. The next day, he summoned the council of priests and placed Paul before them to examine his case. Paul realized that the council had a mixture of Sadducees and Pharisees, so he played upon their differences and declared that he was a Pharisee and was being persecuted because of his belief in the resurrection of the dead. As this caused a division amongst them because the Pharisees found him to be without blame, there was disorder for which the chief captain brought him out from their midst.

The story proceeds to say that there being danger to Paul's life in Jerusalem, the chief captain shifted him to Caesarea to the Governor Felix with a letter informing him of the case. He clearly stated, 'whom I perceived to be accused of questions of their law, but to have nothing laid to his charge worthy of death or of bonds' (The Acts 23:29). The governor heard him in the presence of his accusers wherein Paul gave his defence, again stressing that he had been charged because of his belief in the resurrection of dead. The hearing was deferred and Paul remained imprisoned for two years by the governor because 'He hoped also that money should have been given him.' After two years, Festus became the governor and reopened the case. As he was hearing the two sides, he asked Paul whether he was willing to go to Jerusalem to be judged by him there. Paul replied that he stood before Caesar's judgement seat and so instead of being sent to Jerusalem, he appeals to Caesar. The governor ordered that he be sent to Caesar, as he had appealed to him, though he felt that there was no serious accusation against him and it was only a question of some superstition. Festus has been reported to have stated that he had no case to make to Caesar on the charge against the prisoner but was sending him only because he had appealed to Caesar directly.

Paul was sent in a ship along with other prisoners to Rome. On the way, they were hit by a storm that wrecked the ship.

Some miracles are reported to have been performed by him on the way, but finally on reaching Rome nothing is reported about his appeal to Caesar and what was done to him. It has been stated that the other prisoners were delivered to the captain of the guard 'but Paul was suffered to dwell by himself with a soldier that kept him'. Paul calls the Jews and, while explaining his case to them, preached Christianity, for which many of them believed in him. The entire story finally ends with the following passage.

> And Paul dwelt two whole years in his own hired house, and received all that came in unto him,
> Preaching the kingdom of God, and teaching those things which concern the Lord Jesus Christ, with all confidence, no man forbidding him.
> (The Acts 28:30–31)

The account presents a picture that contains grave contradictions. Paul is reported to have been taken away in chains by the chief captain when he was being assaulted by the people. When he decides to scourge him, Paul asks whether it was lawful to scourge a Roman citizen who was not condemned. At this the Chief Captain is reported to have been afraid and to have removed his bonds. There was, however, no need to put Paul in chains and scourge him because he was the one being assaulted. There was no crime alleged against him; only a point of religious dispute had been raised. The next day, the council of priests is summoned to hear his case. In this, the Pharisees are reported to have taken his side, upon hearing that he was being persecuted for having faith in the resurrection of the dead. This would indicate that the Pharisees were not aware of the charge of preaching against the Law of Moses that had been brought against him by the Jews. If at all they had taken his side, a major part of the council of priests would have found him blameless and the chief captain would have had to release him. Instead it is reported that the Pharisees' support had only resulted in disorder. Subsequently, Paul was shifted to Caesarea because there was danger to his life in Jerusalem. Paul had been in the custody of the Roman authorities and was reported to have been kept in the castle. It would be a poor commentary on the might of the Roman Empire if it is to be believed that there was danger to a prisoner kept in the castle, thus forcing the chief captain to shift the prisoner to Caesarea under a heavy escort of soldiers. In his report to the governor, the chief captain mentions that he was charged on a point of religion and there was no accusation that warranted a penalty of death or imprisonment. If there was no charge against him that warranted even imprisonment, then he should have been allowed to go free, and even if there was danger to his life in Jerusalem, he should have been escorted out of the place. This is, however, not reported to have been done. Paul continued to be held a prisoner. This is against the fact that the Roman Empire was known for its laws and its criminal justice system.

Governor Felix in Caesarea hears his case once, and expecting a bribe, defers it indefinitely and holds him in prison for two years. Apart from the fact that Paul was a poor tent-maker of Tarsus and could not have been rich enough for the governor to expect a bribe from him, the Roman system of justice did not involve such delays. Just a little earlier, the chief captain was reported to be afraid when he finds out that Paul was a Roman citizen who had been put in chains. Now, one is to believe that the governor of Caesarea was holding him in prison for two years without a trial despite the report given to him stating that he was charged on a question of the religious law of the Jews for which death or imprisonment was not warranted.

After Felix had left, the new Governor Festus, in taking up the case, had only asked Paul, 'Wilt thou go up to Jerusalem, and there be judged of these things before me?' Paul replied that he appeals to Caesar and would not like to be delivered to the Jews. It is evident that Festus was only asking whether the venue of the trial could be shifted to Jerusalem. Paul was still to be judged before Festus in Jerusalem. It was only a question and not an order. Neither had he said that he was handing him over to the Jews nor had he decided to shift the place of the trail. Even if he had handed the matter over to the Jews, they did not have the power to kill him, as was evident in the trial of Jesus. The governor had not heard the matter to its conclusion and had not passed a sentence on him inflicting a punishment, yet he agreed to send him to Caesar to refer his appeal. An appeal can be filed against an adverse order passed by a subordinate authority, but in this case no order had been passed by any authority against him. Further, the Romans did have an elaborate criminal justice system, but it did not provide for an appeal to be made to Caesar for petty issues. Paul could not have appealed to Caesar in the given situation. The governor, too, is reported to have sent him to Rome only because he had appealed to Caesar, otherwise he is said to be of the view that he should have been set at liberty. He could not prepare even a report of the offence that had been committed that could be sent to Caesar.

Paul is reported to have been put on a ship with other prisoners to go to Rome. This, again, goes against the known facts about the Roman Empire. Prisoners were not sent to Rome from far-flung areas to be punished there. Each province had its own arrangements for imprisoning people and for inflicting any other punishment. On reaching Rome, Paul is not put in a prison but stays with a soldier who had accompanied him. With this, all mention of contact with the state machinery ends in the story. It has not been stated whether he continued to be a prisoner and what happened to the appeal that he had made to Caesar. It would appear to be odd if being a prisoner he was living with a soldier and not in a prison. Next, it is told, that he called the Jews and explained his case to them and also preached Christ, because of which some believed while the others did not. Just a little earlier, it had been stated that the Emperor Claudius had expelled all Jews from Rome. This was when Paul had gone to Corinth and stayed with a Jew named Aquila, who had moved there from Italy. If all Jews had been expelled from Rome just a few years earlier, how could Paul have found them there to explain his case and to preach?

The Acts of the Apostles concludes with a statement that Paul dwelt in his own hired house for two years and received everyone. He preached Christianity with all confidence with 'no man forbidding him.' How could this be the conclusion of a long and detailed story that had stated so far how Paul was arrested in Jerusalem, how he was being tried and was sent to Rome to appeal to Caesar. After building up all the tension of sufferings for over two years in prison in Judea and facing all the perils of a sea journey to Rome, the story simply evaporates. In Rome, Paul is reported to be initially lodged with a soldier who had accompanied him and then staying in a hired house for two years, freely preaching amongst the people with 'no man forbidding him.' What happened to the appeal for which the governor had sent him over to Caesar? What happened to whatever charges that were against him for which he had been confined in a prison for so long? All this is being claimed in the backdrop of the Roman Empire, which was known for its efficient and fair criminal justice system.

It is, thus, evident that a fiction of martyrdom was developed for Paul. It was built up to a certain point and then left vague with the scope for people to imagine that he was killed after that. The time for which Paul lived in Rome has been specifically stated as two years but what happened at the end of that period is not told, allowing people scope to imagine that the Caesar took up the appeal after two years and executed him. However, his 'execution' could not have been explicitly described because people were aware that he was alive after that. The evidence for the previous statement lies in the fact that Paul had visited certain places and written epistles at a much later date. An illusion was, thus, created without making a committed statement about anything.

The explanation for this, as given by Jerome, is quoted below.

> I only say this, that in the twenty fifth year after our Lord's passion, that is the second of Nero, at the time when Festus Procurator of Judea succeeded Felix, he was sent bound to Rome, and remaining for two years in free custody, disputed daily with the Jews concerning the advent of Christ. It ought to be said that at the first defence, the power of Nero having not yet been confirmed, nor his wickedness broken forth to such a degree as the histories relate concerning him, Paul was dismissed by Nero, that the gospel of Christ might be preached also in the West.
> (*The Writings of the Early Church Fathers*, Vol. 26, Jerome, Lives of Illustrious Men, Chapter 5)

It was known that Paul had preached in Spain and Italy up to a much later time, because of which it had to be stated that he did not die as early as the Acts of the Apostles have suggested. The conclusion of the events reported therein could not, therefore, have been taken to mean that they preceded his death. Thus, his stay in a rented house in Rome for two years has been stated as 'free custody' by Jerome. This could not possibly be explained, so Jerome has just left it at that. If he was in custody, he would have been lodged in an accommodation of his captors. He could not have had the means of paying for the hired house either, if he had been in custody, even if 'free custody' is understood to mean that he had the freedom to meet anyone that came to see him. A forced explanation had to be given for this stay and an explanation offered for the disposal of the appeal, as

Nero is reported to have set him free. This would mean that in the efficient system of the Roman Empire, the Emperor took two years to decide on an appeal wherein no charge had been reported against the prisoner by Festus and he had been sent only because he had appealed. The question would still arise, why the Acts of the Apostles has given such a detailed account of this arrest, if it did not lead to his death, because Paul is claimed to have been arrested seven times in his life and no mention is to be found anywhere of what happened when he was arrested to be finally killed in Rome.

A similar approach has been taken by Paul in his epistles. At several places he has given the impression that he was imprisoned for being a preacher of Christ or was on the verge of being killed. However, at no point has he specified where he was held and who had ordered his arrest. Although he is usually exact in his letters, mentioning even of an individual by name as 'Alexander the coppersmith did me much evil', the complete silence around the details of his imprisonment can suggest that all the statements claiming he was in chains and ready to be executed were only to create an illusion of his martyrdom—a fiction that was created by him to exalt his status.

Though nothing has been mentioned in the Bible to show that Paul was finally killed by the Romans, a very strong belief was developed in the Pauline Church that he and Peter were executed on the same day—Peter crucified with his head down and Paul beheaded. The reports on this that have emerged from the early writings may be seen below.

> Thus Peter, the first of the apostles, having been apprehended and thrown into prison, and treated with ignomy, was last of all crucified at Rome. Likewise also, the renowned Paul, having been often times delivered up and brought in peril of death, having endured many evils, and making his boast in his numerous persecutions and

afflictions, in the same city was also himself beheaded.
   (*The Writings of the Early Church Fathers*, Vol. 6,
   Peter of Alexandria, Canonical Epistle, Canon IX)

And, when Caesar had commanded that Simon should be crucified with his head downwards, as he himself had requested of Caesar, and that Paul's head should be taken off, there was great commotion among the people.
   (*The Writings of the Early Church Fathers*, Vol. 8,
   Ancient Syriac Documents, Teaching of Simon Cephas)

He then, in the fourteenth year of Nero on the same day with Peter, was beheaded at Rome for Christ's sake and was buried in the Ostian way, in the thirty seventh years after our Lord's passion.
   (*The Writings of the Early Church Fathers*, Vol. 26,
   Jerome, Lives of Illustrious Men, Chapter 5)

It is, thus, evident that a consistent belief had been developed that Peter and Paul were executed on the same day under the orders of Nero in the 14th year of his reign, AD 67. It has also been stated by Jerome that it was the 37th year after the passion of Christ, which would fix the crucifixion of Jesus at AD 30. Peter is reported to have been crucified with his head downwards, as per his request, and Paul is reported to have been beheaded. This belief has been built up along with the tradition that Peter and Paul preached together at Rome. The question whether Peter preached with Paul has already been addressed to a large extent, as it has been revealed that Paul was contending against the Apostles. It would emerge further ahead when the claim that Peter was the bishop of Rome and was crucified there would be examined. There are reasons to believe that neither Peter nor Paul were killed by Nero, and the fiction of it being so has been developed by the Pauline Church to add an aura of martyrdom to the two and to add to the importance of Rome as a place of pilgrimage. Nero's documented reputation for erratic behaviour has been taken advantage of in doing so. Paul appears to have been certain that anything can be blamed on Nero and people would believe it.

However, even Nero, with all his idiosyncrasies, cannot be blamed for religious persecution of the Christians because there are reasons to believe that these persecutions did not begin so early. This can be said because Paul and the Pauline Church did not have much of a following even in Rome not only in Paul's time but even a century later, till the times of Irenaeus. It was the Apostolic Church that had its sway all over, including Rome. The Romans did not persecute the Apostolic Church at all. It was only the Pauline Church that was persecuted and that too not for their religious beliefs but for reasons other than that. The reasons for which the Pauline Church was persecuted did not emerge so soon. These three factors taken together themselves lead to a firm conclusion that Peter and Paul were not killed in Rome by Nero, even if one were to ignore the question of Peter not being a fellow preacher of Paul.

The impossibility of Paul having any substantial following in his time emerges not only from the fact that he was contending against the Apostles but also because he was a poor speaker. This has been admitted by him in one of his epistles, as may be seen from the passage below.

> That I may not seem as if I would terrify you by letters.
> For his letters, say they, are weighty and powerful; but his bodily presence is weak, and his speech contemptible.
> (2 Corinthians 10:9–10)

Paul has referred to this weakness of his as 'a thorn in the flesh, the messenger of Satan to buffet me.' As a weak speaker, Paul could not have been a forceful preacher and could not have been able to draw people in any substantial numbers. This is the picture that emerges in his epistles also wherein almost everyone appears to have forsaken him and he continues to write to different groups of people urging them to adhere to him. Though as the centuries rolled by, Paul's writing stood the test of time, while the words of the Apostles were lost, in their own times and at least till the time Irenaeus has given his report, it was the Apostles who were followed by the Christians almost everywhere, including Rome. Around the time for which the Church has built up a belief that Peter and Paul were executed in Rome, Simon Magus, a fellow Christian, had been honoured by the Romans as a god and a statue had been raised for him. The Church has declared Simon Magus as not just a heretic, but an arch heretic, but this was the view of the Pauline Church. While he will come up for examination later, it is sufficient to say that he was a Christian of the Apostolic Church. It was not just Simon Magus but several of his disciples who were very well-received in Rome. This emerges from the following passage.

> In the time of the above-mentioned Roman bishop Hyginus, Valentinus the founder of a sect of his own, and Cedron, the author of Marcion's error, were both well known at Rome. He writes as follows:
>
> 'For Valentinus came to Rome under Hyginus, flourished under Pius, and remained under Anicetus. Cedron also, Marcion's predecessor entered the Church in the time of Hyginus, the ninth bishop, and made confession, and continued in this way, now teaching in secret, now making confession again, and now denounced for corrupt doctrine and withdrawing from the assembly of the brethren.'
>
> These words are found in the third book of the work Against Heresies. And again in the first book he speaks as follows concerning Cedron: 'A certain Cedron, who had taken his system from the followers of Simon, and had come to Rome under Hyginus, the ninth in the episcopal succession from the apostles, taught that the God

proclaimed by the law and prophets was not the father of
our Lord Jesus Christ.'
> (*The Writings of the Early Church Fathers*, Vol. 24,
> Eusebius Pamphilus, Ecclesiastical History,
> Book IV, Chapter 10)

Valentinus, Cedron, Marcion and others, declared heretics by the Church, are all reported to be the followers of Simon Magus. They were all there in Rome and were very well-received by the Romans. Though they have been termed as leaders of their own sects and were declared heretics by the Pauline Church, they were all Christians and never faced any persecution at the hands of the Romans. They were evidently from the Apostolic Church, and their traditions continued long after them. It has been reported by several Church Fathers that the Christians of Churches that were not Pauline, were not persecuted. This emerges from the following passages.

> Such were Simon, the Magus of Samaria and Dositheus, who was a native of the same place, since the former gave out that he was the power of God that is called great, and the latter that he was the Son of God. Now Simonians are found nowhere throughout the world, and yet in order to gain over to himself many followers, Simon freed his disciples from the danger of death, which the Christians were taught to prefer, by teaching them to regard idolatry as a matter of indifference. But even at the beginning of their existence the followers of Simon were not exposed to persecution.
> (*The Writings of the Early Church Fathers*, Vol. 4,
> Origen, Book IV, Chapter 9)

> We understand, dearest brother, and we perceive with the whole light of our heart, the salutary and holy plans of the divine majesty, whence the sudden persecution lately

arose, whence the secular power suddenly broke forth against the Church of Christ and the bishop Cornelius, the blessed martyr, and all of you; so that, for the confusion and beating down of heretics, the Lord might show which was the Church, which is its one bishop chosen by divine appointment, which presbyters are associated with the bishop in priestly honour, which is the united and true people of Christ, linked together in the love of the Lord's flock, who they were whom the enemy would harass, whom, on the other hand, the devil would spare as being his own. For Christ's adversary does not persecute and attack any except Christ's camp and soldiers; heretics, once prostrated and made his own, he despises and passes by.

(The Writings of the Early Church Fathers, Vol. 5, Cyprian, Epistle 57)

Both these references show that it was only the Pauline Church that was being persecuted. The Christians who were not with the Pauline Church suffered no persecution at the hands of the Roman. A hint of the reasons for this persecution has also been indicated. The Church had created a situation wherein the relationship was of hostility with the state. Though it has been projected that it was because of their belief in Christ, this is evidently not true because there were other Christians who shared their beliefs. It was the manner in which the Pauline Church was asking its followers to conduct themselves in the name of true faith, which had resulted in a situation that the Romans adopted harsh measures against them. The Romans were not religious bigots. They not only tolerated all religions but often built temples in Rome to gods of the people they had conquered. There were a number of foreign deities that were worshipped in Rome. Isis, an Egyptian goddess, was a very popular figure amongst them, and some scholars have opined that the cult of Isis holding a baby got adopted in Christianity as the cult of Mary with baby Jesus because of the strong hold it had on the minds of the people in Rome. The reason why Christians other than those of the Pauline Church were not persecuted emerges from the following passage.

> I must not omit an account of the conduct also of the heretics, how frivolous it is, how worldly, how merely human, without seriousness, without authority, without discipline, as suits their creed. To begin with, it is doubtful who is a catechumen and who a believer, they all have access alike, they hear alike, they pray alike, even heathens, if any such happen to come among them. 'That which is holy they will cast to the dogs, and their pearls (although they are not real ones) they will fling to the swine.' This will simply have to consist in the overthrow of discipline, attention to which on our part, they call brotherly. In peace also they huddle up anyhow with all comers; for it matters not to them however different be their treatment of subjects, provided only they can conspire together to storm the citadel of the one only Truth.
>
> (*The Writings of the Early Church Fathers*, Vol. 3, Tertullian, Prescription Against Heretics, Chapter 41)

The difference between the manner in which the Christians of the Pauline Church and those that have been called heretics interacted with others comes out in this statement of Tertullian. Those who have been called heretics were the followers of the Apostolic Church. They have been reported to be 'huddling up' in peace with everyone, allowing everyone free access to their places of worship. Anybody, even if he was a heathen, could join them in their prayers and could listen to their discourses. It was with brotherly affection that they treated everyone. Tertullian's tone of disapproval indicates that this was not what the Pauline Church was doing. It had created a structure of authority for itself in the name of discipline and had separated its followers from the rest of the people, putting them at odds with other people and the state. How this happened emerges in their writings. As a first step, the Church claimed and acquired for itself authority over the believers not only in religious matters but in secular affairs too, thereby becoming an institution parallel to the state. Next, it claimed its diktat to be more influential than that of the state. After reaching this stage, it laid down such rules for its followers that they disturbed the social and political life of the empire. It was for this reason that the Romans reacted so sharply and not for any religious belief that the Christians were professing. The following passages tell of how the church acquired authority for itself.

> Do nothing without the bishop; keep your bodies as the temples of God; love unity; avoid divisions; be the followers of Jesus Christ, even as He is of His Father.
> (*The Writings of the Early Church Fathers*, Vol. 1, Ignatius, Epistle to the Philadelphians, Chapter 7)

> It is well to reverence both God and the bishop.
> (*The Writings of the Early Church Fathers*, Vol. 1, Ignatius, Epistle to the Smyrnaeans, Chapter 9)

> If he begins to boast, he is undone; and if he reckon himself greater than the bishop, he is ruined.
> (*The Writings of the Early Church Fathers*, Vol. 1, Ignatius, Epistle to Polycarp, Chapter 5)

> As to a good shepherd, let the lay person honour him, love him, reverence him as his lord, as his master, as the high priest of God, as a teacher of piety.
> (*The Writings of the Early Church Fathers*, Vol. 7, Apostolic Teachings and Constitution, Book II, Section 20)

> You are to the laity prophets, rulers, governors and kings;

the mediators between God and His faithful people, who receive and declare His word.

(*The Writings of the Early Church Fathers*, Vol. 7, Apostolic Teachings and Constitution, Book II, Section 25)

He is the teacher of piety; and, next after God, he is your father, who has begotten you again to the adoption of sons by water and the Spirit. He is your ruler and governor; he is your king and potentate; he is, next after God, your earthly god, who has a right to be honoured by you. For let the bishop preside over you as one honoured with the authority of God.

(*The Writings of the Early Church Fathers*, Vol. 7, Apostolic Teachings and Constitution, Book II, Section 26)

Esteem your bishop to be the mouth of God. Let the bishop be honoured among you as god, and the deacon as his prophet.

(*The Writings of the Early Church Fathers*, Vol. 7, Apostolic Teachings and Constitution, Book II, Section 30)

Account these worthy to be esteemed your rulers and your kings, and bring them tribute as to kings. By how much, therefore, the soul is more valuable than the body, so much the priestly office is beyond the kingly.

(*The Writings of the Early Church Fathers*, Vol. 7, Apostolic Teachings and Constitution, Book II, Section 34)

Give to the priest what things are due to him, the first fruits of thy floor, and of thy wine-press, and sin-offerings, as to the mediator between God and such as stand in need of purgation and forgiveness.

(*The Writings of the Early Church Fathers*, Vol. 7, Apostolic Teachings and Constitution, Book II, Section 35)

Follow therefore your trades as by the by, for your

maintenance, but make the worship of God your main business.
(*The Writings of the Early Church Fathers*, Vol. 7, Apostolic Teachings and Constitution, Book II, Section 61)

Moreover, it is contained in the ancient law, that whoever has not given obedience to the priests should either be stoned outside the camp by the people, or with his neck beneath the sword should expiate his presumption by his blood.
(*The Writings of the Early Church Fathers*, Vol. 8, Pope Auterus, The Decretals)

It is evident that the attempts of the Pauline Church to gain authority over its followers was initially limited to religious affairs only, as can be seen from the statements of Ignatius. This could have been because there was a constant effort on its part to keep its followers away from the Apostolic Church and to insist that the true teachings could be received only from the persons authorized by it. This, however, did not last very long and very soon the Church claimed authority in secular affairs also, claiming authority parallel to the state. It required the followers to treat their priest as not only their guide and head in religious matters but their ruler, governor and king. Once parallel jurisdictions were claimed by it, the Church declared itself superior to the state because it claimed that it derived its authority directly from God. It could then say that the state had control only over the body of the person, while the Church had control over the soul. It emphasized that obedience to the Church was more important than obedience to the state. This has been stated expressly in the following passages.

For those who are greater than I have said, 'We ought to obey God rather than men.'
(*The Writings of the Early Church Fathers*, Vol. 8, Polycrates, Bishop of Ephesus, Epistle to Victor)

> For the law of God is above all laws; it forbids even those things which are esteemed lawful, that it may fulfil justice.
> (*The Writings of the Early Church Fathers*, Vol. 7, Lactantius, Epitome of the Divine Institutes, Chapter 64)

> Be ye subject to all royal power and dominion in things which are pleasing to God, as to the ministers of God, and the punishers of the ungodly.
> (*The Writings of the Early Church Fathers*, Vol. 7, Apostolic Teachings and Constitution, Book IV, Section 13)

> He that heareth us heareth Christ, and he that heareth Christ heareth His God and Father, to whom be glory for ever.
> (*The Writings of the Early Church Fathers*, Vol. 7, Apostolic Teachings and Constitution, Book VIII, Section 3)

The Pauline Church, thus, assumed authority over its followers in a way that it superseded the state. Obeying God rather than men is a noble concept, but how would anyone know what God has commanded and what is pleasing to Him? This is where the Church came in and took over the role of a mediator between God and men. Thus, what it said became the command of God and the law of God. The believers were to be subject to the royal power and dominion only in things that were pleasing to God. This was propounded despite Paul's epistles, and even those of Peter, noting that the state authorities should be honoured without any reservation. Once the Church had claimed complete authority over the believers, it laid down norms for their behaviour as true Christians, which not only segregated them from the composite social fabric but also put them in direct confrontation with their neighbours and the state. This can be seen in the following passages.

Take heed, therefore, not to join yourselves in your

worship with those that perish, which is the assembly of the Gentiles, to your deceit and destruction. For there is no fellowship between God and devil. Avoid also indecent spectacles: I mean the theatres and the pomps of the heathens; their enchantments, observations of omens, soothsayings, purgations, divinations, observations of birds; their necromancies and invocations. So it is the duty of a believer to avoid the assemblies of the ungodly, of the heathen, and of the Jews, and of the rest of the heretics, lest by uniting ourselves to them we bring snares upon our own souls; that we may not by joining in their feasts be partakers with them in their impiety. You are also to avoid their public meetings, and those sports which are celebrated in them. Abstain, therefore, from all idolatrous pomp and state, all their public meetings, banquets, duels and all shows belonging to demons.
 (*The Writings of the Early Church Fathers*, Vol. 7, Apostolic Teachings and Constitution, Book II, Section 62)

But they say that those are rightly and deservedly punished, who dislike the public rites of religion handed down to them by their ancestors.
 (*The Writings of the Early Church Fathers*, Vol. 7, Lactantius, Epitome of Divine Institutes, Chapter 55)

It remains to speak of public shows, which, since they have a more powerful influence on the corruption of the mind, ought to be avoided by the wise, and to be altogether guarded against, because it is said that they were instituted in celebration of the honours of the gods.
 (*The Writings of the Early Church Fathers*, Vol. 7, Lactantius Epitome of Divine Institutes, Chapter 63)

We might take part in public feasts, if it were proved that the public feasts had nothing wrong in them, and were

grounded upon true views of the character of God. If, however, the so-called public festivals can in no way be shown to accord with the service of God, but may on the contrary be proved to have been devised by men when occasion offered to commemorate some human events, or to set forth certain qualities of water or earth, or the fruits of the earth, in that case, it is clear that those who wish to offer an enlightened worship to the Divine Being will act according to sound reason, and not take part in the public feasts.
   (*The Writings of the Early Church Fathers*, Vol. 4,
   Origen, Against Celsus, Book VIII, Chapter 21)

It has been clearly shown that we are forbidden to take part in these festivals, when we know the difference between the table of the Lord and the table of demons.
   (*The Writings of the Early Church Fathers*, Vol. 4,
   Origen, Against Celsus, Book VIII, Chapter 24)

In the next place, Celsus, urges us 'to help the king with all our might, and to labour with him in the maintenance of justice, to fight for him, and if he requires it, to fight under him, or lead an army along with him.' To this our answer is, that we do, when occasion requires, give help to kings, and that, so to say, a divine help, 'putting on the whole armour of God.' And this we do in obedience to the injunction of the apostle, 'I exhort, therefore, that first of all, supplications, prayers, intercessions, and giving of thanks, be made for all men, for kings, and for all that are in authority.' The more anyone excels in piety, the more effective help does he render to kings, even more than is given by soldiers, who go forth to fight and slay as many of the enemy as they can.
   (*The Writings of the Early Church Fathers*, Vol. 4,
   Origen, Against Celsus, Book VIII, Chapter 73)

And none fight better for the king than we do. We do not indeed fight under him, although he require it; but we fight on his behalf, forming a special army—an army of piety—by offering our prayers to God.
> (*The Writings of the Early Church Fathers*, Vol. 4, Origen, Against Celsus, Book VIII, Chapter 73)

Celsus also urges us to 'take office in the government of the country, if that is required for the maintenance of the laws and the support of religion.' But we recognize in each state the existence of another national organization founded by the Word of God, and we exhort those who are mighty in word and of blameless life to rule over Churches. Those who are ambitious of ruling we reject, but we constrain those who, through excess of modesty are not easily induced to take a public charge in the Church of God. And those who rule over us well are under the constraining influence of the great King, whom we believe to be the Son of God. And if those who govern in the Church, and are called rulers of the divine nation—that is, the Church—rule well, they rule in accordance with the divine commands, and never suffer themselves to be led astray by worldly policy. And it is not for the purpose of escaping public duties that Christians decline public offices, but that they may reserve themselves for a diviner and more necessary service in the Church of God.
> (*The Writings of the Early Church Fathers*, Vol. 4, Origen, Against Celsus, Book VIII, Chapter 75)

These excerpts show what the Pauline Church had pushed the believers into. Rome had a vibrant society with a variety of public activities and celebrations. Unlike the Apostolic Church, which required its believers to freely mix with the rest of the people in brotherly love, the Pauline Church, in the name of Christian discipline, not only segregated its followers from the rest of the people in religious matters but also restrained them from theatres, feasts, sports and all public meetings, declaring them to belong to the demon. All those events may nominally have had some vague religious connotations, but they were essentially social events which were an integral part of the life of the city. They had been objected to because somewhere in their origin there was something of the heathen religion—though it was not known what it was. After disturbing the social life of the empire, the Church then proceeded to restrain the believers from joining the army and civil offices of the government, even if they were asked to do so by the command of the emperor. Origen has given the justifications for their doing so, but these reasons are only to justify an existing situation. Even these reasons appear to be hollow because as soon as the Roman emperor became Christian, the Church changed its stand and asked the believers to join the imperial efforts in all fields, whether it was the army or the civilian government. Origen talks of the existence of 'another national organization founded by the Word of God.' The Church had, thus, become a state within the state and was asking its followers to boycott the real state. Put simply, this was sedition. The Church was exhorting the believers to acts of sedition in the name of Christian discipline, giving them a solemn assurance that the worldly powers could punish them for it only for a short time, as they had control only over the body, while the reward for their soul was eternal bliss in heaven. It was this sedition caused by the Church that led to a violent reaction from the Romans, leading to the persecution of the Christians. No state worth the name could have tolerated what the Church was requiring its followers to do. It is not a surprise that the Romans, who in their liberal beliefs tolerated every religion, could not extend their liberalism to the Pauline Church.

Once persecution broke out, the Church laid great emphasis

on martyrdom and imposed heavy penalties on those who broke down midway, unable to withstand the tortures. It was declared that martyrdom was the time-tested way of going to heaven. Any other method may have an element of doubt in its efficacy, but a martyr dying for the sake of Christ not only had the certainty of going to heaven but also had the power to forgive the sins of others. Several Church Fathers have reported how people used to approach the prospective martyrs in their prison cells and obtain from them letters forgiving their sins and admitting them to the communion of the church if they had been excommunicated. Their relics, too, were believed to possess miraculous powers. Often they would be stolen and churches would be built on top of them. Fake or exaggerated accounts were created and circulated to show how others, including women, had withstood painful tortures to finally achieve the crown of martyrdom so as to encourage people to follow their examples. For those who broke down during the tortures and could not bear them till death, the penalty was excommunication from the Church, with a long and elaborate procedure laid down for being restored. The Apostolic Church maintained a constant appeal to the people and the Pauline Church against martyrdom, declaring that it was of no use and could not lead anyone to heaven, but they were not heard. This is evident in the following passage.

> This among Christians is a season of persecution. When, therefore, faith is greatly agitated and the Church burning, as represented by the bush, then the Gnostics break out, then the Valentinians creep forth, then all the opponents of martyrdom bubble up, being themselves also hot to strike, penetrate, kill.
>
> (*The Writings of the Early Church Fathers*, Vol. 3, Tertullian, Antidote for the Scorpion's Sting, Chapter 1)

This digression on the causes of Roman persecution of the Christians had become necessary as it has been claimed that Nero killed Peter and Paul on the same day in AD 67. It has also been maintained all along by the Church that the persecution of Christians was because of their faith, and an impression has been created that they were innocent victims of religious fanaticism on the part of the Romans. It is evident from the records left by the early Church Fathers that this was not the case. Their statements show that they had taken the lead in disrupting the Roman Empire and had created a state within the state that was hostile to the non-Christian ruling establishment. Roman persecution was only a reaction to this sedition on their part and had nothing to do with their intolerance in religious affairs. This took time to develop and could not have happened as early as the days of Nero. Though all the directions regarding the powers of bishops have been given in a work named *Apostolic Teachings and Constitution*, it has nothing to do with the Apostles and is a later creation. It took more than a century for the Pauline Church to build its governing institutions, only after which could it have been possible to put its followers on a path of sedition against the Roman Empire. Nero may be worthy of blame on many counts and advantage has been taken of this very fact to claim that he killed Peter and Paul, but he certainly cannot be blamed for their deaths. It can be said with certainty that the stories of Peter and Paul getting killed in Rome are not true, as evidence against it from the Bible and available Christian sources is overwhelming.

Apart from developing an aura of apostleship around himself by showing supernatural conditions associated with his conversion to Christianity, the miracles that were claimed to have been performed by him and the martyrdom achieved by him, Paul claimed that Christ spoke through him. In his epistles, he has claimed this on several occasions, which may be seen in below.

> If any man think himself to be a prophet, or spiritual, let him acknowledge that the things I write unto you are the commandments of the Lord.
>
> (1 Corinthians 14:37)

> And all things are of God, who hath reconciled us to himself by Jesus Christ, and hath given to us the ministry of reconciliation;
>
> To wit, that God was in Christ, reconciling the world unto himself, not imputing their trespasses unto them; and hath committed unto us the word of reconciliation.
>
> Now then we are ambassadors for Christ, as though God did beseech you by us: we pray you in Christ's stead, be ye reconciled to God.
>
> (2 Corinthians 5:18–20)

> For we preach not ourselves, but Christ Jesus the Lord; and ourselves your servants for Jesus' sake.
>
> (2 Corinthians 4:5)

> Since ye seek a proof of Christ speaking in me, which to you-ward is not weak, but is mighty in you.
>
> (2 Corinthians 13:3)

It appears that the people sought proof from Paul for his claim that Christ spoke through him. No ready answer has been given as a response in any of his epistles. The issue is shifted, instead, to his usual sermons on the efficacy of faith and the coming of judgement. It was a normal reaction to seek proof for something that was being claimed, especially when the claim was that God spoke through him, but Paul has only mentioned it without providing any satisfactory response. However, he leaves one with the distinct impression that he did give proof that Christ spoke through him to the people of his times, the scope of which has been accepted by later preachers as well.

Raising Paul to the status of an apostle was not enough

for the purpose of establishing Pauline teachings because Paul had never met Jesus in his lifetime but had claimed that he received the truths directly from him in visions and by signs. This would not have been enough to convince the people that what he spoke was preached by Jesus because Jesus had been alive not too long before the time and there were still some people who had been with him in his lifetime and had had the good fortune of following him and listening to him preach. These were the people who had to be believed about what Jesus taught, and if they taught something different from what Paul was claiming he had received from Jesus in visions, his version was liable to be rejected. For Paul it was not possible to acquire the approval of the Apostles for what he was preaching because he was preaching something totally different. He had been with them for 14 years and had preached along with Barnabas at several places. At a stage he developed his own ideas and parted company from them. For him, it became necessary to claim that his teachings did not need the stamp of approval from the Apostles because he had received the truths directly from Jesus. The Pauline Church realized the weakness of this situation very early. It could see that to establish the claim that these were the teaching of Jesus, the people who were with him in his lifetime and were to be trusted for what he taught had to confirm this. The sanction of the Apostles had to be obtained for what Paul had laid down. To achieve this objective, the Pauline Church linked John and Peter to its traditions. It, thus, got established that Paul and the Apostles taught the same things and together laid down all the traditions of a Church, which was essentially only a Pauline Church. This was a master stroke, without which, it is extremely doubtful that the Pauline Church would have survived at all. The significance of this measure can be gauged from the statement of Augustine in the following passage.

Whereas, even in the case of the Apostle Paul, who was called from heaven after the Lord's ascension, the Church would not have believed him, had there not been apostles in life with whom he might communicate and compare his gospel with theirs, so as to be recognized as belonging to the same society. When it was ascertained that Paul preached what the apostles preached, and that he lived in fellowship and harmony with them, and when God's testimony was added by Paul's working miracles like those done by his apostles, his authority became so great that his words are now received in the Church, as if, to use his own appropriate words, Christ were speaking in him.
(*The Writings of the Early Church Fathers*, Vol. 13, Augustine, Contra Faustam, Book XXVIII)

When Paul claimed that Christ spoke in him, the Corinthians did not believe him and sought proof for it, but Augustine believed it because he felt that he preached what the Apostles preached and lived in fellowship with them. That is the importance of this single factor in the survival of the theology of Paul. The attempts of the Pauline Church to assimilate John into its traditions were successful only partially, as when it came in conflict with the Eastern Church, which had the apostolic traditions till then, John continued to remain linked with the Eastern Church. In the case of Peter, the success was complete. The Eastern Church could neither claim legacy from him nor was it able to disprove the claim of the Western Church, which was totally Pauline by then, that its traditions were established by him.

To assimilate John into its traditions, the Pauline Church created works that were ascribed to him and incorporated them in the Bible. There is a gospel that is claimed to have been written by John and also three epistles from him. Apart from these, there is the Book of Revelations, which now forms a part of the Bible, but, in the past, has been rejected by several

Church Fathers. This has been written by a person named John, who is believed by some to be the Apostle, while some think he was a different person with the same name. The gospel ascribed to him is completely Pauline in content and contains several things to provide the support of a gospel to certain beliefs that had developed in the Pauline Church, including that of the Eucharist. As mentioned earlier, the Church of the Apostles did not acknowledge it as a gospel and the report of the occasion when it was written was to counter the belief of the Ebionites that Jesus did not exist before Mary. It has, however, served the purpose of presenting the belief system from an Apostle who has been shown to have recorded the dialogues of Jesus as he heard them in person and the events as he had witnessed them. It was a situation different from Paul whose claim was that he saw and heard Jesus in a vision. Over time, it was lost that the Ebionites, who were the followers of the Church of the Apostles, did not acknowledge it as genuine. As it got treated as a genuine piece of work of the Apostle, the belief system of Paul received the apostolic stamp on it and they became the teachings of Jesus, though John himself remained associated with the Eastern Church, as his being the bishop of Ephesus remained an undisputed fact because of which, unlike as for Peter, the Pauline Church did not build up a myth of any other place as the episcopate for him.

Of the three epistles of John, some of the Church Fathers considered only the first to be genuine. The remaining two were considered to be forged because there was no mention of them in the earlier records. Going by the contents of it, even the first does not appear to be genuine, as it speaks of the end of the world being around the corner and Jesus coming to judge people. It also mentions of a rival belief amongst the Christians, which emerges from the following passage.

Who is a liar but he that denieth that Jesus is Christ? He

is antichrist, that denieth the Father and the Son.

Whosoever denieth the Son, the same hath not the Father: (but) he that acknowledgeth the Son hath the Father also.

Let that therefore abide in you, which ye have heard from the beginning. If that which ye have heard from the beginning shall remain in you, ye also shall continue in the Son, and in the Father.

And this is the promise that he hath promised us, even eternal life.

These things have I written unto you concerning them that seduce you.

(First Epistle of John 2:22–26)

It is evident that there are preachers who were 'seducing' the believers to their faith. These preachers denied that Jesus was Christ and was the Son of God. The writer of this letter believed in the promise of eternal life. This was Paul. The Apostles did not believe in the resurrection of the dead, as this was mentioned in the Epistle to the Hebrews as one of the doctrinal differences that was to be left for a discussion on a future date. This passage shows that the Apostles did not believe in Jesus being Christ either, or being the Son of God. The epistle is clearly Pauline and has been forged in the name of John. The remaining two are very short epistles addressed to two individuals. One of them brings out another doctrinal dispute, while the other speaks of a personal dispute. This may be seen in the passages below.

> For many deceivers are entered into the world, who confess not that Jesus Christ is come in the flesh. This is a deceiver and an antichrist.
>
> (2 John 1:7)

> I wrote unto the Church: but Diotrephes, who loveth to have the preeminence among them, receiveth us not.

> Wherefore, if I come, I will remember his deeds which he doeth, prating against us with malicious words: and not content therewith, neither doth he himself receive the brethren, and forbiddeth them that would, and casteth them out of the Church.
>
> (3 John 1:9–10)

The second epistle raises a doctrinal issue, which evidently was a point of dispute with some other Christian group. This is whether Jesus Christ came in the flesh or not. The last two chapters of the first epistle also refer to this. The people who denied that Christ came in the flesh were the Manicheans and some Gnostic sects. They maintained that Christ was not a body but a spirit, which descended on Jesus as he came out of the water in his baptism, as has been reported in the Bible in the following passage.

> And Jesus, when he was baptized, went up straightway out of the water: and, lo, the heavens were opened unto him, and he saw the Spirit of God descending like a dove, and lighting upon him.
>
> (Matthew 3:16)

The Manicheans and some Gnostic sects maintained that Christ descended on Jesus in his baptism and left him before he was crucified. They believed that while Jesus was born and was crucified, Christ was neither born nor can be born and was not crucified. They, however, emerged two centuries later and were opposed tooth and nail by the Pauline Church, which considered them amongst the worst possible heretics. The last two chapters of the first epistle and the second epistle ascribed to John are, thus, as late as the second century, and with them a statement has been obtained from the Apostle rejecting the views of the Manicheans and these Gnostics. The third epistle ascribed to John in the Bible appears to be an error on the part of the compiler. It has nothing of doctrine mentioned in it but speaks of a personal dispute that could not have been of the Apostle. It appears to be a letter written by some other John, which the compiler added to the ones being put together to form the Bible, perhaps accidentally, making it a part of the Scriptures. The Book of Revelations, if it is taken to be a work of John the Apostle, lays down the concept of the resurrection of the dead in its complete detail. It provides total support to the Pauline theology.

In creating these works in the name of the Apostle, which became a part of the Bible, the Pauline Church brought forward views that were deemed to be the views of John. As he was unlettered and so did not write anything, the Eastern Church did not have any written account of his teachings. In their conflict with the Western Church, though they continued to insist that their traditions had been laid down by John, they could not counter the views of the Pauline Church in view of written documents speaking just the opposite, which were claimed to have been written by him. John, thus, though remained associated with the Eastern Church, his testimony went in favour of the Pauline Church.

In the case of Peter, not even a trace of his being associated with the traditions of the Eastern Church was left. He has been assimilated into the Pauline Church so completely that he is claimed to be its founder. This has been done by creating a myth that he was the founder of the Church of Rome and was its first bishop, remaining so for 25 years, preaching along with Paul. This myth has been created alongside scriptural and other texts that, as in the case of John, would be deemed to be expressing his views. The works that have been created to demonstrate the views of Peter are in the Bible and the epistles of Ignatius. Mark is said to be the disciple of Peter and is reported to have recorded that he wrote what Peter preached. His gospel, however, is not the main segment of the Bible that has been used for expressing the doctrinal beliefs of Peter and the Apostles in support of Paul. The first 12 chapters of the Acts of the Apostles and the two epistles that are claimed to have been written by Peter have been used for the purpose. These 12 chapters of the Acts of the Apostles, except for the references in them concerning Paul, appear to be a later addition by the Pauline Church. This book is ascribed to Luke, who was a disciple of Paul. It seems that he wrote only the Acts of Paul, because the basic purpose was to raise the stature of Paul to that of an apostle. At a later stage, when the Pauline Church felt the necessity of associating the Apostles to its traditions so as to gain credibility, the book was changed from being the Acts of Paul to that of the Acts of the Apostles and things concerning the Apostles in general and Peter, in particular, were mentioned in the beginning up to the twelfth chapter.

The mention of Peter and the other Apostles in the first 12 chapters being a later interpolation is apparent. What Luke wrote has to be understood to be what Paul thought and said. In the later part of the Acts of the Apostles and in his epistles, Paul is visibly hostile to the Apostles and is seen to be denigrating them in general and Peter, in particular. He is found to be referring to them as 'those who seemed to be somewhat, (whatsoever they were, it maketh no matter to me)', 'chiefest of apostles', 'Judaizers' and even 'dogs'. The first 12 chapters of the Acts of the Apostles, however, extol the Apostles in general and Peter, in particular. As Paul had claimed miracles to have been performed by him to prove his apostleship, Peter is shown to be performing miracles in these chapters to establish the point that performing miracles was a sign of being an apostle. The person who introduced these chapters was not even careful to ensure that no contradiction crept in with what Luke had written in his gospel. As already mentioned, a major contradiction is there with Luke's gospel in respect of the time Jesus spent with the Apostles after rising from the dead till he rose to heaven. Luke's account shows that he ascended to heaven on the same day when his sepulchre had been found empty, which is deemed to be the day on which he rose. The Acts of the Apostles states that he was seen by the Apostles for 40 days after his Passion. It is evident that by the time these chapters were incorporated, a large number of stories had been in circulation about the occasions on which Jesus appeared to his Apostles. These could have been far more than those that finally remained in the four gospels. Even Paul, in his epistles, mentions of occasions on which Jesus appeared and of people to whom he appeared after his resurrection that have not been mentioned in the four gospels. Evidently, such a large number of incidents could not be thought to be possible to occur in one single day, leaving the writer with no option than to state a larger timeframe within which they could possibly occur. Even those occasions that have finally been mentioned in the four gospels cannot be accommodated in a single day. Jesus is reported to have met the two Marys and the 11 Apostles in and around Jerusalem as well as in Galilee. Though Jesus, being divine, could have reached both places on the same day, the 11 Apostles could not have walked the distance in a day, as the two places over 150 kilometres apart.

The writer of these interpolations was also unacquainted with the political situation of Judea of the time he was writing about, just as the one who had interpolated the birth of Jesus at Bethlehem in the Gospel of Matthew. As Herod had been mentioned as the king of the Jews, he thought that he had all the sovereign powers and wrote his account accordingly. He was not aware that the area was a part of the Roman Empire and sovereign powers in the area were exercised only by the Romans. Each ethnic group had a leader, who often called himself a king, but his jurisdictions were limited to settling the internal affairs of that ethnic group alone. He had no powers of punishing people by way of imprisonment or death. This is a known historical fact and stands confirmed by the events reported in the Bible relating to the trial and execution of Jesus, which is clearly stated in the following passage.

> Then said Pilate unto them, Take ye him, and judge him according to your law. The Jews therefore said unto him, It is not lawful for us to put any man to death.
> (John 18:31)

The political situation is evident in this interaction. Pilate, the Roman governor, thought that the matter was just an internal dispute concerning religion, which the Jews needed to settle on their own according to their laws. The Jews responded by saying that they did not have the powers under the law to put any man to death and, as they thought that Jesus deserved death, they had brought him before the governor so that a sentence of death could be passed upon him by the Roman authority having the powers to do so. Even after Jesus was sentenced to death by the Roman governor, he was crucified by Roman soldiers and was not left to the Jews. This was the political position in Judea that was not known to the interpolator who went ahead in writing the account deeming Herod to be a real king having all the sovereign powers only because he had been mentioned as the king of Jews, just like the interpolator of the Gospel of Matthew who has reported that all children under the age of two were ordered by Herod to be killed because he could not find Jesus. The reporting in the Acts of the Apostles on this can be seen in the following passages.

> Now about that time Herod the king stretched forth his hands to vex certain of the Church.
> And he killed James the brother of John with the sword.
> And because he saw it pleased the Jews, he proceeded

further to take Peter also. (Then were the days of unleavened bread.)

And when he had apprehended him, he put him in prison, and delivered him to four quaternions of soldiers to keep him; intending after Easter to bring him forth to the people.

(The Acts 12:1–4)

And when Herod had sought for him, and found him not, he examined the keepers, and commanded that they should be put to death. And he went down from Judea to Caesarea, and there abode.

And Herod was highly displeased with them of Tyre and Sidon: but they came with one accord to him, and, having made Blastus the king's chamberlain their friend, desired peace; because their country was nourished by the king's country.

(The Acts 12:19–20)

The absence of the correct information about the political situation in Judea and Phoenicia on the part of the writer is evident. He believed Herod to be a sovereign with all powers over his subjects and with the freedom of dealing with his neighbouring kingdoms as he deemed fit. He also believed that Tyre and Sidon existed as independent entities. Thus, the story he built up says that Herod beheaded James, the brother of John, and imprisoned Peter. It further states that when the angel freed Peter and he went away, Herod ordered the keepers of the prison to be put to death. He did not know that Herod neither had a prison where he could have kept Peter or anyone else nor had he the powers to order anyone to be beheaded or imprisoned. He further thought that Phoenicia was a neighbouring independent country and so has reported that Herod was displeased with them, but they sought peace and obtained it by befriending Blastus, the king's chamberlain. He did not know that both Phoenicia and Judea were a part of the Roman Empire and none of them had the option to be at anything but peace with each other, whether they were pleased or displeased with the other side. He has also mentioned that Herod intended to bring forth Peter before the people after Easter, without realising that Easter was not a festival of the Jews. Paul was not ignorant of these facts because he lived there. Nor could Luke not be knowing all these things, as further ahead in the Acts of the Apostles itself, he has narrated the trial of Paul, both at Jerusalem and Caesarea. These 12 initial chapters of the Acts of the Apostles, excluding the references therein relating to Paul, have, thus, evidently been written by someone away from Judea and at a later date. He knew nothing of what prevailed in Judea and knew only that there was someone with the name of Herod who had been referred to as the king. Deeming Herod to be a sovereign, he wove a story of Peter and the Church being persecuted by him.

Though these chapters in the Acts of the Apostles have given the story of the persecution of the Christians and the Apostles in Jerusalem, which because of it not being in accord with the known political situation of Judea has exposed them to be interpolations, giving this story was not the main purpose of the Pauline Church in interpolating them. The main purpose was to link Peter to the Pauline theology. This was something which Paul never intended throughout the rest of the Acts of the Apostles and his epistles, as Paul has claimed superiority over the Apostles. In the Epistle to the Hebrews, he has addressed them directly and has asked them to submit themselves to him and his teachings. To stress the superiority of Paul, scope has been created for his advent even in the gospels under the authority of Jesus. This can be seen in the following passages.

And I will pray the Father, and he shall give you another Comforter, that he may abide with you forever.

(John 14:16)

But the Comforter, which is the Holy Ghost, whom the Father will send in my name, he shall teach you all things, and bring all things to your remembrance, whatsoever I have said unto you.

(John 14:26)

But these things have I told you, that when the time shall come, ye may remember that I told you then. And these things I said not unto you at the beginning, because I was with you.

(John 16:4)

Nevertheless I tell you the truth; It is expedient for you that I go away: for if I go not away, the Comforter will not come unto you, but if I depart, I will send him unto you.

And when he is come, he will reprove the world of sin, and of righteousness, and of judgement.

(John 16:7–8)

I have yet many things to say unto you, but ye cannot bear them now.

Howbeit when he, the Spirit of truth, is come, he will guide you into all truth: for he shall not speak of himself; but whatsoever he shall hear, that shall he speak: and he will shew you things to come.

He shall glorify me: he shall receive of mine, and shall shew it unto you.

(John 16:12–14)

These things have I spoken unto you in proverbs: but the time cometh, when I shall no more speak unto you in proverbs, but I shall shew you plainly of the Father.

(John 16:25)

Jesus is speaking to the Apostles. He has been reported to have told them that after he has left he would be sending someone, who has been named as 'the Comforter'. This has been amplified to mean the Holy Ghost, and it has also been stated that he would abide with them forever. This addition of the Comforter, meaning the Holy Ghost, is evidently a much later interpolation because Mani, after whom Manichaeism is named, in the third century, claimed on the basis of this statement of Jesus that he was the promised Comforter. If this had already been amplified in the gospel before Mani's time, it would not have been possible on his part to make this claim because the Holy Ghost is a part of the Trinity, being equal in all respects to God the Father and God the Son. The rest of the things that have been stated in these passages, too, do not agree with the meaning of the Comforter being the Holy Ghost, who is at par with Christ in all respects, but here he receives from Jesus and gives to the Apostles. The original intentions were evidently to mention a human being who would come after Jesus had left and who would give the complete message clearly, which Jesus had left incomplete and had conveyed in proverbs only. It has been stated that 'he will guide you into all truth: for he shall not speak of himself; but whatsoever he shall hear, that shall he speak.' It was Paul who claimed that Jesus had spoken to him and had revealed the real truth to him and what he speaks is not what he speaks but what Christ speaks in him. By introducing all these statements of Jesus, it was Paul who was trying to gain the authority of Jesus for his claim to being superior to the Apostles and of imparting his real teachings.

As Paul had no intentions of obtaining the approval of the Apostles for his teachings, having claimed for himself the authority directly from Jesus, the first 12 chapters of the Acts of the Apostles, excluding the portions mentioning Paul, could not have been authored by Luke. These are later interpolations of the Pauline Church that shifted from the stand taken by Paul and thought it necessary to link the Apostles to the Pauline theology so that it could be linked to the teachings of the living Jesus. This was necessary because it was an unconvincing situation to claim that Jesus in his lifetime did not convey his complete teachings and left it to Paul to convey them after he had received them in his visions. In these chapters, apart from speaking of the miracles performed by Peter, his addresses to the people have been recorded. These are of Pauline theology, as may be seen from the passages below.

> Ye men of Israel, hear these words; Jesus of Nazareth, a man approved of God among you by miracles and wonders and signs, which God did by him in the midst of you, as ye yourself also know:
>
> Him, being delivered by the determinate counsel and foreknowledge of God, ye have taken, and by wicked hands have crucified and slain:
>
> Whom God hath raised up, having loosed the pains of death: because it was not possible that he should be holden of it.
>
> (The Acts 2:22–24)
>
> This Jesus hath God raised up, whereof we all are witnesses.
>
> (The Acts 2:32)
>
> But ye denied the Holy One and the Just, and desired a murderer to be granted unto you;
>
> And killed the Prince of life, whom God hath raised from the dead; whereof we are witnesses.
>
> (The Acts 3:14–15)
>
> And he shall send Jesus Christ, which before was preached unto you:
>
> Whom the heaven must receive until the times of restitution of all things, which God hath spoken by the

mouth of all his holy prophets since the world began.
(The Acts 3:20–21)

Be it known unto you all, and to all the people of Israel, that by the name of Jesus Christ of Nazareth, whom ye crucified, whom God raised from the dead, even by him doth this man stand here before you whole.
(The Acts 4:10)

The God of our fathers raised up Jesus, whom ye slew and hanged on a tree.
(The Acts 5:30)

And we are witnesses of all things which he did both in the land of the Jews, and in Jerusalem; whom they slew and hanged on a tree:

Him God raised up the third day, and shewed him openly;

Not to all people, but unto witnesses chosen before of God, even to us, who did eat and drink with him after he rose from the dead.

And he commanded us to preach unto the people, and to testify that it is he which was ordained of God to be the Judge of quick and dead.

To him give all prophets witness, that through his name whosoever believeth in him shall receive remission of sins.
(The Acts 10:39–43)

In these passages, direct testimony of Peter has been created for several beliefs of the Pauline Church—that Jesus rose from the dead; that there would be a Day of Judgement; that God has ordained Jesus to judge everyone on His behalf on that day and those who believe in him shall receive remission of sins. None of these were a part of the belief system of the Apostles, but by recording them as a part of the addresses of Peter to different sets of people, the stamp of apostolic approval has been put on them. These things were fundamental to the belief system that had been built up by Paul, and by making Peter say them, it has been established that Peter and Paul preached the same things and that the theology thus propounded was what had been established by Jesus. Making Peter say 'we are witnesses of all things' is a far stronger testimony than the reporting in the gospels.

Apart from what has been incorporated in the Acts of the Apostles, there are two epistles in the Bible that have been ascribed to Peter. Some of the Early Church Fathers have considered the second to be forged because there is no mention of it in the earlier writings. On the basis of their contents, however, both epistles appear to be forged. The possibility of questioning the genuineness of the first epistle on the ground that Peter, like John, was unlettered, has been stemmed by stating at the end that it had been written by someone else to Peter's dictation. This, too, seems to have been done at a later stage, as the epistle seems to have ended before that, as can be seen in the passage below.

> To him be glory and dominion forever and ever. Amen.
> By Silvanus, a faithful brother unto you, as I suppose, I have written briefly, exhorting, and testifying that this is the true grace of God wherein ye stand.
> (1 Peter 5:11–12)

It is apparent that this epistle was concluded with 'Amen', but as even then doubts were raised on Peter having written it, as it was known that he was unlettered, further additions were made to show that Silvanus wrote for him. The epistle proceeds a little longer to be concluded a second time with an 'Amen' again. In this epistle addressed to 'strangers scattered throughout Pontus, Galatia, Cappadocia, Asia and Bithynia', Peter has written on the lines of what Paul was preaching. The advice he has given to servants, wives, husbands, elders and young to mould their conduct as a Christian is identical to what Paul has written in his epistles. At places, even words and phrases are the same. On the doctrinal side, it speaks of the Pauline theology, as may be seen in the passages below.

> Blessed be the God and Father of our Lord Jesus Christ, which according to his abundant mercy hath begotten us again unto lively hope by the resurrection of Jesus Christ from the dead,
> To an inheritance incorruptible, and undefiled, and that fadeth not away, reserved in heaven for you,
> Who are kept by the power of God through faith unto salvation ready to be revealed in the last time.
> (1 Peter 1:3–5)

> Forasmuch as ye know that ye were not redeemed with corruptible things, as silver and gold, from your conversation received by tradition from your fathers;
> But with the precious blood of Christ, as of a lamb without blemish and without spot:
> Who verily was foreordained before the foundation of the world, but was manifest in these last times for you,
> Who by him do believe in God, that raised him up from the dead, and gave him glory; that your faith and hope might be in God.
> (1 Peter 1:18–21)

It was Paul's theory derived from the apocalyptic literature of the Jews that the world was coming to an end. He has written that it would happen within the lifetime of the people he was addressing and has given the sequence in which those already dead and these alive would be presenting themselves for the judgement. Peter is stating the same things here. The last times are already there, but a great hope has been raised, as the belief in resurrection has been proved to be correct by

Jesus rising from dead, and for the believers in him, heaven is an assured inheritance for all times to come. The claim of the Pauline Church that Peter and Paul had no differences gets confirmed with Peter having been reported to have written the same things that Paul had propounded.

In the second epistle of Peter, a direct affirmation has been given to what Paul had preached and written in his epistles. This may be seen in the passage below.

> And account that the long suffering of our Lord is salvation; even as our beloved brother Paul also according to the wisdom given unto him hath written unto you;
>
> As also in all his epistles, speaking in them of these things; in which are some things hard to be understood, which they that are unlearned and unstable wrest, as they do also the other scriptures, unto their own destruction.
>
> (2 Peter 3:15–16)

This is a complete ratification of everything that Paul had said or written. Nothing is left out as a matter of dispute, and Paul is called a beloved brother with whom there could not possibly have been any dispute. Though the genuineness of this epistle has been questioned even by some Church Fathers, yet it being a part of the Bible had its effect on the minds of the believers. The epistle also seems to be in response to people questioning why the world had not come to an end even by then, though it had been preached that it would end in the lifetime of people long dead. Though no satisfactory reply is given, the epistle would have been used for claiming the unity between Peter and Paul and in proving that the Pauline teachings were identical to those of Peter and so of Jesus, as Peter has given a certificate to this effect.

Apart from the text thus created, which is now a part of the Bible to show the doctrinal unity between Peter and Paul, some more epistles have survived that seem to have been generated with the same purpose. Main amongst these are the Epistles of Barnabas and the Epistles of Ignatius. Though now nobody believes this Barnabas to be the same as the Apostle who accompanied Paul, yet in the early years that was the impression. Ignatius succeeded Peter as the bishop of Antioch. This emerges from the following passages.

> But since I have mentioned Peter, I have perceived a fifth crown woven from him, and this is that this man succeeded to the office after him. For just as any one taking a great stone from a foundation hastens by all means to introduce an equivalent to it, lest he should shake the whole building, and make it more unsound, so accordingly, when Peter was about to depart from here, the grace of the Spirit introduced another teacher equivalent to Peter, so that the building already completed should not be made more unsound by the insignificance of the successor.
> (*The Writings of the Early Church Fathers*, Vol. 18, John Chrysostom, Eulogy, On the Holy Martyr St. Ignatius)

> As did also Ignatius, who was chosen bishop of Antioch, second in succession to Peter.
> (*The Writings of the Early Church Fathers*, Vol. 24, Eusebius Pamphilus, Ecclesiastical History, Book III, Chapter 36)

> Ignatius, third bishop of the Church of Antioch after Peter, the Apostle, condemned to the wild beasts during the persecution of Trajan, was sent bound to Rome.
> (*The Writings of the Early Church Fathers*, Vol. 26, Jerome, Lives of Illustrious Men, Chapter 16)

> You have no doubt heard of the illustrious Ignatius, who received episcopal grace by the hand of the great Peter,

and after ruling the church of Antioch wore the crown of martyrdom.
(The Writings of the Early Church Fathers, Vol. 26, Theodoret, The Diologues, Dialogue I, The Immutable)

He would have been a close and prominent disciple of Peter and so what he wrote would be believed to be the teachings of Peter, though in his epistles he is presented as a disciple of John. This has perhaps been done because the Pauline Church tried to efface the connection of Peter with Antioch and created an impression that the Eastern Church followed the traditions laid down by John. Several of his epistles have come down to us, of which seven—to the Ephesians, Magnesians, Trallians, Romans, Philadelphians, Smyrnaeans and Polycarp— are generally considered to be genuine, while the rest, which are quite a few, are considered to be fake. Someone else has written an account of his martyrdom, which accompanies these epistles. Ignatius has mentioned in his epistles how he was condemned by Trajan. As per the account that emerges from these, Trajan, in the ninth year of his reign, visited Antioch. He was persecuting Christians and was forcing them to worship demons. Ignatius was brought before him and questioned of his faith. As he confessed to being a Christian, Trajan ordered 'we command that Ignatius, who affirms that he carries about within Him that was crucified, be bound by soldiers, and carried to the great Rome, there to be devoured by the beasts, for the gratification of the people.' All the epistles of Ignatius are reported to have been written by him during his journey from Antioch to Rome as a prisoner. It is further reported that after he was devoured by the beasts, his bones were brought back to Antioch, where they were deposited in the Church as his relics.

The story that has been woven around Ignatius is such that if the Church of Antioch had questioned the genuineness of his epistles on the ground that there was no record of them in their Church, it stood explained. Similarly, if they had questioned the claim that he had been taken away to Rome to be killed because his grave was there at Antioch, even this stood explained. However, all epistles that are there in his name are forged and have been generated only to establish that the Apostles preached what Paul had propounded. Apart from their contents, this can be said for a number of reasons. No epistle was written by Ignatius while he was living in peace in Antioch, for which there should not have been a reason for him to write them while he was being transported as a prisoner. These epistles are not small notes or letters but are very long and put together can be treated to be almost a treatise. He could not have had the means of writing them while being taken in a bound state to Rome. Next, Trajan has been reported to be persecuting Christians and to have ordered his execution as a part of this. As already mentioned in the case of Paul, Roman persecution of Christians began when the Pauline Church created a situation of sedition, which happened much later. Romans were not persecuting Christians in Trajan's time. In fact, around this time one of Ignatius's fellow Christians, Simon Magus, had been declared to be a god by the Romans. Trajan has a record of being a very philanthropic emperor, and several Church Fathers have reported that John the Apostle was alive during his time. John lived in Ephesus, which was very much a part of the Roman Empire. He suffered no persecution in his life and lived to a ripe old age to die a natural death. Further, as per historical records, Trajan ascended the throne in AD 98. As Ignatius is reported to have been condemned by him in the ninth year of his reign, it would be AD 107. Roman records show that Trajan did visit Antioch but that was in AD 113, as he led an expedition against the Parthians. He returned from the east in AD 115 and died on his way back to Rome. It is evident that the person who forged these epistles was aware that Trajan had been to Antioch but had lost track of the correct dates, for which he has given a story of Ignatius being condemned by Trajan in Antioch in a year when Trajan did not visit that city. Even otherwise, the Romans did not have the custom of transporting prisoners from outlying areas to Rome. They were executed at the place where they were sentenced. Ignatius, thus, could not have been required to be taken to Rome, even if Trajan had ordered his execution in Antioch.

Apart from giving an impossible story of Ignatius having been killed by Trajan, the person writing his epistles has not taken care to see to whom such epistles could have possibly been addressed. One of the epistles is addressed to the Ephesians. John the Apostle, as already mentioned, was stationed in Ephesus. He was alive around the time Ignatius has been reported to have been killed. The epistle addressed to the Ephesians on proper Christian beliefs and conduct would amount to Ignatius writing to John the Apostle, giving him advice on the subject.

Though these forged epistles of Barnabas and Ignatius have disappeared into oblivion for centuries now, as the debate over what were the teachings of the Apostles and what were the teachings of Paul is long over, but at the time when the issue was alive, these would have played an important role in silencing the followers of the Apostles, as is apparent from the wholesome praise Chrysostom showers on Ignatius. These epistles are significant in what they are opposing because that would reflect the belief system of the Apostles and the Apostolic Church. The epistle of Barnabas has given stress on giving up animal sacrifices and the Jewish customs of fasting, circumcision, Sabbath, etc., as laid down in the Law of Moses. This is the same as what Paul stated in his Epistle to the Hebrews so far as animal sacrifice is concerned and what he stated everywhere against Judaizing.

Ignatius, in his epistles, has laid great stress on respecting the bishops and deacons, stressing that nothing should be done without their approval, and honouring them as Christ.

Evidently, these are works of a time when the Pauline Church was making a conscious effort to acquire authority over the believers not only in religious matters but also in secular affairs. He has also stressed that what was being written was the faith of the Apostles. Apart from the usual sermons against following the customs of Judaism and stating the Jesus rose with his body in his resurrection, a major thing that he has pointed out is that the false followers do not believe in Eucharist. This can be seen in the following passage.

> They abstain from the Eucharist and from prayer, because they confess not the Eucharist to be the flesh of our Saviour Jesus Christ, which suffered for our sins, and which the Father, of His goodness, raised up again. Those, therefore, who speak against this gift of God, incur death in the midst of their disciples. But it were better for them to treat it with respect that they also might rise again. It is fitting, therefore, that ye should keep aloof from such persons, and not to speak of them either in private or in public, but to give heed to the prophets, and above all, to the Gospel, in which the passion of Christ has been revealed to us, and the resurrection has been fully proved.
>
> (*The Writings of the Early Church Fathers*, Vol. 1, Ignatius, Epistle to the Smyrnaeans, Chapter 7)

This is significant as it shows that the rival Christians, who would have been the Christians of the Apostolic Church, did not have the Eucharist as a part of their rituals. They did not believe that the bread became the flesh of Christ and wine mixed with water, his blood. This was one of the most important, if not the most important, ritual of the Church. The bread after prayers is believed to have become the body of Christ and wine mixed with water, his blood. The bread thus broken and dipped in wine mixed with water is eaten by all believers, with which it is believed that they have become one with Christ. Ignatius stating that it was not so believed by the Apostolic Church is supported by the fact that the said Church had animal sacrifice as a part of its rituals, as has already emerged earlier. The Eucharist, in all probability, was introduced in the Pauline Church as a replacement of animal sacrifice. Paul has written in his Epistle to the Hebrews that, for the Christians, Jesus offered the ultimate sacrifice of his body, which once offered, had cleansed them forever and no further blood need be shed. However, support for the Eucharist can be found in the gospels themselves, as Christ is reported to be speaking of it, as can be seen in the following passages.

> And as they were eating, Jesus took bread, and blessed it, and brake it, and gave it to the disciples, and said, Take, eat; this is my body.
> And he took the cup, and gave thanks, and gave it to them, saying, Drink ye all of it;
> For this is my blood of the new testament, which is shed for many for the remission of sins.
> (Matthew 26:26–28)

> And as they did eat, Jesus took bread, and blessed, and brake it, and gave to them, and said, Take, eat: this is my body.
> And he took the cup, and when he had given thanks, he gave it to them: and they all drank of it.
> And he said unto them, This is my blood of the new testament, which is shed for many.
> (Mark 14:22–24)

> And he took bread, and gave thanks, and brake it, and gave unto them saying, This is my body which is given for you: this do in remembrance of me.
> Likewise also the cup after supper, saying, This cup is the new testament in my blood, which is shed for you.
> (Luke 22:19–20)

Verily, verily, I say unto you, He that believeth on me hath everlasting life.

I am that bread of life.

Your fathers did eat manna in the wilderness, and are dead.

This is the bread which cometh down from heaven, that a man may eat thereof, and not die.

I am the living bread which came down from heaven: if any man eat of this bread, he shall live for ever: and the bread that I will give is my flesh, which I will give for the life of the world.

The Jews therefore strove among themselves, saying, How can this man give up his flesh to eat?

Then Jesus said unto them, Verily, verily, I say unto you, Except ye eat the flesh of the Son of man, and drink his blood, ye have no life in you.

Whoso eateth my flesh, and drinketh my blood, hath eternal life; and I will raise him up at the last day.

For my flesh is meat indeed, and my blood is drink indeed.

He that eateth my flesh, and drinketh my blood, dwelleth in me, and I in him.

As the living Father hath sent me, and I live by the Father: so he that eateth me, even he shall live by me.

This is that bread which came down from heaven: not as your fathers did eat manna, and are dead: he that eateth of this bread shall live for ever.

(John 6:47–58)

It is evident that these passages were not there in the gospels at the time the epistles of Ignatius had been written because if they had been there, no Christian could have refused to believe in the Eucharist, as has been reported by him, and even Ignatius, while defending the same, would have referred to the authority of the gospels for it. He does not say that Jesus said this himself in his lifetime but gives his own reasons for the belief.

Though it was known to the Eastern Church that Ignatius was the disciple and successor of Peter, as has been recorded by Chrysostom and other Church Fathers, his epistles are Pauline in their leanings. Apart from their contents, the statement in the following passage is noteworthy.

> Ye are initiated into the Gospel with Paul, the holy, the martyred, the deservedly most happy, at whose feet may I be found, when I shall attain to God; who in all his epistles makes mention of you in Christ Jesus.
> (*The Writings of the Early Church Fathers*, Vol. 1, Ignatius, Epistle to the Ephesians, Chapter 12)

Along with these texts that were created to link Peter and thereby all the Apostles to the Pauline theology, a myth was created that Peter moved from Antioch to Rome and was the bishop there for 25 years. He was, thus, said to have established the Church of Rome, which had emerged as the principal centre of the Pauline Church. As Paul was also there at that time, the two are said to have preached together and laid down the traditions of that Church. At the end, both were said to have been killed on the same day under the orders of Nero—Peter by being crucified with his head down, while Paul by being beheaded. Mention of these beliefs is found at several places. Some may be seen in the following passages.

> We do this, I say by indicating that tradition derived from the apostles, of the very great, the very ancient, and universally known Church founded and organized at Rome by the two most glorious apostles, Peter and Paul.
> (*The Writings of the Early Church Fathers*, Vol. 1, Irenaeus, Against Heresies, Book III, Chapter 3)

While Peter publicly preached the Gospel at Rome before some of Caesar's equites, and adduced many testimonies to Christ, in order thereby they might be able to commit to memory what was spoken.

(*The Writings of the Early Church Fathers*, Vol. 2, Clement of Alexandria, Comments on the First Epistle of Peter)

After such things as these, moreover, they still dare a false bishop having been appointed for them by heretics to set sail and to bear letters from schismatic and profane persons to the throne of Peter, and to the chief church whence priestly unity takes its source, and not to consider that these were the Romans where faith was praised in the preaching of the apostles.

(*The Writings of the Early Church Fathers*, Vol. 5, Cyprian, Epistle 54, To Cornelius)

The city of Rome, and all Italy, and Spain, and Britain, and Gaul, together with all the rest of the countries round about them, received the apostles' ordination to the priesthood from Simon Cephas, who went up from Antioch; and he was ruler and guide there, in the Church which he had built there, and in the places round about it.

(*The Writings of the Early Church Fathers*, Vol. 8, Ancient Syriac Documents, The Teachings of the Apostles)

And when there was great rejoicing at his teaching, he built churches there, in Rome and in the cities round about, and in all the villages of the people of Italy; and he served there in the rank of the Superintendence of Rulers twenty-five years.

(*The Writings of the Early Church Fathers*, Vol. 8, Ancient Syriac Documents, The Teachings of Simon Cephas)

All these Church Fathers and many more have stated in unequivocal terms that Peter shifted from Antioch to Rome and preached there for 20 years before being killed along with Paul under the orders of Nero. It has already emerged earlier that the contention that Nero killed Paul is not correct. The same reasons would negate the claim for Peter having been killed by him. In his case, even the claim that he preached in Rome along with Paul for 25 years is false. He may or may not have visited Rome, but he certainly did not stay there for 25 years preaching with Paul and establishing the traditions of the Church of Rome. It is Simon Magus and his disciples who are reported to have been very well-regarded in Rome, which shows that initially Simon established the Apostolic Church there. Their dominance, however, did not last very long and very soon Rome emerged as the main centre of the Pauline Church and all traces of the Apostolic Church were wiped out.

There are several reasons for disbelieving the claim that Peter preached in Rome for 25 years and established the Church there, being its first bishop. Had this been so, he and Paul would have been preaching together, as is claimed. This does not emerge from the epistles of Paul. In his epistles, Paul has usually mentioned the people who were with him and conveyed their greetings while himself blessing the recipients. In none of the epistles has he mentioned that Peter was with him and conveyed his blessings or greetings to the people to whom the epistle was being addressed. It is an impossibility that a person of the stature of Peter should not have been mentioned by Paul, had he been there. Further, in his epistles at times Paul mentions that most of the Churches had ceased to have communion with him. He has also given a long list of people who had forsaken him, giving the impression that he had been left alone, with the exception of Luke, for company. If Peter and Paul had been together and had they being preaching as one, as is claimed, this would become applicable to Peter also.

If all the Churches had ceased to have communion with Peter and Paul, and had all Christians forsaken both of them, who would have been left for them to have communion with? The manner in which Paul has claimed he received his gospel and got it confirmed by the Apostles also does not match with the claim that Paul and Peter preached together at Rome. Paul has stated categorically that he received nothing from the Apostles but Jesus Christ revealed everything to him directly. He has also stated that it was only after 14 years that he went over to them to compare his gospel with what they taught, and after it had been found to be in order by them, it was decided that Peter would preach amongst the Jews, while Paul would preach amongst the Gentiles. Though stray meetings of Paul with the Apostles have been reported, this shows that he was not interacting with them on doctrinal issues. Even after his gospel had been found to match with that of the Apostles 14 years after he had started preaching, Paul went away on a mission distinct from that of Peter.

There is an interesting difference in the text of one Paul's epistle, as recorded by Chrysostom and as is found in the King James Version of the Bible that has a bearing on this issue. This can be seen in the passages below.

> 'Paul and Timothy, servants of Christ Jesus, to all the saints in Christ Jesus which are at Philippi, fellow-Bishops and Deacons.'
>
> (*The Writings of the Early Church Fathers*, Vol. 22, John Chrysostom, Homilies on Philippians, Homily 1)

> Paul and Timotheus, the servants of Jesus Christ, to all the saints in Christ Jesus which are at Philippi, with the bishops and deacons.
>
> (*The Bible*, King James Version, Philippians 1:1)

There is a crucial difference in the text of the opening lines of Paul's epistle to the Philippians. Chrysostom, in the text of the epistle, has recorded that Paul addressed them as 'Fellow Bishops.' The present text of the Bible does not show this. It is evident that the original version of the Bible that was available with John Chrysostom had Paul addressing them as 'fellow bishops.' Over the ages, with different translations, this has been changed because the address 'fellow bishops' would mean that Paul was also a bishop. He is claimed to be stationed at Rome for most of the time and could have been a bishop only of Rome. This was an inconvenient position because a myth had been developed that Peter was the first bishop of Rome. If this myth had to be made acceptable, it would have become necessary to efface all references that showed that Paul was the bishop there. Though there is nothing to show any such thing, apparently, there was a claim that Paul claimed himself to be the bishop of Rome. This seems to have been the accepted position in Chrysostom's times because he has explained the use of a plural for a bishop, stating that the bishop and presbyters together have been called bishops, though there was only one bishop in Philippi, but has not made any comment on his addressing them as 'fellow bishops'. Evidently, they were his fellow bishops.

The impression that emerges from Paul's epistles about Peter not being associated with Rome finds support from the epistles of Ignatius. Amongst his epistles, one is addressed to the Romans. The opening address of this epistle may be seen in the passage below.

> Ignatius, who is also called Theophorus, to the Church which has obtained mercy, through the majesty of the Most High God, the Father, and of Jesus Christ, His only-begotten son; the Church which is sanctified and enlightened by the will of God, who formed all things that are according to the faith and love of Jesus Christ, our God and Saviour;

the Church which presides in the place of the region of the Romans, and which is worthy of God, worthy of honour, worthy of the highest happiness, worthy of praise, worthy of credit, worthy of being deemed holy, and which presides over love, is name from Christ, and from the Father, is possessed of the Spirit, which I also salute in the name of Almighty God, and of Jesus Christ His son: to those who are united, both according to the flesh and spirit, to every one of His commandments, who are filled inseparably with all the grace of God, and are purified from every strange taint, I wish abundance of happiness unblameably, in God, even the Father, and our Lord Jesus Christ.

(*The Writings of the Early Church Fathers*, Vol. 1, Ignatius, Epistle to the Romans)

A lot of things have been written in this salutation. The Church of Rome has been deemed to be worthy of honour, praise and happiness, etc., purified from every strange taint, but not a word has been mentioned that could even remotely link it to Peter in any way, leave aside it having been founded by him. Even in the rest of the epistle no such thing has been mentioned. The epistles of Ignatius had been forged to link Peter to the Pauline theology so as to obtain his stamp as they being the teachings of Jesus. The persons who wrote them knew that Peter was the bishop of Antioch and was the founder of that Church. With this knowledge, they selected Ignatius to be the person in whose name these epistles were to be named, as he had succeeded Peter at Antioch and so would be believed to be conveying his teachings. These people had no inkling that in course of time Peter would be believed to have founded the Church of Rome, having been the bishop there for 25 years. Evidently, this myth had not been created at the time when these epistles had been forged. A situation has, thus, been created that a person who was the successor of Peter

ACQUIRING APOSTOLIC AUTHORITY • 197

in Antioch is shown to have written a letter to the Church of Rome, whose bishop would have been the successor of Peter there, without any reference to this special relationship with the common teachings from a common teacher. It is a letter that could have been addressed by Ignatius or any other priest of any Church anywhere, if he was about to be killed in that city. He mentions that he would be killed there very soon and urges them not to try to save him in any manner, giving his reasons for wanting to be martyred, but does not mention Peter or that being the place of his martyrdom or that of Paul and he wanting to follow them. It is evident that the persons who wrote the epistles of Ignatius had the sole objective to write things in the name of Ignatius, which would have been written by a bishop of the Pauline Church. The Church of Rome had to be addressed, as Ignatius was supposed to go there to be killed as per their story. Thus, an epistle was forged addressed to them also and all usual things were written in it which a man condemned to death and travelling to that city to be executed would have written, though in doing so, they showed that the followers of Ignatius had the means to travel to Rome faster than what was at the disposal of the Roman emperor who had sent him, as the epistle reached before him. This perhaps was of no consequence to them. However, as the other myth that Peter founded the Roman Church and was the bishop there for 25 years before being crucified under the orders of Nero had not been developed by then, they cannot be blamed for not taking care to incorporate this also in their forgery.

The evidence emerging from Irenaeus is of interest. He lived between AD 120 and AD 202 and has written a book in five volumes with the title *Against Heresies.* Though in its third volume, it has been mentioned, as already quoted, that the Church of Rome had been founded and organized by 'the two most glorious apostles, Peter and Paul', this appears to be a later interpolation, as this does not match with what has been stated by him in the preface and the rest of the book. It has been reported that Irenaeus, who later became the bishop of Lyons in France, was a presbyter when he had been sent to Rome with letters of remonstrance against the rising pestilence of heresy there. Eleutherus is reported to be the bishop of Rome at that time and he is reported to be patronising the Montanist heresy. The Valentinian heresy is also reported to have been very strong there at that time. On return from Rome, Irenaeus became the bishop of Lyons, as his predecessor had died. He took up the writing of his book at this stage to counter Gnosticism in its different forms that had all been declared to be heretical. Its first two chapters contain a description of the tenets of various heretical sects, with his remarks on their absurdity and being opposed to the truths laid down by the Bible. The remaining three chapters set forth the true doctrines of Christianity and how they were not in accord with the views held by the Gnostic teachers. In the beginning, he has written a short preface, giving the reasons for his writing it. As it is not an epistle but a book and, therefore, is not addressed to anyone in particular, the preface shows that it was primarily addressed to the Church of Rome and the Christians there. In this preface, he refers to the Gnostics and the disciples of Valentinus as evil interpreters having the pretence of superior knowledge, 'using language that resembles ours' while having sentiments that are very different, etc., but then he proceeds to offer the defence as his own without mentioning that they as Romans had received them directly from Peter. The concluding paragraph of the preface gives a clear impression that the Church of Rome had no special claim in its background to be in any way superior to that of Lyons. This may be seen in the following passage.

> Thou wilt not expect from me, who am resident among the Keltae, and am accustomed for the most part to use

a barbarous dialect, any display of rhetoric, which I have never learned, or any excellence of composition which I have never practiced, or any beauty and persuasiveness of style, to which I make no pretensions. But thou wilt accept in a kindly spirit what I in a like spirit write to thee simply, truthfully, and in my own homely way; whilst thou thyself (as being more capable than I am) wilt expand those ideas of which I send thee, as it were, only the seminal principles; and in the comprehensiveness of thy understanding, wilt develop to their extent the points on which I briefly touch, so as to set with power before thy companions those things which I have uttered in weakness. In fine, as I (to gratify thy long-cherished desire for information regarding the tenets of these persons) have spared no pains, not only to make these doctrines known to thee, but also to furnish the means of showing their falsity; so shalt thou, according to the grace given to thee by the Lord, prove an earnest and efficient minister to others, that men may no longer be drawn away by the plausible system of these heretics, which I now proceed to describe.

(*The Writings of the Early Church Fathers*, Vol. 1, Irenaeus, Against Heresies, Book I, Preface)

Irenaeus, while admitting his limitations because of his being a resident among the Celts, speaks of several advantages that the Romans had over him, which include 'as being more capable than l am,' having 'the comprehensiveness of thy understanding' and with 'the grace given to thee by the Lord', but does not include the benefit of having being taught by Peter or Paul. It is evident that till the second century, the myth of Peter having been the bishop of Rome for 25 years and of having established the Church of Rome had not emerged. The mention of this in the third chapter of the book *Against Heresies*, as earlier stated, could not have been written by Irenaeus and is an interpolation, because if he had believed it to be so, he would have mentioned in the preface something regarding Peter's teachings to them that had to be followed as against what was being propounded by the heretics. There is no mention of Paul either, which raises another question, whether Paul was really stationed in Rome for all the time that emerges from his writings. The Acts of the Apostles and the epistles of Paul give an impression that he spent a major part of his preaching career in Rome and perhaps had that as his base once he was established as a preacher. Irenaeus not acknowledging his direct role in the faith of the Romans gives an impression that this not true. It would then be only another myth that Paul has created around himself. The absence of strength on the part of the Pauline Church in Rome is reflected by the fact that Eleutherus, the bishop of Rome in the times of Irenaeus, is reported to be patronising the Montanist heresy. The Valentinian heresy has also been reported to have been very strong there at that time. Montanus and Valentinus are both reported to have been disciples of Simon Magus, who was of the Apostolic Church. It seems likely that Simon Magus, for whom the Romans had installed a statue after declaring him to be a god, had established a Church at Rome. Montanus and other Gnostics followed him, because of which, at the time when Irenaeus was sent from Lyons with letters of remonstrance, Rome is reported to have had a bishop who was patronising a heresy.

The efforts of linking Peter to the Church of Rome continued for very long. Several centuries later, the grave of Peter was claimed to have been discovered and the main altar of the Cathedral of St. Peter's at the Vatican was claimed to be built over it. Modern historians, however, have expressed doubts about Peter being linked with Rome and having been killed there, though his grave has created a doubt for them. This can be seen in the following passages.

> Scripture says nothing to link Peter and his death to Rome, and the suspicion does linger that the story of Peter's martyrdom there was a fiction based retrospectively on the undoubted death of Paul in the city. Nevertheless there are strong witnesses in tradition and archaeology that at least as early as the mid-second century the Christians of Rome were confidently asserting that Peter was buried among their dead, in a cemetery across the Tiber beyond the western suburbs of Rome. The leadership of the Western Church went on to build on that memory or claimed memory over a thousand years, to create one of Christianity's most noble and dangerous visions, the Roman papacy. Their building was literal, in the massive shape of the Basilica of St Peter above Peter's supposed grave site.
>
> (Diarmaid Macculloch, A History of Christianity, Chapter 3)

> Sometime in the 160s a shrine was built for Peter at the place of his burial, perhaps to commemorate a hundred years passing since his death. The remains of it, directly under the high altar of the present basilica, were recovered during the twentieth century in a sensational series of archaeological investigations. The shrine was a modest structure, but its very existence in a public urban cemetery speaks of a community determined to stake its claim to an open existence in the capital. It is unclear whether Peter had actually played the role of bishop in the Church of Rome, even if he did indeed die in the city, and the names traditionally provided for his successor bishops up to the end of the first century are no more than names. They are probably the result of later second-century back projection to create a history for the episcopal succession in the era when episcopal succession had become significant.
>
> (Diarmaid Macculloch, A History of Christianity, Chapter 4)

It is, thus, evident that the myth of Peter being the bishop of Rome and of having been crucified there has been developed by the Pauline Church systematically over the ages. Though there is no reference in the writings of the early Church Fathers of a shrine having been built for Peter at the place of his burial in the 1600s, as late as the twentieth century, it has been declared to have been recovered directly under the high altar of the Basilica of St Peter's in the Vatican in a series of sensational archaeological investigations. Even when the said basilica was being built several centuries earlier, nobody mentioned that a shrine had been built for Peter in the 160s or any trace was there at that time, yet the archaeologists in the twentieth century declared that they had found its remains directly under the high altar, without explaining what led them to dig under the high altar of a functioning cathedral. The earliest mention about Peter having been buried in Rome is of the fourth century, which may be seen in the passage below.

> It is, therefore, recorded that Paul was beheaded in Rome itself, and that Peter likewise was crucified under Nero. This account of Peter and Paul is substantiated by the fact that their names are preserved in the cemeteries of that place even to the present day.
>
> It is confirmed likewise by Caius, a member of the Church, who arose under Zephyrinus, bishop of Rome. He, in a published disputation with Proclus, the leader of the Phrygian heresy, speaks as follows concerning the places where the sacred corpses of the aforesaid apostles are laid: 'But I can show the trophies of the apostles. For if you go to the Vatican or to the Ostian way, you will find the trophies of those who laid the foundation of this Church.'
> (*The Writings of the Early Church Fathers*, Vol. 24, Eusebius Pamphilus, Ecclesiastical History, Book II, Chapter 25)

This statement of Eusebius is significant. It shows that by the fourth century, the belief developed was only that the cemeteries of Rome had a record that Peter and Paul had been buried there. There was no belief even by that time that a shrine had been erected in honour of Peter at the place where he had been buried, remains of which have been claimed in the twentieth century to have been found directly under the high altar of the present basilica. It also mentions of an earlier work of Caius, who is reported to have been a member of the Church and to have written in a dispute with the Phrygian heretics that he could show where the bodies of the two apostles had been buried. Apart from confirming that there was no shrine built for Peter at the place where he was buried, it shows that at such an early date the Apostolic Church disputed the claim that Peter was the founder of the Church of Rome and that he lay buried there. Had Peter, and perhaps even Paul, been buried in Rome, all Christians, irrespective of whether they were of the Pauline or the Apostolic Church, would have known from the very beginning where they were so buried. It would not have been necessary for Caius, or anybody else, to state where lay buried in support of an argument. It is evident that the Pauline Church, to which Caius belonged, developed this myth, for which, while others did not know, Caius claimed he knew where these apostles lay buried. However, even Caius did not know that a shrine would be claimed to have been built in honour of Peter in the 1600s at the place where he was buried. MacCulloch has stated in his work that he was not writing on the basis of original research. Evidently, he has mentioned of the shrine having been found on the basis of the claims made. Though the success of the Pauline Church in linking Peter meant the fading away of Paul in its traditions and in Rome, this was crucial in its conflict with the Apostolic Church in the coming centuries. By the early third century, this myth got established, for which it became a very crucial element of its arsenal when an open conflict broke out in the next century with the Eastern Church. This claim has also been used by the Papacy to assert its position as the leading Church of Christianity worldwide, as it has made the claim that it is the successor to the throne of Peter.

4

THE MARCH TO SUPREMACY

The Apostles had a stature of their own, because of which, during their lifetime, despite being unlettered, they were not affected by the propaganda of Paul and held sway over the believers everywhere. The statements of Paul in his epistles reporting of the large number of Churches not having communion with him and of people who had forsaken him are all a testimony of their success in withstanding the onslaught of Paul. However, despite the Apostolic Church being dominant, the Pauline Church did survive in the West, though perhaps only in small pockets. As Paul had written a lot, which was made a part of the scriptures by the Pauline Church, a mass of scriptural text was created by it despite its limited support base. After Paul, his supporters added to what he had left and included things in the Bible to show that the Apostles propounded the same beliefs and had inspected and approved of the gospel that Paul had received directly from Christ. For several centuries thereafter, the Pauline Church took the liberty of modifying or interpolating things in the Bible to create scriptural support for its point of view in disputes that arose with rival groups. The apostolic nature of the Apostolic Church was gradually replaced by the Pauline theology, with the gradual adoption of the Pauline scriptures by the Churches in more and more areas. It was a situation wherein the fact that the Apostles were unlettered, for which they wrote almost nothing, became a major handicap for the apostolic teachings because on one side was the Pauline theology with a mass of written scriptures claimed to be from the Apostles and, on the other, were the apostolic teachings that were only in an oral tradition from them. Though quite a lot was written on their side also, which has not survived but finds mention elsewhere, this was only by their disciples and not by the Apostles themselves. Though, while the Apostles were alive there may have been a segregation between the Pauline Churches and the Apostolic Churches, as several of these Churches are reported to be not having communion with Paul, once they were no more, this separation seems to have faded away and the Pauline scriptures found their way into the Apostolic Churches. What happened thereafter was a silent takeover by the Pauline theology. It would have been possible for the Apostolic Church to retain its apostolic nature only if it had been able to identify the Pauline contents in the Bible and to have rejected them even if they stood in the name of the Apostles. As it failed to do so and to hold on only to the limited written text that the Apostles had left and to their oral teachings as recorded by their immediate disciples, the Pauline belief system was bound to take over and to become the religion of all Christians in the centuries to come. Christianity today is Pauline because of this reason wherein Jesus is worshipped as the Son of God, but his teachings have been lost. The struggle for supremacy, thus, was not a struggle of two Churches as external physical entities but between two theologies within the same body of the Church.

In the conflict between the two theologies, it became possible for the Pauline side to ascribe the apostolic teachings to the disciples of the Apostles who had recorded them and had left written texts. It was not in dispute that those written works were of persons other than the Apostles. It was only claimed and believed that it was what the Apostles taught, but wherever there was a contradiction with what had been stated in the Pauline scriptures, the claim in these works that it was a recording of what had been preached by the Apostles got rejected and it was declared to be an innovation of the writer, who in turn was declared to be a heretic. By this process, the teachings of the Apostles and, therefore, of Jesus became a heresy for the Christian Church because they were contradictory to what the written Scriptures stated. The spread of the Pauline theology began from the West. It had to be so because Paul and the Pauline scriptures were in the West. Very soon the myth that Peter was the bishop of Rome for 25 years and laid the traditions of the Church there was developed and Rome started becoming a major centre of the Pauline Church. The East took longer to be converted, as the Pauline scriptures took longer to reach there, for which reason the apostolic traditions got more time to settle down, because of which it took longer for the Pauline theology to uproot them despite the support of the written text. Though the actual cause of this takeover remained the same, as in the West, with the written scriptures overruling oral traditions, and the process also remained the same, with the apostolic teachings getting ascribed to others and getting declared heretical, the East witnessed a lot many things, as the Roman Emperor Constantine triggered a chain of events in his attempt to have a common faith declared for all Christians. The West, by then, had become Pauline, while the East still had strong apostolic traditions, because of which it became a conflict between the East and the West, with all the associated ill will and bloodshed that followed.

In the West, the first name that emerges as a heretic is of Simon Magus. He appears to have been the founder of the Apostolic Church in Rome and to have been a great preacher of his times. His importance can be gauged from the fact that the Pauline Church felt it necessary to have an incident incorporated in the Bible itself to show that Peter noticed him to be evil very early and to have cursed him. This may be seen in the passage below.

But there was a certain man, called Simon, which before time in the same city used sorcery, and bewitched the people of Samaria, giving out that himself was some great one:

To whom they all gave heed, from the least to the greatest, saying, This man is the great power of God.

And to him they had regard, because that of long time he had bewitched them with sorceries.

But when they believed Philip preaching the things concerning the kingdom of God, and the name of Jesus Christ, they were baptized, both men and women.

Then Simon himself believed also: and when he was baptized, he continued with Philip, and wondered, beholding the miracles and signs which were done.

Now when the apostles which were at Jerusalem heard that Samaria had received the word of God, they sent unto them Peter and John:

Who, when they were come down, prayed for them, that they might receive the Holy Ghost:

(For as yet he was fallen upon none of them: only they were baptized in the name of the Lord Jesus.)

Then laid they their hands on them, and they received the Holy Ghost.

And when Simon saw that through laying on of the apostles' hands the Holy Ghost was given, he offered them money,

Saying, Give me also this power, that on whomsoever I may lay hands, he may receive the Holy Ghost.

But Peter said unto him, Thy money perish with thee, because thou hast thought that the gift of God may be purchased with money.

Thou hast neither part nor lot in this matter: for thy heart is not right in the sight of God.

Repent therefore of this thy wickedness, and pray God,

if perhaps the thought of thine heart may be forgiven thee.

For I perceive that thou art in the gall of bitterness, and in the bond of iniquity.

Then answered Simon, and said, Pray ye to the Lord for me, that none of these things which ye have spoken come upon me.

(The Acts 8:9–24)

This is a part of the first 12 chapters of the Acts of the Apostles, which are interpolations. The story has been incorporated only to denigrate Simon and to distance him from the Apostles, though contradictions in it have been left. Simon has been reported to be a sorcerer in Samaria, where Philip the Apostle was preaching. Some Church Fathers have doubted that this Philip was the Apostle and have stated that he was a deacon. This does not seem to be true, as immediately after the story of Simon, Philip is reported to have gone south to baptize the eunuch of the queen of Ethiopia and that story is about the Apostle only. Here, Simon has been reported to have been baptized by Philip and to have accompanied him as a believer. After some time, the Apostles from Jerusalem send Peter and John. There could not have been any reason to send Peter and John to Samaria, as an Apostle with all apostolic powers and authority was already there. These two are reported to have prayed that the Holy Ghost may be received by the new converts as they had been baptized only but the Holy Ghost had not fallen upon them. They then proceeded to lay their hands on the persons who had been baptized, by which the new converts received the Holy Ghost. This is not a logical statement. Laying of hands is a part of baptism and with it, it is believed, that the Holy Ghost is received by the person being baptized. The account amounts to saying that Philip was not baptising the people correctly with the complete requirements. Even if this was true, there was no necessity for Peter and John to have come to Samaria to lay their hands on the believers. They could have corrected Philip and he could have completed the process by laying of his hand. He was an Apostle and so had the same divine grace as was with Peter and John. Chrysostom had felt the difficulty in explaining this position, as can be seen from the passage below.

> Why had not these received the Holy Ghost, when baptized? Either because Philip kept this honour for the Apostles; or, because he had not this gift (to impart); or, he was one of the Seven: which is rather to be said. Whence, I take it, this Philip was one of the Apostles. But observe; those went not forth: it was providentially ordered that these should go forth and those be lacking, because of the Holy Ghost: for they had received power to work miracles, but not to impart the Spirit to others: this was the prerogative of the Apostles. And observe (how they sent) the chief ones: not any other, but Peter (and John).
> (*The Writings of the Early Church Fathers*, Vol. 20, John Chrysostom, Homilies on the Acts, Homily 18)

It is evident that Chrysostom was under the compulsion to explain a text, each word of which he had to uphold as true. Here an incident had been reported wherein Philip had baptized people but they had not received the Holy Ghost. For this Peter and John had come over. He is, therefore, under compulsion to say that Philip had the powers to perform miracles, as he had been reported to be performing them, but he did not have the power to impart the Spirit to others, as this was the prerogative of only the Apostles. While stating that he believed that this Philip was one of the Apostles, he opines that because of his not being able to impart the Spirit, he must have been one of the Seven other disciples chosen by Jesus but not one of the 12 Apostles. Though later all priests had the power to impart the Holy Ghost on the person being baptized by them, here

Chrysostom had to state that this was the prerogative of only the Apostles. He could not say that this was in contradiction with the rest of the narrative, as Philip is clearly one of the Apostles and everyone received the Holy Ghost on baptism, whether he was baptized by one of the Apostles or by any other priest. He could not have said that this was an interpolation, which it clearly is, and has been brought in to delink Simon Magus from the Apostles in the strongest possible manner, with Peter cursing him to perish.

Next, the story says, Simon offered money to Peter to receive the power that on laying of his hand, the Holy Ghost may fall on the person, and Peter cursed him. This is odd, as Simon had not asked for something rare, as this power that on laying of hand during baptism the Holy Ghost descends on the person is believed to be with every priest who baptizes. Having woven an illogical story, the interpolator has proceeded to record Peter saying 'thy heart is not right in the sight of God.' Evidently, this was the purpose, showing Peter to be declaring that Simon was not worthy of being a Christian, leave aside being a close and prominent disciple of the Apostles.

Though the Bible has not mentioned Simon Magus any further and an impression has been left that he ceased to be a Christian, having been denounced by no other than Peter himself, references from the other writings show that he did remain a Christian till the end and had a huge following, particularly in Rome. He and his followers have been called heretics, which shows that they were opposed to the Pauline Church. The extent to which he is reported to have had a following and influence emerges from the following passages.

> Simon the Samaritan was the magician of whom Luke, the disciple and follower of the apostle mentions.
>
> He, then, not putting faith in God a whit the more, set himself eagerly to contend against the apostles, in order

that he himself might seem to be a wonderful being, and applied himself with still greater zeal to the study of the whole magical art, that he might the better bewilder and overpower multitudes of men. Such was his procedure in the reign of Claudius Caesar, by whom also he is said to have been honoured with a statue, on account of his magical power. This man was then glorified by many as if he were a god; and he taught that it was himself who appeared among the Jews as the Son, but descended as the Father in Samaria while he came to other nations in the character of the Holy Spirit. He represented himself, in a word, as being the loftiest of all powers, that is, the Being who is the Father over all, and he allowed himself to be called by whatsoever title men were pleased to address him. Now this Simon of Samaria, from whom all sorts of heresies derive their origin, formed his sect out of the following materials.

(*The Writings of the Early Church Fathers*, Vol. 1, Irenaeus, Against Heresies, Book I, Chapter 23)

Cerdo was the one who took his system from the followers of Simon and came to live at Rome in the time of Hyginus, who held the ninth place in the episcopal succession from the apostles downward.

Marcion of Pontus succeeded him, and developed his doctrine.

At present, however, I have simply been led to mention him, that thou mightiest know that all those who in any way corrupt the truth, and injuriously affect the preaching of Church, are the disciples and successors of Simon Magus of Samaria. Although they do not confess the name of their master, in order all the more to seduce others, yet they do teach his doctrines. They set forth, indeed, the name of Christ Jesus as a sort of lure, but in various

ways they introduce the impieties of Simon.
> (*The Writings of the Early Church Fathers*, Vol. 1, Irenaeus, Against Heresies, Book I, Chapter 27)

Simon Magus was the first who said that he himself was God over all and the world was formed by his angels.
> (*The Writings of the Early Church Fathers*, Vol. 1, Irenaeus, Against Heresies, Book II, Chapter 9)

This spiritual man shall also judge the vain speeches of the perverse Gnostics by showing that they are the disciples of Simon Magus.
> (*The Writings of the Early Church Fathers*, Vol. 1, Irenaeus, Against Heresies, Book IV, Chapter 33)

These passages from Irenaeus, who wrote in the second century, are significant because they show what happened to the Apostolic Church in the West as early as the second century. The heretic Christians are reported to be in a significant number and have been shown to be spread over a large area, as a person from Pontus is reported to be a believer amongst them. Such a large following could not have been of Simon Magus but only of the Apostles. The Pauline Church, however, branded them to be the followers of Simon Magus, who had already been denounced by no less an authority than Peter. The second passage above shows that these believers did not think that they were the followers of Simon Magus but believed that they were following Christ Jesus, but Irenaeus insists that they were his disciples and were using the name of Christ only as a lure for others.

Simon Magus's belief system has been recorded here by a hostile adversary, because of which it appears to be offensive. Translated into Sanskrit, what he has been reported to have claimed would be '*Aham brahm Asmi*', or 'I am God', which is the belief system of the Upanishads. This, as would emerge ahead, was the belief system of the Apostles and, therefore, of Jesus. The miracles performed by him have been stated to be acts of magic, with nothing to do with the divine, though it has been reported that during his lifetime many people believed him to be a god. Irenaeus also mentions that the Emperor Claudius honoured him with a statue. This reflects the approach of the Romans towards Christianity in the early years as long as the Apostolic Church had its sway in Rome. It is in line with the writings of several Church Fathers who have reported that the heretics lived in peace with the people around them and were never persecuted by the Romans. It also confirms the fact that the Romans did not persecute the Christians because of their religious beliefs but did so only when the Pauline Church pushed the believers into acts that fell within the ambit of sedition. Nero had succeeded Claudius as the emperor and is claimed by the Pauline Church to have killed both Peter and Paul. Irenaeus does not mention that they were so killed, though an interpolated passage in his work states only that Peter and Paul preached in Rome and the Church there was founded by them. His testimony here shows that it was not these two but Simon Magus who was the leading Christian preacher in Rome and was held in very high esteem by the emperor preceding Nero. He had a very large following and these were the Christians who have been reported even by the Pauline Christians to have never suffered persecution because they lived in peace with the people around them. This testimony would absolve Nero from any possible blame of having killed Peter and Paul and the Roman Empire of indulging in the persecution of the Christians from the very beginning because of their religious beliefs.

After Irenaeus, several other writers have also mentioned of the large following that Simon Magus had and the honour that was given to him by the Romans. Some of these are in the passages below.

And, thirdly, because after Christ's ascension into heaven the devils put forward certain men who said that they themselves were gods, and they were not only not persecuted by you, but even deemed worthy of honours. There was a Samaritan, Simon, a native of the village called Gitto, who in the reign of Claudius Caesar, and in your royal city of Rome, did mighty acts of magic, by virtue of the art of the devils operating in him. He was considered a god, and as a god was honoured by you with a statue, which statue was erected on the river Tiber, between the two bridges, and bore this inscription in the language of Rome 'Simoni Deo Sancto' or 'To Simon the holy God'. And almost all the Samaritans and a few even of other nations, worship him and acknowledge him as the first god.

And a man, Menander also a Samaritan, a disciple of Simon, and inspired by devils, we know to have deceived many while he was at Antioch by his magical art. He persuaded those who adhered to him that they should never die, and even now there are some livings who hold this opinion of his. And there is Marcion, a man of Pontus, who is even at this day alive and teaching his disciples to believe in some other god greater than the Creator. And he, by the aid of the devils, has caused many of every nation to speak blasphemies, and to deny that God is the maker of this universe, and to assert that some other being, greater than He. All who take their opinions from these men, are, as we before said, called Christians.

(*The Writings of the Early Church Fathers*, Vol. 1, Justin Martyr, First Apology of Justin, Chapter 26)

When you install in your pantheon Simon Magus, giving him a statue and the title of Holy God, as though your ancient deities are in reality no better, they will still think

themselves affronted by you, that the privilege, antiquity
conferred on them alone, has been allowed to others.
(*The Writings of the Early Church Fathers*, Vol. 3,
Tertullian, The Apology, Chapter 13)

To those I betake myself who have chosen to make the
gospel the starting point of their heresies.

Of these the first of all is Simon Magus, who in the
Acts of the Apostles earned a condign and just sentence
from the Apostle Peter. He had the hardihood to call himself
the Supreme Virtue, that is the Supreme God.
(*The Writings of the Early Church Fathers*, Vol. 3,
Tertullian, Against All Heresies, Chapter 1)

Simon was at that time so celebrated, and had acquired by
his jugglery such influence over those who were deceived
by him, that he was thought to be the great power of
God. But at this time, being amazed at the wonderful deed
wrought by Philip through the divine power, he reigned
and counterfeited faith in Christ, even going so far as to
receive baptism. And what is surprising, the same thing
is done even to this day by those who follow his most
impure heresy.
(*The Writings of the Early Church Fathers*, Vol. 24,
Eusebius Pamphilus, Ecclesiastical History,
Book II, Chapter 1)

We have understood that Simon was the author of all
heresies. From his time down to the present those who
have followed his heresy have reigned the sober philosophy
of the Christians.
(*The Writings of the Early Church Fathers*, Vol. 24,
Eusebius Pamphilus, Ecclesiastical History, Book II,
Chapter 13)

The inventor of all heresy was Simon Magus. This man

after he had been cast out by the Apostles, came to Rome, and gaining over one Helena a harlot, was the first that dared with blasphemous mouth to say that it was himself who appeared on Mount Sinai as the Father, and afterwards appeared among the Jews, not in real flesh but in seeming, as Christ Jesus, and afterwards as the Holy Spirit whom Christ promised to send as the Paraclete. And he so deceived the city of Rome that Claudius set up his statue, and wrote beneath it, in the language of the Romans 'Simoni Deo Sancto' which being interpreted signifies, 'To Simon the Holy God.'

In this man first the serpent of wickedness appeared, but when one head had been cut off, the root of wickedness was found again with many heads. For Cerinthus made havoc of the Church, and Menander, and Carpocrates, Ebionites also, and Marcion that mouthpiece of ungodliness.

(*The Writings of the Early Church Fathers*, Vol. 30, Cyril, Lecture VI, Concerning the Unity of God)

These passages show that all people who have been stated to be disciples of Simon Magus considered themselves to be Christians. Simon Magus himself is also stated to have begun his belief from the gospel. The spread of the believers in his heresy has been stated to be as far as Antioch and Samaria, though it is reported to have originated in Rome. The believers of his heresy are also reported to be present till several centuries later, and all heresies, including that of the Ebionites, have been stated to have originated from him. It is evident that in Rome and the West, the followers of the Apostles and the Apostolic Church were branded as the followers of Simon Magus by the Pauline Church. The Ebionites, as has already come up for mention earlier, were the Jewish Christians who were the followers of the Church of James at Jerusalem. Though Apostle James was the brother of Jesus and was the bishop of the first Church that was established after the death of Jesus, the followers of his Church were branded as heretics by the Pauline Church much before the time of Cyril, who, in his lecture quoted above, has stated that even they received their heresy from Simon Magus. This shows that the teachings of Simon Magus were identical with the beliefs of the Ebionites.

Though during the lifetime of the Apostles, the Apostolic Church seems to have had complete ascendency all over, including Rome, but just in about a century or so the Pauline Church appears to have made sufficient inroads in the West and to have acquired a lot of strength in Rome. This shows that by the end of the second century AD, the Pauline scriptures had acquired considerable hold in the West and had been able to uproot the apostolic teachings to a very large extent in that area. The stratagem of declaring the followers of the Apostolic Church to be the followers of Simon Magus worked very well with Simon already villainized and delinked from the legacy of the Apostles. Simon Magus is reported to have written things in the name of Jesus. Apparently, these would have been the teachings of Jesus, as Simon would have received them from the Apostles, but as they were written by him, they were declared to be originating from him and to be having nothing to do with the Apostles or Jesus, as they were shown to be contradictory to what was presented as the teachings of the Apostles in the written text. The handicap of the Apostolic Church in having so little in writing from the Apostles themselves became a fatal factor, as there was nothing with them to prove that what had been written by Simon Magus was in line with what they had taught. The Pauline theology was in a position of advantage with the written text from Paul to support it and to which additions had been made to provide the concurrence of the Apostles.

Despite the initial attempts of the Pauline Church to

denigrate Simon Magus by incorporating a story about him in the Acts of the Apostles, his stature appears to have been such that further efforts were required to delink him from the Apostles. The story in the Acts of the Apostles was of the time when Simon Magus had just been baptized by Philip. At that stage, he was cursed to perish with his money by Peter. He was also declared to be wicked in the eyes of God. Though this gives an impression that he did not remain a Christian thereafter, as already stated, the facts do not support this. He was a widely respected Christian preacher so much so that the Emperor Claudius had installed his statue and called him a Holy God. His link with Christianity could not be broken because his followers continued to call themselves Christians and continued to be baptized in the name of Christ. This required a new story to be invented to delink him further from the Apostles with a later incident when Simon Magus had reached maturity as a believer and was at the end of his career as a preacher. A story was, thus, invented to show that he was brought down or killed by Peter in Rome. This emerges from the following passages.

> They have nevertheless hastened to give up their father's mode of life and attach themselves to Christian faith. For they had seen the chariot of Simon Magus, and his fiery car, blown into pieces by the mouth of Peter, and vanish when Christ was named.
> (*The Writings of the Early Church Fathers*, Vol. 6, Arnobius, Against the Heathens, Book II)

> Now when he was in Rome, he mightily disturbed the Church and subverted many, and brought over to himself, and astonished the Gentiles with his skill in magic, insomuch that once, in the middle of the day, he went into their theatre, and commanded the people that they should bring me also by force into the theatre, and promised

he would fly in the air, and when all the people were in suspense at this, I prayed by myself. And indeed he was carried up into the air by demons and did fly on high in the air, saying that he was returning into heaven, and that he would supply them with good things from thence. And the people making acclamations to him, as to a god, I stretched out my hands to heaven, with my mind and besought God through Lord Jesus to throw down this pestilent fellow and to destroy the power of those demons that made use of the same for the seduction and perdition of men, to dash him against the ground, and bruise him, but not to kill him. And then, fixing my eyes on Simon, I said to him, 'If I be a man of God, and a real apostle of Jesus Christ, and a teacher of piety, and not of deceit, as thou art, Simon, I command the wicked powers of the apostate from piety, by whom Simon the magician is carried, to let go their hold, that he may fall down headlong from his height, that he may be exposed to the laughter of those that have been seduced by him.' When I had said these words, Simon was deprived of his powers and fell down headlong with a great noise, and was violently dashed against the ground, and had his hip and ankle bones broken, and the people cried out saying, 'There is one only God, whom Peter rightly preaches in truth.' And many left him, but some who were worthy of perdition continued in the wicked doctrine. And after this manner the most atheistic heresy of the Simonians was first established in Rome.

(*The Writings of the Early Church Fathers*, Vol. 7, Apostolic Teachings and Constitution, Book VI, Section I)

So, then, through the visit of the divine word to them, the power of Simon was extinguished, and immediately was destroyed along with the man himself. And such a ray of godliness shone forth on the minds of Peter's hearers that they were not satisfied with the once hearing or with the unwritten teaching of the divine proclamation.

(The Writings of the Early Church Fathers,
Vol. 24, Eusebius Pamphilus, Ecclesiastical
History, Book II, Chapter 15)

As the delusion was extending, Peter and Paul, a noble pair, chief rulers of the Church, arrived and set the error right; and when the supposed god Simon wished to shew himself off, they straightway shewed him as a corpse. For Simon promised to rise aloft to heaven, and came riding in a daemon's chariot on the air, but the servants of God fell on their knees, and having shewn the agreement of which Jesus spake, that If two of you shall agree concerning anything that they shall ask, it shall be done unto them, they launched the weapon of their concord prayer against Magus and struck him down to the earth. And marvelous though it was, yet no marvel. For Peter was there, who carrieth the keys of heaven: and nothing wonderful, for Paul was there, who was caught up to the third heaven and into Paradise, and heard unspeakable words, which it is not lawful for a man to utter. These brought the supposed god down from the sky to earth, thence to be taken down to the regions below the earth.

(The Writings of the Early Church Fathers, Vol. 30,
Cyril, Lecture VI, Concerning the Unity of God)

For, at that time, our divine religion had obtained a wide prevalence in the city. Peter was there executing the office of bishop and Paul, too, after he had been brought to Rome, on appealing to Caesar from the unjust judgement of the governor. Multitudes came together to hear Paul, and these, influenced by the truth which they were given to know, and by the miracles of the apostles, which they then so frequently performed, turned to the worship of God. For then took place the well-known and celebrated encounter of Peter and Paul with Simon. He, after he had flown up into the air by his magical arts, and supported by two demons (with the view of proving that he was a god), the demons being put to flight by the prayers of the apostles, fell to the earth in the sight of all the people, and was dashed to pieces.

(*The Writings of the Early Church Fathers*, Vol. 34, Sulpitius Severus, Sacred History, Book II, Chapter 28)

These stories about Simon Magus having being killed, in some by Peter alone, while in others by Peter and Paul together, are evidently false and were developed later. Irenaeus and Justin Martyr have not mentioned any such thing, though they have written about him and have blamed him to be the source of all heresies. In these stories, too, there are obvious contradictions that expose the falsehood. The second passage has Peter directly reporting of the incident himself. It is stated that he prayed that Simon should be bruised but not killed. Thereafter he prayed that he falls down headlong, and he did fall down headlong with a great noise and was violently dashed against the ground. Despite falling violently headlong, his hip and ankle bones are reported to have been broken. The writer did not feel it necessary to examine which bones should break if a person fell headlong because his purpose was limited to showing that Peter considered Simon Magus to be an adversary. The writer has continued to state that despite this, some people continued to follow his wicked doctrine and this was the manner in which his heresy was first established in Rome. It was of no relevance for him to explain that it was not just a few people who were his followers but even the Emperor Claudius, who had got a statue installed in his honour calling him a Holy God. No writer has stated that after Peter alone or Peter and Paul together had been able to expose the delusion of Simon Magus and to have injured or killed him, his statue was pulled down by Claudius or his successor Nero. Cyril and Severus have stated that Peter and Paul together killed Simon by combining their powers and prayers. Severus has given even the occasion when this happened. As per his statement, it happened when Paul had been brought to Rome on his appeal against the unjust judgement of the governor, while Peter was already the bishop there. Paul's arrival in Rome for his appeal to Caesar has been described in the Acts of the Apostles along with how he was arrested and what transpired before the governor. The account ends with saying that he lived in a hired house for two years and preached to all who came to him. There is neither a mention of Peter being present in Rome, leave aside his being a bishop there, nor of Simon Magus. It is evident that these were the types of stories that had been developed by the fourth century AD to combine the legacy of Peter and Paul, and to distance Peter from Simon Magus, with whom the Apostolic Church and the followers of the Apostles had been linked in Rome and the West.

After Simon Magus, a few more names have been mentioned by different writers, who seem to have been prominent Christian preachers of the Apostolic Church in the West. They all have been called the disciples of Simon Magus or to have taken their doctrine from him. Valentinus is named very prominently amongst them. Comments from Irenaeus about him are in the passage below.

> I should bring to light the Valentinian doctrines, concealed as their votaries imagine, that I should exhibit their diversity and compose a treatise in refutation of them, therefore have undertaken, showing that they spring from Simon, the father of all heretics, to exhibit both their doctrines and succession.
> (*The Writings of the Early Church Fathers*, Vol. 1, Irenaeus, Against Heresies, Book III, Preface)

It is evident that Valentinus and others were all branded as the followers of Simon Magus in the West, though, in fact, they were the followers of the Apostolic Church. This was essentially an exercise on the part of the Pauline Church to establish that it was the real Christian Church preaching what had been taught by the Apostles, while those teaching something different were in no way connected with Jesus Christ. The number of such Christians has, however, been reported to be so large that they could have been the followers of the Apostolic Church only. No preacher, whether it was Simon Magus or Valentinus, could have been able to have such a large following of people, all of whom firmly believed that they were Christians. The presence of these Christians in a large number emerges from the following passage.

> The Valentinians, who are no doubt a very large body of heretics, comprising as they do so many apostates from the truths, who have a propensity for fables, and no discipline to deter them there from, care for nothing, so much so, as to obscure what they preach, if indeed they can be said to preach, who obscure their doctrine. The officiousness with which they guard their doctrine is an officiousness which betrays their guilt.
> (*The Writings of the Early Church Fathers*, Vol. 3, Tertullian, Against the Valentinians, Chapter 1)

Two things have been mentioned about the Valentinians, apart from they being in a very large number. They do not have discipline and that they keep their doctrine secret, keeping it obscure, so that it may not be known to a person to whom they did not wish to impart it. The second point of keeping the doctrine obscure so as to keep it secret and prevent it from being known to undesirable people is an important link of their being from the Apostolic Church and would come up ahead. The mention of an absence of discipline in the Apostolic

Church gives a clue to its failure to withstand the onslaught of the Pauline theology. It shows that in the apostolic traditions, the clergy had a weak organizational set-up in which the believers were left with a lot of liberty. The priests seem to have been concerned only with religious matters. On the other hand, the Pauline traditions seem to have developed a strong organizational structure of the Church. Initially, this would have been because of the necessity of ensuring that the believers believed exactly and only what it taught, but gradually it would have enveloped every facet of life, thus creating a regimental discipline for itself. As the Pauline theology gradually spread and erased the apostolic teachings and as this would have happened in each Church and groups of believers individually, the fact that the Pauline clergy was well-organized and regimentalized, would have given it another great advantage over its disorganized rivals. Though prominent preachers kept emerging on the apostolic side, all of them got clubbed as heretics and could not get associated with the legacy of the Apostles. Some such names emerge from the following passages.

> Menander, who succeeded Simon Magus, showed himself in his conduct another instrument of diabolical power, not inferior to the former. He also was a Samaritan and carried his sorceries to no less extent than his teacher had done, and at the same time reveled in still marvelous tales than he. For he said that he was himself the Saviour, who had been sent down from invisible aeons for the salvation of men.
> (*The Writings of the Early Church Fathers*, Vol. 24, Eusebius Pamphilus, Ecclesiastical History, Book III, Chapter 26)

> Accordingly there proceeded from that Menander, whom we have already mentioned as the successor of Simon, a certain serpent-like power, double-tongued and two-headed, which produced the leaders of two different

heresies, Saturnius, an Antiochian by birth and Basilides an Alexandrian. The former of these established schools of godless heresy in Syria, the latter in Alexandria.

Irenaeus states that the false teaching of Saturnius agreed in most respects with that of Menander, but that Basilides, under the pretext of unspeakable mysteries, invented monstrous fables, and carried the fictions of his impious heresy quite beyond bounds.

(*The Writings of the Early Church Fathers*, Vol. 24, Eusebius Pamphilus, Ecclesiastical History, Book IV, Chapter 7)

In writing about these Christians, who have been called heretics, Eusebius has given an account of only what they conceived God to be and how they thought the world to have been created. Even by the other writers, other aspects of their system and practices have either been mentioned just in passing or have been left out completely. Even what has been recorded, has been done as a hostile critic with the intention of proving them to be false and absolutely against reason, making it difficult to reconstruct their belief system on the basis of the Christian writings alone. They also seem to have been clubbed with the Jews in the West and appear to have suffered persecution at the hands of their fellow Christians of the Pauline Church rather early. This emerges from the following passage.

> For when it was reported that a synagogue of the Jews and a conventicle of the Valentinians had been burnt by Christians at the instigation of the bishop, an order was made while I was at Aquileia that the synagogue should be rebuilt and the monks punished who had burnt the Valentinian building.
>
> (*The Writings of the Early Church Fathers*, Vol. 33, Ambrose, Letter XLI)

Here a conventicle of the Valentinians has been reported to have been burnt along with the synagogue of the Jews by Christians at the instigation of the bishop. The Roman authorities are reported to have ordered that the synagogue be rebuilt and those responsible for the burning of the conventicle of the Valentinians be punished. This shows not only the aggressive stance of the Pauline Church wherever it was strong but also the fact that the Valentinians, though they claimed to be Christians, were treated like the Jews by this Church. This would be a further evidence of the Valentinians being the followers of the Apostolic Church because it is known that the Apostolic Church was Jewish in character.

The process of the Pauline theology replacing the apostolic teachings everywhere got initiated with the acceptance of the Pauline scriptures. It is only the Ebionites who have been reported to have declared Paul to be an apostate and to have rejected all his works. They were the followers of the Church of Jerusalem that had been founded by James, an Apostle and the brother of Jesus. As they had received their traditions from a person who was a witness to what Paul was attempting to do and had also written an epistle questioning Paul's theory that faith alone is sufficient, they had a clarity that Paul and anything Pauline had to be rejected. No other Church could realize this, because of which Pauline scriptures got accepted everywhere. Once these scriptures had been accepted, the takeover by the Pauline theology was an automatic process, which went totally unnoticed. The Churches could not even realize when they had ceased to follow the apostolic teachings and when their theology had become Pauline. In fact, they continued to believe that there had been no change and what they were practising was the same as had been practised in their Church since inception, claiming everything to have come down to them in an unbroken tradition from the times of the Apostles. This would have been an obvious conclusion because their beliefs and practices were in line with the written texts of the scriptures that they had, which clearly stated that Peter and Paul taught the same things. The oral traditions, once they were found to be in contradiction to the written text, would have been rejected and given up without any hesitation because there was no way to know that they were from the Apostles and Paul was their adversary. As in the case of Simon Magus, if any person raised an issue of belief that was a part of his belief system as received in the oral traditions, he was declared to be a heretic and the point raised by him was treated to be a heresy propounded by him. The manner in which Churches became Pauline unnoticed emerges from the case of Alexandria. There is clear evidence that this Church was Jewish when it was established by Mark. This emerges from the following passages.

> So, taking the gospel which he himself composed, he went to Egypt and first preaching Christ at Alexandria he formed a Church so admirable in doctrine and continence of living that he constrained all followers of Christ to his example. Philo, most learned of the Jews, seeing the first Church at Alexandria still Jewish in a degree, wrote a book on their manner of life as something creditable to his nation telling how, as Luke says, the believers had all things in common at Jerusalem, so he recorded that he saw was done at Alexandria, under the learned Mark.
> (*The Writings of the Early Church Fathers*, Vol. 26, Jerome, Lives of Illustrious Men, Chapter 8)

> Philo the Jew, an Alexandrian of the priestly class, is placed by us among the ecclesiastical writers on the ground that, writing a book concerning the first church of Mark, the evangelist at Alexandria, he writes to our praise, declaring not only that they were there, but also that they were in many provinces and calling their habitations monasteries. From this it appears that the church of those that believed

in Christ at first, was such as now the monks desire to imitate.

> (*The Writings of the Early Church Fathers*, Vol. 26, Jerome, Lives of Illustrious Men, Chapter 11)

Jerome has recorded the testimony of Philo the Jew, who was of the first century. This is very significant as it gives a picture of the times when the Apostles were alive and that too from a source that was external to Christianity. His statement has to be accepted as correct on how the Apostles established the Churches and what traditions they laid down. Two things are marked in this account, the Church was Jewish in character and monasticism was the core of the religion. That the Apostolic Church was Jewish has already come up earlier. Monasticism was the core of the teachings of Jesus would emerge ahead. The Church of Alexandria was, thus, an Apostolic Church when it was established. The founder, too, by all accounts, was Mark, a close disciple of Peter, who also translated the Gospel of Matthew into Greek, though it came to be known as his gospel. How and when this Church became Pauline was never noticed, but by the third century it had contributed a lot to the development of the Pauline Church, and when finally an open confrontation broke out between the two theologies, it was at the epicenter with the bishop on one side and a presbyter on the other.

By the beginning of the fourth century, the Pauline scriptures had percolated the West completely, because of which the West had become the stronghold of the Pauline Church, with Rome emerging at the head. It had started calling itself as the Catholic Church. In the East, the Pauline scriptures had started penetrating but their percolation had not been complete. The teachings of the Apostles, as received by oral traditions and the writings of people who came after the Apostles, were still very strong there. The contradictions in what they believed because of their past teachings and what they needed to believe because of the written text that was coming in would have baffled even the best of the priests. That the Pauline scriptures were in the process of being imbibed by the East in the fourth century emerges from the following passage.

> To many persons this Book is so little known, both it and its author, that they are not even aware that there is such a book in existence. For this reason especially I have taken this narrative for my subject, that I may draw to it such as do not know it, and not let such a treasure as this remain hidden out of sight. For indeed it may profit us no less than even the Gospels; so replete is it with Christian wisdom and sound doctrine, especially in what is said concerning the Holy Ghost.
> (*The Writings of the Early Church Fathers*, Vol. 20, John Chrysostom, Homilies on Acts, Homily 1)

These are the opening words of Chrysostom as he begins to comment on the Acts of the Apostles. Chrysostom (AD 349–407) was the bishop of Antioch and Constantinople at different times in his chequered career that finally ended with his death in exile. His statement is very significant because it shows that not only the Acts of the Apostles but even its author, Luke, was little known in the East even up to the end of the fourth century. This would mean that even the Gospel of Luke was unknown in the East till the fourth century. The controversies that arose during the period also confirm the fact that the Pauline scriptures, though they had reached the East, had not percolated deep enough to efface the apostolic teachings because if they had been able to do so, the belief system of the East would have been based on them and issues that were raised could not have been raised or would not have found acceptance by such a large number of people. As already stated, the pattern of the conflict between the Pauline theology and the apostolic teachings in the East remained the same as it had been in the West, though because of the presence of two new factors, the manner in which it unfolded created a lot of conflicts. As in the West, in the East also the beliefs of the Apostolic Church, as they came in conflict with the beliefs of the Pauline theology, were branded to be the new beliefs propounded by the person who raised them. In the process that person was branded as a heretic and the belief he was advocating was declared to be his heresy. Thus, just as the West had Simon Magus, Valentinius, Marcion and others, who, though they were preaching what they had received from the Apostles, were declared to be heretics and the apostolic teaching being taught by them were declared to be their heresies, the East had their counterparts in Arius, Nestorius and others, who were declared heretics in a similar way and the beliefs they had brought forward were condemned as heresies propounded by them, though there are overwhelming reasons to believe that what was declared to be the heresy propounded by these persons was, in fact, the teachings of the Apostles. The takeover of the Apostolic Churches of the East by the Pauline theology would have been as silent and uneventful a process as it had been in the West had it been left to the normal acceptance of the Pauline scriptures in that area, as that was the only real cause by which it happened. Though it did happen only because of this reason and not anything else, two factors created a conflict, with its associated bitterness and violence, which left scars for centuries thereafter. One of these was the involvement of the Roman Empire in the affairs of Christian theology and the other was the consolidation by them of the Pauline theology in the Churches of the West, because of which they, led by Rome, became its vociferous advocates. The combination of these two factors made the conflict, which was essentially between the oral traditions received from the Apostles and the written text of the Pauline theology, a conflict between the Western Church and the Eastern Church. If these two factors had not been there, the apostolic theology would have met as quite a burial in the East just as it had in the West.

It all started with Constantine becoming a Christian and wanting to do whatever he possibly could for the Christian cause. As the basic belief of the religion presented to him was that faith was all that was required for salvation, he felt that this faith must be in the right beliefs. As he found the Christians in his empire to be having diverse beliefs, he felt it necessary to intervene and to have all the Churches to sort their differences out and arrive at a consensus on what the correct Christian belief was, in which he and other seekers of salvation could have faith. There were two issues before him, one was the Paschal question or the manner in which Easter should be observed by the Christians and the other was the Arian controversy. For this, he convened a council of bishops in AD 325 at Nicea in Bithynia, which falls in modern Turkey. With this began the trend of convening councils to settle disputes of theology that were raised. A total of seven such councils, which are called ecumenical, were convened, in which attempts were made to finally define the Christian faith or Creed as it is called. As the acceptance of the Pauline scriptures was the actual cause of the end of the apostolic traditions and this was working unnoticed in the background, when this process was complete, the questions of faith stopped cropping up and the need for convening such councils ended. However, as the issue had been forced at a time when the East was not ripe for the switchover, it created debates, acrimony and bloodshed for several centuries.

If the two issues that were before Constantine for convening the Nicene council are examined, it would be evident that the conflict was between the Apostolic Church and the Pauline

Church. The first issue was the Paschal question. The churches in the West observed Easter on a Sunday and celebrated it as an occasion of festivity, as it was believed that Jesus rose from the dead on that day. The churches of the East, on the other hand, observed the Passover of the Jews in the manner of the Jews on the fourteenth day of the moon. They observed it as an occasion for mourning and kept a fast, as Jesus had been crucified on that occasion. This is brought out in the passages below.

> But before this time another most virulent disorder had existed, and long afflicted the Church, I mean the difference respecting the salutary feast of Easter. For while one party asserted that the Jewish custom should be adhered to, the other affirmed that the exact recurrence of the period should be observed, without following the authority of those who were in error and strangers to gospel grace. Accordingly, the people being thus in every place divided in respect of this and the sacred observances of religion remained confounded for a long period.
> (*The Writings of the Early Church Fathers*, Vol. 24, Eusebius Pamphilus, Ecclesiastical History, Book III, Chapter 5)

> A question of no small importance arose at that time. For the parishes of all Asia, as from an older tradition, held that the fourteenth day of the moon, on which day the Jews are commanded to sacrifice the lamb, should be observed as the feast of the Saviour's Passover. It was necessary to end their fast on that day whatever day of the week it should happen to be.
> (*The Writings of the Early Church Fathers*, Vol. 24, Eusebius Pamphilus, Ecclesiastical History, Book V, Chapter 23)

Constantine was also deeply grieved at the diversity of opinion which prevailed concerning the celebration of the Passover, for some of the cities of the East differed on this point, although they did not withhold communion with one another, they kept the festival more according to the manner of the Jews, and as was natural by this divergence, detracted from the splendor of the festal sacrifice.

(The Writings of the Early Church Fathers, Vol. 25, Hermias Sozomen, Ecclesiastical History, Book I, Chapter 16)

For as the bishops of the West did not deem it necessary to dishonor the tradition handed down to them by Peter and by Paul, and as, on the other hand, the Asiatic bishops persisted in following the rules laid down by John the evangelist, they unanimously agreed to continue in the observance of the festival according to their respective customs, without separation from communion with each other.

(The Writings of the Early Church Fathers, Vol. 25, Hermias Sozomen, Ecclesiastical History, Book VII, Chapter 19)

Let the prudence consistent with your sacred character consider how grievous and indecorous it is that on the same days some should be observing fasts, while others are celebrating feasts; and after the days of Easter some should indulge in festivities and enjoyments, and others submit to appointed fasting.

(The Writings of the Early Church Fathers, Vol. 25, Socrates Scholasticus, Ecclesiastical History, Book I, Chapter 9)

Quartodecimans affirm that the observance of the fourteenth day was delivered to them by the Apostle John, while the Romans and those in the Western part assure us that their usage originated with the Apostles Peter and Paul. (*The Writings of the Early Church Fathers*, Vol. 25, Socrates Scholasticus, Ecclesiastical History, Book V, Chapter 22)

These passages bring out the difference in the perception of the Churches of the East and the West regarding Easter and the manner in which it was to be observed. As it was a continuing practice of the East and had not been propounded by anyone in recent times, it could not be blamed on anyone and be called a heresy in his name. The practice was evidently universal in the East. There were several differences with the practices of the West in this. First was the day on which it was to be celebrated and what was believed about it. The West celebrated it as Easter and observed it on a Sunday, as that was the day on which Christ was believed to have risen from the dead, while the East observed it on the fourteenth day of the moon, like the Jews observed it, not as Easter, but as the Passover. Next, the West celebrated it with festivities as it was an occasion for rejoicing, as Christ had risen from the dead. The East observed it with fasting, like the Jews, and had mourning attached to it, obviously because as per the teachings of the Apostles, Jesus was crucified on that occasion. They did not have the concept of his having risen from the dead to start with when the traditions of the manner in which this occasion was to be observed were laid down. Apparently, the Christians in the East were celebrating it as a Passover only and not something in the manner of the Passover because the Apostles were Judaizing the Gentiles while converting them to Christianity. As the Passover is a major Jewish festival, the Christians, on being Judaised, were also celebrating it in the same manner and on the same day as the Jews were. However, as Jesus had been crucified on that day, it became an occasion for mourning also. With the resurrection of Jesus not being a part of their early beliefs, the matter ended there and no cause for rejoicing or festivities could be thought of. This perception of the occasion is an obvious perception if the resurrection of Jesus is not a part of the belief system, as the Saviour, who in this case would be perceived as the founding teacher of the believers, was killed on that day. As people following him were converted to Judaism, as that was the religion he followed, they observed all the rituals and festivals of that religion.

When the matter came up before Constantine, it has been stated that the East claimed that they did so because it had been laid down by John, while the West claimed that they were following the traditions laid down by Peter and Paul. Evidently, the myth that Peter was the bishop of Rome for 25 years and lay buried there after being killed by Nero had been developed so completely that it had erased the association of Peter with the East. The East could not claim his legacy, even though it was admitted that he was the bishop of Antioch before moving to Rome. It is on occasions like this that the wisdom of the Pauline Church in giving up the hostility, which Paul showed towards the Apostles in his lifetime, and associating Peter to its traditions becomes evident. If Peter had not been linked to the traditions of the Pauline Church, it is extremely doubtful that the West would have carried the day. With the authority of Peter and Paul on one side and that of John on the other, and the hostility towards the Jews added to it as they carried the blame for having killed Jesus, the outcome was a foregone conclusion. Constantine decided that it was unbecoming on the part of the Christians to be following the Jews as they were refused the grace of God to have not been able to recognize the divine in Jesus and to have killed him. He issued an imperial edict directing the East to observe Easter in the manner in which the West did.

The Paschal question, though on its face, does not seem to

be having any theological angle involved in it, as it appears to have been a dispute only about when and how Easter was to be celebrated, but deep within it had the question of the belief in the resurrection of Jesus. The East observing the occasion with mourning shows that it did not believe in the resurrection of Jesus, just as the Apostles did not. However, when the issue came up before the emperor, they have not been reported to have said so. Evidently, the debate did not go into the reasons why the West celebrated it with festivities and the East observed it with mourning but was limited to how these traditions got established. The Pauline scriptures, too, by then seem to have reached far enough in the East to prevent them from denying the resurrection of Christ.

The other issue before Constantine was theological. It has been called the Arian Heresy. Arius was a presbyter in the Church of Alexandria, while his bishop was Alexander. It was reported to the bishop that Arius was preaching things different from the Church beliefs. When he was asked about the same, he explained what he was preaching and how he believed that it was the true Christian doctrine. This was totally against what Alexander believed and what he found written in the Scriptures. As his attempts to persuade Arius to correct himself failed, he excommunicated him from the Church and wrote a long account to the other Churches of what had happened and how the views expressed by Arius were contrary to the laid down Christian beliefs. This virtually split the Churches of the East and the West, and was the cause of their final rupture a few centuries later. While the West supported the bishop Alexander and concurred with his views, the East came out in support of Arius and felt that his excommunication was not proper. After the Paschal question, this controversy over the views of Arius was the next issue that Constantine was attempting to resolve in the Council of Nicea.

All along, in the history of Christianity, this has been called the Arian Heresy and it has been projected that Arius was the originator of these views and a lot many people became a victim of his heresy, which was ultimately extinguished by the true Christian doctrine. This does not appear to be true. When the wide support and following of the Arian view is seen, it becomes obvious that these people had not fallen a victim to the Arian Heresy by being influenced by him but that it was their belief system that had been articulated by Arius when it came in conflict with the doctrines of the Pauline Church. Its wide prevalence shows that this was the belief system of the Apostles that had survived till then in an oral tradition in the East and now was in conflict with the Pauline theology that had the support of written texts and was gradually moving from the West, where it had already uprooted the Apostolic Church with the adoption of Pauline scriptures much earlier. Adoption of these scriptures being the actual cause by which Pauline theology replaced the apostolic teachings everywhere, their effect needed time to mature for a smooth takeover because, over a period of time, what was found written by an Apostle long ago would have been deemed to be correct over what was stated by the immediate teacher with the claim that it had come down to them in an oral tradition. Even if some disciples of the Apostles had written something after their teachings, their testimony would stand to be rejected in front of the direct statements of the Apostles that were claimed in the Pauline scriptures. As the East was not given the time by which this process could ripen and the apostolic teachings could be silently replaced unnoticed because the Roman emperor intervened to force an immediate acceptance of an agreed belief system, the next few centuries witnessed the phenomenon of issues being raised in the East that were branded as heresies in the name of the person who raised them and ecumenical councils being convened to find answers, leading finally to the Churches of the East and the West parting ways with each other. What happened in the East was in the same lines as what had already happened in the West. The first person in the East to have been blamed to have raised a heresy was Arius, just as in the West Simon Magus had been projected to be a heretic and the teachings of the Apostles were ascribed to him. As in the case of Simon Magus a huge following spread over a large area was reported for him, it gets revealed that what was being stated to be his following was, in fact, of the Apostolic Church. In the case of Arius also the same huge following betrays the fact that what has been claimed as the Arian heresy was the belief system of the Churches of the East that they had received from the Apostles, which had not till then been uprooted by the Pauline theology as the Pauline scriptures had made an entry not very long ago. The massive following that has been reported for Arius before and after Nicene emerges from the passages below.

> For ye yourselves are taught of God, nor are ye ignorant that this doctrine, which hath lately raised its head against the piety of the Church, is that of Ebion and Artemas; nor is it aught else but an imitation of Paul of Samosata, bishop of Antioch, who by the judgement and counsel of all the bishops, and in every place, was separated from the Church. To whom Lucian succeeding, remained for many years separate from the communion of three bishops. And now lately having drained the dregs of their impiety, there have arisen amongst us those who teach this doctrine of a creation from things which are not, their hidden sprouts, Arius and Achilles, and the gathering of those who join in their wickedness. And three bishops in Syria, having been in some manner, consecrated on account of their agreement with them, incite them to worse things.
> (*The Writings of the Early Church Fathers*, Vol. 6, Alexander of Alexandria, Epistles on the Arian Heresy, Epistle 1)

> But since Eusebius, the present bishop of Nicomedia, imagining that with him rest all ecclesiastic matters, because having left Berytus and cast his eyes upon the Church of the Nicomedians, and no punishment has been inflicted upon him, he is set over these apostates, and has undertaken to write everywhere commending them, if by any means he may draw aside some who are ignorant to his most disgraceful and anti Christian heresy.
> (*The Writings of the Early Church Fathers*, Vol. 6, Alexander of Alexandria, Epistles on the Arian Heresy, Epistle 2)

> On his death the doctrine which had been set forth at Nicea was subjected to renewed examination. Although this doctrine was not universally approved, no one during the life of Constantine had dared to reject it openly. At his death, however, many renounced this opinion, especially those who had previously been suspected of treachery. Of all these Eusebius and Theognis, the bishops of the province of Bithynia did everything in their power to give predominance to the tenets of Arius.
> (*The Writings of the Early Church Fathers*, Vol. 25, Hermius Sozomen, Ecclesiastical History, Book III, Chapter 1)

> Eusebius, your brother bishop of Caesarea, Theodotus, Paulinus, Athanasius, Gregorius, Aetius and all the bishops of the East, have been condemned because they say that God had an existence prior to that of His son.
> (*The Writings of the Early Church Fathers*, Vol. 26, Theodoret, Ecclesiastical History, Book I, Chapter 4)

> All these bishops (of Antioch) secretly clung to the Arian heresy.
> (*The Writings of the Early Church Fathers*, Vol. 26, Theodoret, Ecclesiastical History, Book I, Chapter 21)

And before Nicene Council took place, similar statements were made by Eusebius and his fellows, Narcissus, Patroplilus, Maris, Paulinus, Theodotus and Athanasius of Anazarba. And Eusebius of Nicomedia wrote over and above to Arius to this effect, 'Since your sentiments are good, pray that all may adopt them; for it is plain to anyone, that what has been made was not before its origination, but what came to be has a beginning of being.' And Eusebius of Caesarea in Palestine, in a letter to Euphration the bishop, did not scruple to say plainly that Christ was not true God.
(*The Writings of the Early Church Fathers*, Vol. 27, Athanasius, Councils of Ariminum and Seleucia, History of the Councils)

For the conflagration which has devoured a great part of the East is already advancing by slow degrees into our own neighbourhood and after burning everything round about us is trying to reach even the Churches of Cappadocia.
(*The Writings of the Early Church Fathers*, Vol. 31, Basil, Letters, Letter 222)

Nearly all the East (I include under this name all regions from Illyricum to Egypt) is being agitated, right honourable father, by a terrible storm and tempest. The old heresy sown by Arius the enemy of the truth, has now boldly and unblushingly reappeared. Like some sour root, it is producing its deadly fruit and is prevailing. The reason for this is, that in every district the champions of right doctrine have been exiled from their Churches by calumny and outrage, and the control of affairs has been handed over to men who are leading captive the souls of the simpler brethren.
(*The Writings of the Early Church Fathers*, Vol. 31, Basil, Letters, Letter 70)

It is with a full knowledge of the dangers and passions of the time that I have ventured to attack this wild and godless heresy, which asserts that the Son of God is a creature. Multitudes of Churches in almost every province of the Roman Empire have already caught the plague of this deadly doctrine; errors, persistently inculcated and falsely claiming to be the truth, has become ingrained in minds which vainly imagine that they are loyal to the faith.
(*The Writings of the Early Church Fathers*, Vol. 32, Hilary of Poiters, Contra Arianos, Book VI)

After this, when the Arian heresy had spread through the whole world and was especially powerful in Illyria, and when he, almost single handed was fighting, he established a monastery for himself in Milan.
(*The Writings of the Early Church Fathers*, Vol. 34, Sulpitius Severus, On the Life of St, Martin, Chapter 6)

But then the Arians, seeing that stratagem did not succeed, determined to proceed by force.
Moreover, they were by the consent of all unconquerable; for almost all the bishops of the two Pannonias, and many of the Eastern bishops, and those throughout all Asia, had joined in their unfaithfulness.
(*The Writings of the Early Church Fathers*, Vol. 34, Sulpitius Severus, Chronicle, Book II, Chapter 38)

So also when the Arian poison had infected not an insignificant portion of the Church but almost the whole world, so that a sort of blindness had fallen upon almost all the bishops of the Latin tongue circumvented partly by force partly by fraud and was preventing them from seeing what was most expedient to be done in the midst of so much confusion, then whoever was a true lover and worshipper of Christ, preferring the ancient belief to the novel misbelieve, escaped the pestilent infection.

(*The Writings of the Early Church Fathers*, Vol. 34, Vincent of Lerius, Against Profane Novelties of All Heresies, Chapter 4)

These passages give an idea of how widely accepted were the beliefs that have been dubbed in the name of Arius and have been called a heresy. The first passage has linked it to Ebion, which is a reference to the Ebionites, the Jewish Christians of the Church of Jerusalem that had James as its first bishop. Though the followers of James had begun to be branded as heretics in the Christian Church much before this time, this reference shows that what has been ascribed to be an innovation brought about by Arius was in reality what James had preached. There is also a mention of three bishops of Syria having the same view. The next passage speaks of Eusebius, the bishop of Nicomedia. There were two brothers at that time, both named Eusebius and both very prominent. One was the bishop of Nicomedia and the other of Caesarea, the latter of the two has also written the *Ecclesiastical History*. Both are reported to be following and supporting the Arian Heresy. The bishop of Nicomedia held a more prominent position in the Christian world at that time. Alexander, the bishop of Alexandria with whom the controversy with Arius had broken out, is the writer of this passage, which is from an epistle to the bishops of other Churches. He has complained that Eusebius, the bishop of Nicomedia, has taken the lead of the apostates and has written letters to the other Churches in support of the doctrines that have been claimed to have been propounded by Arius and has recommended to all that they may be accepted. The third passage gives the position of the times after the death of Constantine, who had got the Council of Nicea to reject the Arian Heresy and had got a formal declaration made of what the correct Christian faith was. This passage shows that it was the imperial authority of Constantine that had overawed the people into accepting the Nicene Creed. It was accepted as long as he was alive, but as soon as the fear of him had ceased, the bishops in the East renounced it and very prominent bishops are reported to have been promoting the Arian Heresy. The next few passages mention the prominent bishops of the East of the time who were with the Arian doctrine and were condemned by the Pauline Church. The list includes some very noteworthy names, including that of Eusebius of Caesarea and the bishops of Antioch. The further passages speak of the entire East to be with Arius and to have exiled the priests of the Pauline Church from their area. The last passage is significant as it is not speaking of the East but of the West. It has been stated that the Arian poison had infected almost the whole world and almost all the bishops of the Latin tongue were with it. Latin was the language of the Western Church. This mention by Vincent of Lerins that almost all the bishops of the West were with the Arian Heresy shows that up to the fourth and fifth centuries the apostolic theology had not totally died even in the West. The Pauline theology had taken over but somewhere the apostolic theology were also there, because of which when someone brought them forward and people sided with them.

A perusal of these accounts of the support enjoyed by the doctrine that has been stated to have been propounded by Arius shows that this could not have been anything but what the Apostles preached. Arius was only a presbyter of Alexandria. He was not even a bishop. It is not possible that something propounded by him, which if it had been alien to the existing beliefs of the East, would have received an immediate acceptance by all the prominent theologians and bishops of the East, and in course of time found acceptance even in the West. It is obvious that the belief system that he had brought forward before Alexander, his bishop at Alexandria, was the belief system of the entire East at that time, because of which as soon as it became an issue and was raised, the entire East stood by him. Since it was the belief system of the entire East, and in course of time almost all the bishops of the West also agreed with it, it has to be concluded that this was based on the teachings of people far greater than Arius, who could be only the Apostles. The Pauline Church, just as it distanced the apostolic theology from Christianity in the West by dubbing them as the teachings of Simon Magus, started the same process in the East, the first such person being Arius. The belief system that was of the entire East at the time and was also found to be acceptable by almost all bishops of West has been dubbed as the Arian Heresy and has been distanced from Christianity.

That the Arian Heresy was the belief system of the entire East in the fourth century emerges also from the manner in which the Nicene council was conducted and what has been reported happened after it. A general impression has been created that the Council of Nicea was a conference of bishops in which, after a free debate, a consensus was arrived at, which was declared as the true Christian faith. This is not the correct picture. It was evidently an exercise to force the East to agree to the belief system of the West, which by then had become completely Pauline. The council was attended by about 250 bishops and many more presbyters and deacons, of whom only five were from the West. It was presided by Hosius the bishop of Cordoba in Spain, when the emperor was not attending it. It lasted for 67 days, beginning on the 19 June and concluding on 25 August. During these long deliberations no consensus could be arrived at. Apparently, during this period the bishops of the East would have been required to establish the correctness of their beliefs received through their traditions on the touchstone of the written Scriptures, which the Western bishops would have presented. As no conclusion seemed to emerge from the deliberations for such a long time,

Constantine is reported to have taken the chair on the final day. Though Hosius was presiding in his absence and normally he should have been asked to present the agreed draft of the declaration of faith, but as there was no such agreed draft, Constantine asked the Eastern bishops to present the draft. On behalf of the East, Eusebius, the bishop of Nicomedia, presented a draft declaration of their faith. This is reported to have been summarily torn and rejected by Constantine. Eusebius of Nicomedia then presented the second draft. This was accepted by the emperor after adding one word, which is translated as 'consubstantial' in it, on the advice of Hosius, stating the Father and the Son to be consubstantial. All the bishops and others present were asked to sign the declaration as a token of their agreement to it. While 318 signed, five refused to do so and were exiled, these included Eusebius, the bishop of Nicomedia. The frustration of Eusebius, the bishop of Caesarea, too, is evident in the following passage.

> This we have been forced to transmit to you, Beloved, as making clear to you the deliberation of our inquiry and assent, and how reasonably we resisted even to the last minute as long as we were offended at statements which differed from our own, but received without contention what no longer pained us, as soon as, on a candid examination of the sense of the words, they appeared to us to coincide with what we ourselves have professed in the faith which we have already published.
> (*The Writings of the Early Church Fathers*, Vol. 27, Eusebius Pamphilus, Letter of Eusebius to the people of his Diocese)

The fact that Eusebius was compelled to write a letter to the believers in his diocese to explain that what had been agreed was in some way the same that they had always believed and that they had, even to the last minute, resisted what they found offending is a clear evidence that the East had been forced to accept something they did not believe, having been overawed by the authority of the emperor. The first draft that was presented by Eusebius, the bishop of Nicomedia, was summarily rejected. This would have contained their real beliefs, perhaps modified to an extent on being compared with the written text of the Scriptures presented by the West. No writer has mentioned anything on what this contained. It seems very likely that this would have contained the doctrines that have been dubbed as the Arian Heresy. Evidently, Constantine was not prepared to permit any further debate. The council had been in session for over two months, during which the East had the opportunity to compare its beliefs with the written Scriptures and with what the West believed. The emperor, too, does not seem to be having an open mind. A decision had to be taken, which was already there in the emperor's mind, but it had to come from the East and had to come on that day itself. After a struggle of over two months with the Western bishops and the written scripture that they presented along with the claimed legacy of Peter on their side, the East evidently capitulated in front of the imperial authority of the first Christian emperor to sign and ratify the Nicene Creed.

Religious beliefs cannot be changed by imperial edicts, therefore, it would be wrong to say that Nicene replaced the Apostolic Church by the Pauline theology in the East. It was only the fear of the emperor that kept the people from openly questioning it during his lifetime. A passage has already been quoted that shows that immediately on the death of Constantine many renounced the Nicene Creed. Though in present times some of the opponents to this are opposed to only the word 'consubstantial', this was not the case in the fourth century. There were some who were opposed to this word only, while there were others who rejected the entire Nicene Creed outright. Even the Church of Jerusalem rejected the Nicene Creed completely. The complete rejection of this by some emerges from the following passage.

> Those who deny the Council altogether, are sufficiently exposed by these brief remarks; those, however, who accept everything else that was defined at Nicea, and doubt only about the Coessential, must not be treated as enemies, nor do we here attack them as Ariomaniacs, nor as opponents of the Fathers, but we discuss the matter with them as brothers with brothers, who mean what we mean and dispute only about the word.
> (*The Writings of the Early Church Fathers*, Vol. 27, Athanasius, Councils of Ariminum and Seleucia, Part I)

The views of Arius that were considered to be heretical by Alexander, the bishop of Alexandria, may be seen in the passage below.

> For since they call in question all pious and apostolic doctrine, after the manner of the Jews, they have constructed a workshop for contending against Christ, denying the Godhead of our Saviour, and preaching that He is only the equal of all others.
>
> Wherefore without delay, brethren beloved, I have stirred myself up to show you the faithlessness of these men who say that there was a time when the Son of God was not; and that He who was not before, came into existence afterwards, becoming such, when at length He was made, even as every man is wont to be born.
>
> For He did not choose Him as having by nature anything specially beyond His other sons, for no one is by nature a Son of God, as they say; neither as having any peculiar property of His own; but God chose Him who was of a mutable nature, on account of the carefulness of His manners and His practice, which in no way turned to

that which is evil; so that if Paul and Peter had striven for this, there would have been no difference between their sonship and His.

(The Writings of the Early Church Fathers, Vol. 6, Alexander of Alexandria, Epistles on the Arian Heresy, Epistle I)

This belief of Arius is similar to that of the Ebionites that Jesus was born as an ordinary human being like everyone else. He was not by nature the Son of God with any divinity attached to him. It was 'on account of the carefulness of His manners and His practices, which in no way turned to that which is evil' that he achieved divinity. If Paul and Peter or for that matter anybody else would have striven for this in the like manner, he would achieve the same divinity and that would not be in any way different from what had been achieved by Jesus. In effect, it means that nobody is born with any special qualities but by 'the carefulness of manners and practices', everyone can achieve divinity and achieve what Jesus had achieved. This is a part of a larger theological system that would come up for examination ahead. Alexander has raised only a very small component of it that came in conflict with the Pauline theology directly, which propounded that simply having faith in Jesus being the Son of God and that He rose from the dead was sufficient for salvation. The other elements of this belief system, as they did not come in conflict with the Pauline theology directly, were not raised by Alexander.

Nicene decided the Jesus was the Son of God and that the Father and Son were consubstantial. The matter could not have ended there because in the Trinity, the belief is of God the Father, the Son and the Holy Ghost. Nicene had only mentioned a belief in the Holy Ghost. It had not declared Him to be consubstantial with the Father and the Son, so a dispute arose whether He was so. While the West believed that the Holy Ghost was also consubstantial with the Father and the Son, the East had no such belief. As the East had already sought a rethinking of the Nicene Creed, this issue got added to the differences between the two sides. The differences in the views of the two sides over the belief in the Holy Ghost emerges from the following passages.

> To place briefly before your Grace the differences between the errors of the Arians and the Donatists, the Arian say that the Father, the Son and the Holy Ghost are different in substance; whereas the Donatists do not say this but acknowledge the unity of substance in the Trinity.
> (*The Writings of the Early Church Fathers*, Vol. 13, Augustine, Treatise Concerning the Correction of the Donatists)

Question was renewed at this juncture which had previously excited much inquiry and now more, namely, whether the Holy Ghost is or is not to be considered consubstantial with the Father and the Son. Many contentions and debates ensued on this subject, similar to those which had been held concerning the nature of God the Word. Those who asserted that the Son is dissimilar from the Father, and those who insisted that He is similar in substance to the Father, came to one common opinion concerning the Holy Ghost, for both parties maintained that the Holy Ghost differs in substance, and that He is but the Minister and the third in point of order, honour and substance. Those on the contrary, who believed that the Son is consubstantial with the Father, held also the same view about the Spirit.
(*The Writings of the Early Church Fathers*, Vol. 25, Hermias Sozomen, Ecclesiastical History, Book VI, Chapter 22)

> But on the subject of the Holy Spirit the blasphemy is plain

and unconcealed, he says that He is not to be ranked with the Father or the Son, but is subject to both.

(*The Writings of the Early Church Fathers*, Vol. 28, Gregory of Nyssa, Against Eunomius, Book I, Chapter 15)

The next major issue that cropped up was regarding Mary. The West had developed the belief of Jesus being the Son of God much earlier, because of which they considered Mary to be the Mother of God. The East was still in the process of accepting Jesus as the Son of God as the Arian beliefs were still very strong, which insisted that Jesus was a mere man and everybody had the potential of becoming what he had become. In such a situation, they considered Mary to be the mother of Jesus but not the Mother of God. When this issue cropped up, it was dubbed as a heresy propounded by Nestorius and is called the Nestorian Heresy. Nestorius was the bishop of Constantinople who got condemned as a heretic in the Council of Ephesus and was thereafter sent into exile. Though the heresy linked to him is regarding not accepting Mary as the Mother of God, in essence the question was the same as was raised by Arius, Pelegius and others, whether Jesus was the Son of God by nature or he acquired divinity by his efforts. If Jesus was born as the Son of God, obviously, his mother would have to be believed to be the Mother of God, but if he was born a mere human and acquired divinity by his efforts, then Mary could be called only the mother of Jesus and not the Mother of God. This common thread in all these heresies has been noticed by Cassian, as emerges from the following passage where he is discussing the Nestorian doctrine.

> You say then that Christ was born a mere man. But certainly this was asserted by that wicked heresy of Pelegius, as we clearly showed in the first book, that Christ was born a mere man. You add besides, that Jesus Christ the Lord of all should be termed a form that received

> God, i.e. not God, but the receiver of God, so that your view is that He is to be honoured not for His own sake because He is God, but because he receives God into Himself. But clearly this also was asserted by that heresy of which I spoke before, by that Christ was not to be worshipped for His own sake because He was God, but because owing to His good and pious actions He won this, viz. To have God dwelling in Him.
>
> (*The Writings of the Early Church Fathers*, Vol. 34, John Cassian, Seven Books Against Nestorius, Book V, Chapter 1)

Just as in the case of Simon Magus and Arius, the wide support that Nestorius is reported to have enjoyed shows that what has been alleged to have been a heresy propounded by Nestorius was, in fact, the belief of the East that had come in conflict with the Pauline belief system being advocated by the West. This wide support in the East is again a pointer to it being a tradition received from the Apostles that had survived till then despite the Pauline scriptures having come in. The support Nestorius had emerges from the following passage.

> When we had assembled, according to the religious decree of the Emperor, in the metropolis of Ephesus, certain persons, a little more than thirty in number, withdrew from amongst us, having for the leader of their schism John, Bishop of Antioch. Their names are as follows...
>
> These men, having no privilege of ecclesiastical communion on the ground of a priestly authority, by which they could injure or benefit any person, since some of them had already been disposed, and since from their refusing to join in our decree against Nestorius, it was manifestly evident to all men that they were all promoting the opinions of Nestorius and Celestius, the Holy Synod, by one common decree, deposed them from all ecclesiastical communion,

and deprived them of all their priestly power by which they might injure or profit any persons.

> (*The Writings of the Early Church Fathers*, Vol. 37, The Canons of the Two Hundred Fathers Who Met At Ephesus)

This record of the Council of Ephesus shows that more than 30 bishops, all from the East, refused to condemn Nestorius and left the conference. These bishops are reported to have met in a separate council that was attended by 43 bishops and was presided over by John, the Bishop of Antioch. It held the view that Nestorius could not be condemned without giving him an opportunity of presenting his defence. It also proceeded to depose Cyril of Alexandria who was the leading figure in all the deliberations and declarations of Ephesus. All others who had given consent to the decisions in that council were also excommunicated. The reaction on the part of these 43 bishops of the East shows not only the wide support that the views of Nestorius had in the East but also how strongly his supporters felt about them. Ephesus was a council convened on the orders of the emperor, who was bound to put its decision into effect, if need be, by an imperial edict. These bishops not only took the risk of being themselves condemned as heretics by the said council but went ahead to hold a parallel council to excommunicate all bishops of the other council. Amidst all these wrangling, a stage was reached wherein the East and the West ceased to meet each other and started having separate councils to determine questions of religion. Things worsened further with both sides excommunicating each other and becoming separate Churches, often hostile, a hostility which reached an unfortunate level when the Pope ordered a crusade against the Eastern Church and Christian armies from Italy attacked Constantinople, destroying the Eastern Churches there and killing the clergy and believers en masse in the city.

These unfortunate centuries in the history of Christianity were not a necessary requirement for the Pauline theology to dislodge the apostolic traditions. By the eighth century, the Eastern Church had also become Pauline. The differences that remained between the East and the West after that and that are there amongst the different Churches now are of no real consequence. They are either a legacy of the past or are a question of authority, as the Pope, being the Bishop of Rome, claims to be the supreme head of all Churches of the world by virtue of being the successor to the throne of Peter. However, all substantial points of differences in the theology died out by the eighth century, not because of any number of councils that were held or the debates that took place between the East and the West. No amount of sermons from the West or edicts from the Roman emperors could possibly have been successful in dislodging the apostolic traditions. This could happen only by a silent process that remained unnoticed once the Pauline scriptures had been adopted, the written texts overruling whatever was not in line with them in the traditions received with no textual support from the Apostles. The efforts of the Roman emperors, which eventually led to forcing issues before the time was ripe for them, may have hastened the process by hastening the spread of the Pauline scriptures and requiring the people to re-examine their tradition-based beliefs in the light of the written texts, but beyond this they do not seem to have contributed to the process. Pauline theology crept into all Churches on the strength of its written texts, without anybody even noticing it, making Christianity the world over Pauline and only Pauline, in a way proving true the words of God as claimed by Paul to have been spoken to him 'My grace is sufficient for thee' (2 Corinthians 12:9).

5

RETRIEVING THE LOST TEACHINGS

The urge to search for the teachings of Jesus cannot end, even if it is has been established that they have been submerged by the Pauline theology in all surviving Churches. The study of how Paul contended with the Apostles and how Pauline theology replaced the traditions left by the Apostles gives an idea of where they need to be looked for. It is the beliefs of the people who were declared heretics and the Gnostics of the East that have to be taken into account for this purpose. As the beliefs of the Apostles, as established by an oral tradition, were superseded by the Pauline theology with its written text, whatever has been suppressed or was attempted to be suppressed by the Pauline Church has to come within the ambit of examination as being likely to have been the teaching of Jesus. The Eastern Church, the present-day Orthodox Church, which continued with the apostolic traditions for a longer time and withstood the onslaught of the Pauline theology much longer, could also be of help in this regard, especially on points on which it differs from the Catholic Church, now the Church of Rome. A lot has been written by the early writers about these heretics, making it possible to reconstruct the belief system propounded by Jesus to a very large extent, if not completely. These writers, however, have written as hostile critics, aiming to discredit the heretics, so their beliefs emerge from these writing in a distorted and disjointed manner. It would be easier if a parallel belief system that was in the area is understood, with which the beliefs of

Jesus appear to be having a marked degree of similarity. Once this belief system is understood, all the essential elements of this belief system can be looked into for what Christianity has suppressed or tried to suppress in the name of heresy, over the ages, to become Pauline.

The parallel religious beliefs of the area having similarity with the beliefs of Jesus are of a remarkable group of people clubbed under the name of Aryans. A segment of these people fortunately came to India, where alone their religious literature and beliefs survived almost in their original form. Based on the evidence that emerges from the Vedas of the Hindus and the Avesta of the Zoroastrians, a broad historical account of these people has been brought out in another book by the author—*An Aryan Journey*. It emerges therein that before the last Ice Age, the entire land mass of at least Europe and Central Asia had very dangerous animals that made it very difficult for man to survive. In search of safety, some groups of humans tried to move away and moved north till they reached the Arctic Circle. It is here that they survived for several thousand years, till the end of the Ice Age. The Ice Age killed all the dangerous animals and humans that had stayed back on land, as their food disappeared with the entire land mass going under ice. The people in the Arctic Circle survived because they were not dependent on land for food. Their food was from water that was below the ice on which they were living. With food remaining available where they had always found it and having been acclimatized with the Arctic cold for several thousand years before the onset of the Ice Age, these people could weather those terrible conditions and survived to trickle down south after the Ice Age was over, only to find no other human race in their long journey till they reached the Arabian Sea.

The delta of the river Ili near Lake Balkhash in modern Kazakhstan was a place of great importance in the history of these people. They stayed there for a long time and there is evidence to show that at least by this time they had built up a remarkable system of religious beliefs. Here they also developed differences amongst themselves over certain religious practices and split into two fiercely hostile rival groups, calling themselves Devs and Asurs. The impact of this split and its consequences for the history of the world has not been appreciated because the events have been lost in antiquity. These two inimical groups, the Devs and the Asurs, after fighting a series of battles amongst themselves, at times with the support of neighbouring people, finally got uprooted from the delta of Ili River, which has been called Arjika in the Vedas and Airyana Vaego in the Avesta. The Vedas mention these people next in the delta of the river Amu Dariya in modern Uzbekistan. The river Oxus, as this was known in the past, remained the main habitation of the Devs for long. With the growth of population, they migrated in several directions from there. The early records mention the area east of the Caspian Sea as Devasthan, which gives the impression that this also would have been their homeland for a long period. The Asurs, as a population block, seem to have parted ways from the Devs from the Amu Dariya area, because of which the Vedas cease to mention them with a historic perspective, though they continued to haunt them in their mythology and a small segment from amongst them stayed behind to keep their religious beliefs alive. The area, south of what was termed as Devasthan, has been called Asuristan in the Eastern sources and Babylon in the Western sources. The name Asuristan, where the Assyrian Empire was established with several of its emperors using the word Asur as either a prefix or suffix to their names, like Asur Banipal, Asur Hadden etc., gives an impression that this is where the Asurs went after parting ways from the Devs. There is, however, no evidence in the Vedas to support this except that from a position of complete ascendency in the Amu Dariya area, the Asurs suddenly appear to have completely lost ground. The issue would need to be examined from other sources to arrive at a firm conclusion.

So far as the teachings of Jesus are concerned, it is not relevant whether the Assyrians were the Asurs of the Vedas as it is the religious system of the Devs that is material on this issue. The Devs, in the Vedas, are next noticed in the capital of the Persians kings, as their priests. It emerges therein that though the writers of the Vedas were in Iran, mainly as priests, but Iran was not their homeland. Their homeland was to the north, which has been named Turan in the Zoroastrian sources. The Dev religion was, however, the religion of the kings and the people of Iran also, for which these Devs were their priests. At a stage, Zoroaster, who was of the Asur religion, emerged on the scene. For some time, he advocated his religion before the king and the people without success. He is reported to have been imprisoned by the king of Iran. The Zoroastrian sources state that Vistasp, the king of Iran, because of certain miracles, got converted to Zoroastrianism and released Zoroaster from the prison to make him the chief priest. It is, however, possible that Vistasp had political reasons for his decision, as Iran and Turan had become inimical neighbours, having fought two wars already between themselves, so the king must have felt it to be a dangerous situation to have religious leaders and priests of the religion of the people being sympathetic to the enemy. Vistasp's decision to convert the entire population of Iran to Zoroastrianism led to the persecution of the priests and believers of the Dev religion. Evidence from the Zoroastrian sources shows that, amongst other places, these people fled to Greece and India. The Vedas confirm their coming to India alone.

The Indus Valley Civilization was flourishing at that time and had a flourishing trade with the West. The fleeing Dev population came to India in Indian trade ships as refugees, as has been brought out in the aforementioned book

An Aryan Journey. Their coming to India has to be called fortunate because, though only a very small segment of the Dev population came here while the bulk stayed back in Central Asia, it is only in the peaceful and tolerant environment of India that their religious literature has survived. These are the Vedas and the Vedic literature, which includes the Brahmans and the Upanishads. It is the religion of the Vedas that was a parallel religion of Central and West Asia with which the teachings of Jesus have a marked degree of similarity and that needs to be understood before its features are searched for in what has been stated to be the views of the Christians declared heretics by the Pauline Church in its march to supremacy. In Central Asia, this religious system survived throughout and surfaced later as Sufism, but its link to its ancient past was lost. In India, too, it was restated in Buddhism.

The first element in the Vedic religion is that it has two mutually exclusive streams, one is for the common followers, which, like all other religions, involves rituals and prayers, etc. In the commentaries of the Vedas, this part of the religion is contained in the Brahman literature. For a common believer, the purpose of religion is limited to ensuring that he leads a virtuous life and that the hope for a better tomorrow is kept alive in all circumstances because so long as hope is alive, man is able to go through even the worst of times. For this, a concept of God is created, who is a benefactor and a dispenser of justice. As human nature is the only nature known to man, while creating God for his religion, he imputed human nature on Him. God in religion, thus, likes people with a good conduct, people who humble themselves before Him, people who flatter Him and people who give plenty of gifts, etc. All prayers and rituals in religions are moulded on these lines, with an added emphasis on an ethical code of conduct. Like man, God is believed to be pleased or incited to anger as a reaction to something done by the believer. This brings in the necessity of ensuring that He is never angry and, if possible, is always favourably disposed. If something adverse happens, it is believed that it was because of the disfavour of God, which could be changed by appeasing Him, thus keeping a hope for a better tomorrow alive. The Vedic religion had this component in it for the common followers who sought only worldly things in life and were satisfied with them. The Vedic rishis, however, knew that this was not the relevant part of the religion, so this belief could be in any form as long as the basic purpose of ensuring that an ethical life was led and hope was not lost, is achieved. The second stream in the Vedic religion was its very core, which was not for the common followers but only for those who were more spiritually inclined, who may be called the elect, the monks, etc. In the commentaries of the Vedas, this part of the religion is contained in the Upanishads. Though the followers of this path were family people also, it was desirable for the person on this path to renounce the world. The core teachings of Jesus have a marked degree of similarity with this, which was the heart of the religion, the ritualistic side being of no real relevance, its variance is of no real value. It is, thus, the Upanishadic religion, the very core of the Vedic religion, that needs to be understood in this context.

A very important feature of the practices of the people of the Upanishadic religion was that its precepts were kept secret. They were not disclosed to anyone except a disciple who had been initiated into it. A long process of observation and testing was gone through before deciding whether a person wanting to join the order was worthy to be allowed to be initiated into it. If he was found wanting in any respect, he was not initiated. It was only after this that the real secrets were disclosed to him, the ceremony of initiation already having required him to take an oath that he would not divulge the secrets to anybody. For the rest of the people, the beliefs and practices of these people, therefore, remained a closely guarded mystery. To prevent secret teachings from getting divulged to undesirable elements, they were normally not reduced to writing but were communicated by word of mouth from the teacher to the disciple. If ever they were written, it was in a coded language and was mixed with several other things, because of which an uninitiated person could not understand them even if he got access to the text. A teacher was, thus, essential to disclose the key to the code in which the book was written, without which nobody could correctly navigate through it, as the apparent meaning would mislead the reader.

The next element in this system was the belief that there is only one true Reality. Everything that is seen or felt to exist was only an expression of this Reality. Their existence was only relative to other similarly existing things. In absolute terms, nothing had any existence but was only an illusion of existence. The implication of this belief is that there is no distinction between the Creator and the created. They are one. There is, thus, no benefactor or dispenser of justice in God, as God and man are not distinct from each other, the distinction being felt only because of the illusion of creation in which man feels he is a real entity. To start with, there does not appear to have been the concept of an individual soul but only of an all-pervading Supreme Reality, as what became a soul later is referred to as 'Atman' or the 'Self', being the true self of the person as distinct from the perceived self. However, with the repeated use of the same term 'Atman', it developed an identity of 'atma' or soul. However, in essence, it remains the same as the Supreme Reality, God. An individual goes through a cycle of births and deaths, in which the 'karma' or the deeds that he does in life determine his next birth, which could be in any form—man, animal or plant. All rewards or punishments that an individual may earn by his deeds are to be received in this world itself, either in this life or in a future life, but there is no heaven or hell as designated places for the same. Thus, the objective for a follower of this path cannot be obtaining heaven and staying away from hell.

The objective for a follower of this path is going out of the cycle of births and deaths, which is called 'moksha'. It means freedom, the freedom from births and deaths, and has been translated as salvation. The realization of one's true self leads to a realization that the individual does not exist. What exists is God and God alone. It was only God that was existing as the individual's true self, but he had not been able to recognize Him. With the realization of one's true self, the human ceases to exist and the individual becomes God, which he always was but did not know. This realization must not be confused with understanding. It means direct perception. Seeing by the faculty within the self within and seeing that this self that is within is the Creator and is pervading everything without. Though in Hinduism three paths have been mentioned for achieving this realization—the path of knowledge, the path of works and the path devotion—the Upanishads lay stress on the path of knowledge alone, the 'Gyan Marg' as it is called.

Along with the practical side of guiding a follower to the path of salvation, the Upanishads talk also of philosophy. This tries to explain the concept of God and how creation came into existence. For a practitioner of this path, philosophy is irrelevant. Its irrelevance can be gauged from the fact that Buddha refused to even speak about it. The Christian writers have, however, written very frequently of what the heretics believed to be God and how they thought creation took place. As this has been spoken very often by them, the similarity of the views of the so-called heretic Christians with the philosophy of the Upanishads can also be a pointer to what Jesus believed. The Christian writers have repeatedly written on this subject, perhaps because the Pauline Christianity laid a lot of stress on faith in Jesus being the Son of God and he having risen from the dead. It would have required the believers to have the right faith. As this was not a very closely guarded belief of the heretics, the concept of God and the manner in which creation took place would have been known to the other side, also giving an opportunity to the Church Father to discuss it and show how it differed from the laid down beliefs in the Scriptures.

The philosophies based on the Vedas are classed as the six systems of Indian philosophy. These are the interpretations given by different people of what they understood had been stated in the Vedas and the Upanishads. Two prominent schools of thought in these are the 'Sankhya' and the 'Vedanta'. 'Sankhya' believes in the existence of two mutually exclusive entities, the 'Purush' and 'Prakriti'. These can loosely be translated as consciousness and matter. Both are eternal and uncreated. As long as they remain separated from each other, no creation exists. When these two mingle with each other, creation begins and, in stages, the entire universe is created. When these two separate again, the entire creation dissolves back into them and nothing is left. Though the dominant view in 'Sankhya' believes in the multiplicity of 'Purush', as it believes every soul to be an independent 'Purush', this seems to have been an error that crept in at a later stage. The Bhagavad Gita, however, speaks of 'Purush' in the singular, which shows that this must have been the real belief. Against this dualism of the 'Sankhya', the 'Vedanta' speaks of non-dualism. It does not consider the two entities of consciousness and matter to be eternal and uncreated but believes that there is another entity beyond these two that transcends both of them and from which everything emerges. It names this supreme entity to be 'Brahma' or the Supreme God. When not involved in the creation, this Supreme God exists only as consciousness and bliss. At this stage, He is bereft of all qualities as He has shed all of them. When He decides to create the universe, He acquires qualities in Himself. When He has acquired qualities, He has been called 'Ishwar', which can be translated as the Inferior God, inferior only in relation to the Supreme, with no connotation of the word inferior attached to Him. It is this Inferior God that creates the world, which has been called 'Maya'. This word means illusion, which the universe has been called because it has no real existence. When it is time for the world to come to an end, this illusion comes to an end. The Inferior God, too, sheds His qualities and becomes 'Brahma' or the Supreme God.

The fundamental elements of this belief system are listed out below before a search for them in the beliefs of the heretics is made.

1. The religion had two distinct streams, one for the common believers and the other for the spiritually inclined, and it was the practices of the latter that formed the core of the religion.
2. Secrecy was maintained about the core teachings. People were admitted to this order only after being tested for a long period and only after that the real truths were divulged to them. The teacher was, thus, an essential requirement to begin with.
3. There was no difference between the Creator and the creation. The unbridgeable chasm between God and man, as it exists in other religions, was not there in it.
4. There was a belief in rebirth, with the soul going through a cycle of births and deaths, in which the next birth was determined by the deeds done in the previous birth. This is the theory of 'Karma'. In this, it is possible for the soul to go out of this cycle of births and deaths, which is called 'Moksha' or salvation.
5. The objective of the practitioner was to go out of this cycle of births and deaths and become free. This is achieved by a realization that I and God are the same. I do not exist, only God does. And when this is achieved,

man ceases to identify himself as man and does so with God.
6. There were two philosophical thoughts prevalent, one was the dualism of 'Sankhya' and the other was the non-dualism of 'Vedanta'.

The first element of the Vedic religion that needs to be looked for in the teachings of Jesus is the presence of two distinct streams in them, one for the common followers and the other for the spiritually inclined, with the latter being the core. In effect, one for those who sought worldly things through God and the other for those who sought God. Evidence of the presence of this in Christ's teachings comes directly from Jesus himself, as recorded in the passage below.

> And, behold, one came and said unto him, Good Master, what good things shall I do, that I may have eternal life?
>
> He said unto him, Why callest thou me good? there is none good but one, that is, God: but if thou wilt enter into life, keep the commandments.
>
> He saith unto him, Which? Jesus said, Thou shalt do no murder, Thou shalt not commit adultery, Thou shalt not steal, Thou shalt not bear false witness,
>
> Honour thy father and they mother: and, Thou shalt love thy neighbour as thyself.
>
> The young man saith unto him, All these things have I kept from my youth up: what lack I yet?
>
> Jesus said unto him, If thou wilt be perfect, go and sell that thou hast, and give to the poor, and thou shalt have treasure in heaven: and come and follow me.
>
> (Matthew 19:16–21)

Mark and Luke, too, have reported this incident. It is evident that Jesus was asking the common people to follow the Law of Moses, but he had something more to offer. He has told the youth 'if thou wilt be perfect, go and sell that thou has, and give to the poor' and follow him. It is evident that he was asking him to renounce the world and become a monk. There were, thus, two distinct paths that he had laid down, one for the common people, whom he asked to observe the tenets of Judaism in their right spirit, and the second, for those who sought perfection, whom he asked to renounce the world and become a monk before he could give them further guidance. Though this passage has no ambiguity, the Church has not explained this on these lines. It has been explained to mean that if someone wished to enter the world, he should remain a Jew and follow the tenets of Judaism, but if he wanted to become perfect, he should become a Christian. This would bring in a very major difficulty, as it will make 'selling of all possessions and giving them away to the poor' a precondition for becoming a Christian. This is not something that even the Church wanted, as such a percept cannot be for common people. There was, thus, a necessity to explain it in a different manner, which led to laying a lot of stress on charity and on donating to the Church liberally. In trying to meet the difficulties created by this interpretation, various explanations were given to an obvious statement, as can be seen in the passage below.

> So also let not the man that has been invested with worldly wealth proclaim himself excluded at the outset from the Saviour's list provided he is a believer.
>
> But well knowing that the Saviour teaches nothing in a mere human way, we must not listen to His utterances casually.
>
> He does not bid him to throw away the substance he possessed, but bids him to banish from his soul the notions about wealth and morbid feelings about it.
>
> It is not outward act but the stripping off the passions from the soul itself.

He does not bid them part with their property, but applying the just and removing the unjust judgement.

But by offering to all in turn that need, you must of necessity by all means find some one of those who have power with God to save.

One can obtain your pardon from God, another comfort you when sick, another teach some of the things useful for salvation.

Wherefore it is by all means necessary for thee, who art rich, to set over thyself some man of God as a trainer and governor. Let him pass many sleepless nights for thee, interceding for thee with God, influencing the Father with the magic of familiar litanies.

(The Writings of the Early Church Fathers, Vol. 2, Clement of Alexandria, Who is the Rich Man that Shall be Saved)

Jesus, however, meant the renunciation of the world, if someone wanted to be perfect, is established by the fact that he has repeated the same sentiment twice. This may be seen in the following passages.

And he said to them all, If any man will come after me, let him deny himself, and take up his cross daily, and follow me.

(Luke 9:23)

If any man come to me, and hate not his father, and mother, and wife, and children, and brethren, and sisters, yea, and his own life also, he cannot be my disciple.

(Luke 14:26)

These passages have no ambiguity, as Jesus is requiring a person wanting to follow him to deny himself and to cease to love even his closest possible relatives. He is asking him to renounce the world and become a monk. This is not something that can be made a prerequisite for a common believer. It is only the few who can pay this price. This makes it evident that there were deeper secrets in the teachings of Jesus that were reserved only for these few who could prove their worth. For the common people, it was just the usual things that all religions prescribe and because Judaism was the religion of the people amongst whom he was preaching, he required them to be a good Jew by following its percepts not only in letter but also in spirit. It has been noticed by Origen that Jesus had two sets of teachings for two types of followers. This emerges from the passages below.

> Such, indeed, was the abounding love which He had for men, that He gave to the more learned a theology capable of raising the soul far above all earthly things; while with no less consideration He comes down to the weaker capacities of ignorant men, of simple woman, of slaves, and, in short, of all those who from Jesus alone could have received that help for the better regulation of their lives which is supplied by his instructions in regard to the Divine Being, adopted to their wants and capacities.
> (*The Writings of the Early Church Fathers*, Vol. 4, Origen, Contra Celsum, Book VII, Chapter 41)

'And straightaway He constrained the disciples to enter into the boat and to go before Him unto the other side, till He should send the multitudes away.' It should be observed how often in the same passages is mentioned the word, 'the multitudes,' and another word, 'the disciples,' so that by observing and bringing together the passages about this matter it may be seen that the aim of the Evangelists was to represent by means of the Gospel history the differences of those who came to Jesus; of whom some are the multitudes and are not called disciples, and the others are the disciples who are better than the multitudes.

Jesus separated the disciples from the multitudes, and constrained them to enter into the boat and to go before

Him unto the other side until He Himself should send the multitudes, for the multitudes were not able to go away to the other side and to pass beyond things seen and material, as temporal, and to go on to the things unseen and eternal.

Only, the disciples were not able to go before Jesus to the other side, but when they had got as far as the middle of the sea, and the boat was distressed 'because the wind was contrary to them', and they were afraid when about the fourth watch of the night Jesus came to them. And if Jesus had not gone up into the boat neither would the wind which was contrary to the disciples who were sailing, have ceased, nor would those who were sailing have gone across and come to the other side.

He having judged that they should make trial of the waves and of the contrary wind, which would not have been contrary if they had been with Jesus, put on them the necessity of being separated from Him and entering into the boat.

But as for the multitudes, who because they were weaker, did not make trial of the boat and the waves and the contrary wind, them He sent away, and went up into the mountain apart to pray.

(*The Writings of the Early Church Fathers*, Vol. 9, Origen, Commentaries on Matthew, Book IX)

While explaining a passage of the Bible, Origen has very clearly brought out the difference between the multitudes and the disciples as mentioned by Matthew in his gospel. In reading the Bible, this distinction is often missed, but once Origen has pointed it out, the subject becomes clear. Jesus had the multitudes coming to him who were not capable of going to the other side and to pass beyond the material and go on to the spiritual and eternal. To these followers, he gave what they could take for the better regulation of their lives, adapting the

Divine Being to their wants and capacities. These were the people whom he blessed, healed and fed but thereafter sent away. They were not required to take the test of the boat and to face the waves and the contrary winds. This was the test for the few, the disciples. Though it was possible for Jesus to accompany them, yet he separated himself from them and sent them away in a boat at night to cross over on their own. He was there to save them and to help to cross over to the other side when in the middle of the sea they were caught in contrary winds and strong waves, yet this was the test they had to go through. It is a situation of a teacher guiding his disciples to move forward on a spiritual path. The teacher can only guide, but after that it is the disciple and the disciple alone who has to navigate the path facing the contrary winds and the waves. The teacher is there if a difficulty arises to further guide and encourage, but beyond that no help is available.

The presence of two distinct streams, one for the common followers and the other for the spiritually advanced, in the teachings of Jesus emerges also from the fact that monks existed in Christianity from a very early date. A passage from Jerome has already been quoted that has reported the observations of Philo the Jew about the Church of Alexandria as established by Mark. He has reported that the Christians there led a life that would be like that of a monk. This shows that monasticism was at the core of the teachings of Jesus, and Mark had established only a monastery at Alexandria, which got converted into a Church with the Pauline theology taking over. Jesus prescribing monasticism for the few emerges from the following passage.

> His disciples say unto him, If the case of man be so with wife, it is not good to marry.
>
> But he said unto them, All men cannot receive this saying, save they to whom it is given.
>
> For there are some eunuchs, which were so born from

their mother's womb: and there are some eunuchs, which were made eunuchs of men: and there be eunuchs, which have made themselves eunuchs for the kingdom of heaven's sake. He that is able to receive it, let him receive it.
(Matthew 19:10–12)

That the Apostles were also stressing on a monastic life is borne out in the following passage.

Now the Spirit speaketh expressly, that in the latter times some shall depart from the faith, giving heed to seducing spirits, and doctrines of devils;
Speaking lies in hypocrisy; having their conscience seared with a hot iron.
Forbidding to marry, and commanding to abstain from meats, which God hath created to be received with thanksgiving of them which believe and know the truth.
(1 Timothy 4:1–3)

Paul is referring to his rival preachers, the Apostles. He has stated that they forbid to marry and command to abstain from certain meats. The Jews consider certain animals to be unclean and are forbidden to eat their meat. As the Apostles were Judaizing the Gentiles while converting them to Christianity, this practice of the Jews would have been prescribed by them, which has been mentioned by Paul. The other thing he mentions is that they forbid marriage. It is obvious that this cannot be a prescription for the common believers of a religion, as it would end the entire race if it is followed by everyone. It can be a requirement only for the few, which as a hostile critic, Paul has mentioned in a way that it appears to be the main focus of the teachings of his rivals. Paul has mentioned this with disapproval elsewhere, too, in his epistles, which shows what the two sides thought about it. Evidently, the Apostles prescribed monasticism for the few, while Paul opposed it.

The presence of monks in large numbers, especially in the East where Pauline scriptures reached late, is brought out in the writings of several Church Fathers. Their presence in such large numbers in the area where the apostolic traditions survived much longer is an evidence of monasticism being an integral part of the teachings of Jesus and there being two distinct sets of prescriptions in them for two different audiences. The presence of monks in such large numbers at a very early date is brought out in the following passages.

> It is said that Philo in the reign of Claudius became acquainted at Rome with Peter.
>
> And since he describes as accurately as possible the life of our ascetics, it is clear that he not only knew, but that he also approved, while he venerated and extolled, the apostolic men of his time, who were as it seems of the Hebrew race, and hence observed, after the manner of the Jews most of the customs of the ancient.
>
> In the work to which he gave the title, On a Contemplative Life or Suppliants, he says that these men were called Therapeutae and the women that were with them Therapeutrides. He bears witness that first of all they renounce their property and give up their goods to their relatives, and then, renouncing all the cares of life, they go forth beyond the walls and dwell in lonely fields and gardens, knowing well that intercourse with people of a different character is unprofitable and harmful, practicing in emulation the prophet's mode of life.
>
> Philo bears witness to facts very much like those here described and then adds the following account, 'Everywhere in the world is this race found. For it was fitting that both Greek and Barbarian should share in what is perfectly good. But the race particularly abounds in Egypt, in each of its so-called nomes, and specially about Alexandria. The best men

from every quarter emigrate, as if to a colony of Therapeut's fatherland, to a certain very suitable spot which lies above lake Maria upon a low hill excellently suited on account of its security and mildness of the atmosphere.'

And then a little further, after describing the kind of houses which they had, he speaks as follows concerning their churches which were scattered about here and there 'In each house there is a sacred apartment which is called sanctuary and monastery, where, quite alone they perform the mysteries of the religious life. The whole interval, from morning to evening, is for them a time of exercise. For they read the holy scriptures, and explain the philosophy of their fathers in an allegorical manner, regarding the written words as symbols of hidden truth which is communicated in obscure figures. They have also writings of ancient men, who were the founders of their sect, and who left many monuments of the allegorical method. These they use as models and imitate their principles.

'They not only spend their time in meditation, but they also compose songs and hymns to God in every variety of metre and melody, though they divide them of course, into measures of more than common solemnity.

'Having laid down temperance as a sort of the foundation in the soul, they build upon it the other virtue. None of them takes food before sunset and some forget to take food for three days.'

(The Writings of the Early Church Fathers,
Vol. 24, Eusebius Pamphilus, Ecclesiastic
History, Book II, Chapter 17)

This passage from Philo that has been quoted by Eusebius is very significant because it reveals what Jesus had intended and what the Apostles were preaching. He is speaking of people who acknowledged Jesus and have been understood to have been

Christians by Eusebius. Philo was a contemporary of Jesus and the Apostles. He was a Jew and remained a Jew till the end. This passage shows that in his view the followers of Jesus were leading a monastic life, but their sect had a long and continuing tradition in which they had scriptures received from their fathers. Though they followed Jesus, Philo is distinctly appreciative of them as they followed all Jewish traditions and customs. Philo has also extolled the Apostles who were following all Hebrew customs. This shows that neither Jesus nor the Apostles had any intention of propounding a new faith. For the common believers, Judaism was to be followed in its true spirit and even those converted were to be converted to Judaism. It is an irony that Christians have persecuted the Jews throughout the centuries, as it is Judaism that the Apostles seem to have wanted them to follow, while Jesus does not appear to have had any interest in preaching to anyone but the Jews. The importance of Jesus to his disciples was on the spiritual side, where he had crossed all frontiers and reached the ultimate stage and was in a position to guide others in the same journey. This is the picture that emerges also from Philo's account of the Church established by Mark at Alexandria as has been mentioned earlier. Mark has been reported to have established a church in which Christians lived like monks. Though it was a continuing tradition, as has been brought out by Philo, something coming first-hand from a teacher would have made things much easier than understanding them from obscure writings that had been written in an allegorical manner. Though Philo has called them Christians, he has stated 'everywhere in the world this race is found' and 'it particularly abounds in Egypt, in each of its so-called nomes, and specially about Alexandria.' The presence of these monks and monasteries in such a widely spread area as early as the times of Philo shows that this was an old and well-established tradition at that time and could not have been originated by Jesus. In a continuing tradition, Jesus had come as a recent teacher who had succeeded in the struggle and gave a fresh understanding of all the ancient precepts that had become obscure by then, because of which all these monks acknowledged him as a teacher.

The presence of monasteries for centuries amongst the Christians is brought out in the following passages.

> Not far from the desert, and close to the Nile, there are numerous monasteries. For the most part, the monks there dwell together in companies of a hundred; and their highest rule is to live under orders of their Abbot, to do nothing by their own inclination, but to depend in all things on his will and authority. If it so happens that any of them form in their minds a lofty ideal of virtue, so as to wish to betake themselves to the desert to live a solitary life, they do not venture to act on this desire except with the permission of the Abbot.
> (*The Writings of the Early Church Fathers*, Vol. 34, Sulpitus Severus, Dialogue I, Chapter X)

> I, for my part, departed from Mount Sinai, and returned to the river Nile, the banks of which, on both sides, I beheld dotted with numerous monasteries.
> (*The Writings of the Early Church Fathers*, Vol. 34, Sulpitus Severus, Dialogue I, Chapter XVII)

The presence of monks in such large numbers in Egypt, Palestine and other places in the East for several centuries confirms that the teachings of Jesus had two distinct streams for two different categories of followers. This is further established by the early writers speaking of these two categories directly. This emerges from the following passages.

> For each one is capable of both types of transgression, namely that of an adept and that of an ordinary person.
> (The Nag Hammadi Library, The Interpretation of Knowledge)

> While he who is in a state of knowledge, being assimilated as far as possible to God, is already spiritual, and so elect.
> (*The Writings of the Early Church Fathers*, Vol. 2, Clement of Alexandria, Stromata, Book IV, Chapter 26)

> But that this name is given to such as are also called Hearers, on the supposition that they cannot observe what are considered the higher and greater commandments, which are observed by those whom they think right to distinguish and honour by the name of Elect.
> (*The Writings of the Early Church Fathers*, Vol. 13, Augustine, Treatise for Correction of Donatists, Book III, Chapter 17)

These references are about the Christians who were declared heretics by the Pauline Church. The first two are about Gnostics, while the third is of Manicheans. In all of them, there is a reference of ordinary believers or hearers and Adepts or Elects. It also emerges from these that there were higher and greater commandments that were to be observed only by the Elect. The Hearers or the ordinary believers had a different set of commandments that were lighter and lower than those and, for them, it was enough to follow these only.

The relationship between the Pauline Church and the monasteries was hostile from the beginning. The monks had sentiments of disapproval of the Church, while the Church considered them to be adversaries and went all out to suppress and destroy their beliefs and practices. The views of monks need to be considered as the views of the Apostolic Church, as monasticism was the core of its teachings. The views of the monks and the Gnostics about the beliefs of the Pauline Church and the hierarchy of priests created by it emerges from the following passages.

> God created man and men created God. That is the way it is in the world—men make gods and worship their creation
> (The Nag Hammadi Library, The Gospel of Philip)

> Just as God willed that the inner man be created according to his image, in the very same way, man on earth creates god according to his likeness.
> (The Nag Hammadi Library, Asclepius)

> And there shall be others of those who are outside our number who name themselves bishop and also deacons, as if they have received their authority from God. They bend themselves under the judgement of the leaders. Those people are dry canals.
> (The Nag Hammadi Library, Apocalypse of Peter)

These are the words of the Gnostics. Apart from disapproving the manner in which the Church had created the image of God with all human attributes, they have called the bishops and deacons dry canals and have also said for them 'those who are outside our number'. This was a natural reaction of the people who had the core teachings of Jesus for those who were unacquainted with them and yet had assumed positions of authority and were claiming to be the true guides of the believers. That the spirituals, who constituted the core of the Apostolic Church, had such sentiments for the Pauline Church is confirmed by the other writers also, as evident in the passage below.

> Animal men, again, are instructed in animal things; such men are established by their works and by a mere faith, while they have not perfect knowledge. We of the Church, they say, are these persons. Wherefore also they maintain that good works are necessary for us, for that otherwise it is impossible we should be saved. But as to themselves, they hold that they shall be entirely and undoubtedly saved,

not by means of conduct, but because they are spiritual by nature.

(*The Writings of the Early Church Fathers*, Vol. 1, Irenaeus, Against Heresies, Book I, Chapter 6)

The earlier passages were from the Nag Hammadi Library, which would lead to a conclusion that those were the sentiments of the Gnostics of Egypt. This passage from Irenaeus is about the heretics of Rome in the second century. It has already been mentioned that the people called heretics in Rome at that time were the followers of the Apostolic Church. Their sentiments towards the Pauline Church are the same as were in Egypt. They considered them to be at the animal level, for whom only carnal things could be prescribed.

Though the hostility of the priests towards monks is understandable because the monks raised a question on the very existence of the clergy, there is a stark difference in the manner in which the Western Church, which is the Catholic Church, and the Eastern Church, which is the Orthodox Church, dealt with monasteries and the subject of monasticism. The Western Church approached the monasteries with complete hostility and brought them under the control of bishops and they were either destroyed or at least the basic essence of monasticism was destroyed in them. The Eastern Church, on the other hand, treated monasticism as an integral part of their religion and supported the monasteries, leaving them independent in their functioning. The hostility of the Western Church to the monasteries emerges from the following passage.

> Our most crafty foe, who fearing our good fame and desiring to obscure it, hath dispersed on every side so many hypocrites under the garb of monks, strolling about the provinces, no where sent, no where fixed, no where standing, no where sitting. Where so ever they be found

out in their evil deeds, or in whatever way they become
notorious, under the general name of monks, your purpose
is blasphemed.

> (*The Writings of the Early Church Fathers*, Vol. 12,
> Augustine, Of the Works of Monks)

This passage from Augustine shows that the adversaries
of the Pauline Church were moving around as monks in
every direction. He has stated that their deeds were evil
and that they blasphemed the religion of Christ. With this
hostility towards monks and monasteries, the Pauline Church
endeavoured to bring monks and monasteries under the
control of bishops. With bishops in command, they made a
conscious effort to check the belief system of the monks and
declared them heretical whenever they were found to not be
in accord with the beliefs of the Church. More often than
not, the beliefs of the monks were not in line with those of
the Church, at least as long as the apostolic theology was
alive. This led to a lot of persecution of the monks at the
hands of the priests. The efforts of the church to bring the
monks under the control of the bishops emerges from the
following passages.

> Let those who truly and sincerely lead the monastic life be
> counted worthy of honour, but as certain persons using the
> pretext of monasticism bring confusion in the cities, it is
> decreed that no one anywhere build or found a monastery
> or oratory contrary to the will of the bishop of the city, and
> that the monks in every city and district shall be subject
> to the bishop, and embrace a quiet course of life.
>
> (*The Writings of the Early Church Fathers*, Vol. 33,
> XXX Canons of the Fourth Synod of Chalcedon, Canon IV)
>
> And those who, without the above-mentioned causes,
> venture forth of their convents, are first of all to be shut

up in the said convent even against their wills and then are to cure themselves with fasting and other afflictions.

(The Writings of the Early Church Fathers, Vol. 37, Canons of the Council in Trullo, Canon 41)

The Western Church in the ecclesiastical councils, thus, took decisions regarding the control of monks and monasteries. They not only placed them under the control of bishops but even provided for shutting up people in monasteries and convents against their will. This gave the priests the right to decide what activities could take place and what beliefs could be held by the people living in them. In effect, people who were to follow the superior and secret teachings of Jesus, which were reserved for the disciples, were placed under the control of those who received his teachings that were meant for the multitudes. This had to lead to the persecution of the monks and the end of the true spirit of the monastic order. The persecution of monks at the hands of priests emerges from the following passage.

What lamentable supplications Luminosus, abbot of the monastery of Saints Andrew and Thomas, in the city of Ariminum, has poured out to us, appears from the text of the subjoined petition. For from his account we learn that in very many monasteries the monks have suffered many prejudices and annoyances from prelates.

(The Writings of the Early Church Fathers, Vol. 36, Gregory the Great, Epistles, Epistle 41)

Though, over time, the control of monasteries by the clergy brought an end to monasticism in the Western Church, it could not stop people from leaving the normal mode of life to look for something beyond. A new form of pietism had to be found for these people, as several spiritual activities had disappeared with the monasteries thus controlled. This was found in education, healthcare, care for the poor and missionary activities. All the people who had come forward essentially to become monks devoted their lives in these activities and several earlier monasteries became centres of learning.

In contrast to the hostility towards monasticism that is to be seen in the Western Church, the approach of the Orthodox Church towards it has always been of respect. Because of this, monasteries of the Orthodox Christians have survived till date, the most celebrated of them being at Mt Athos, a Greek island. This difference in the dealing of monasteries and monasticism by the Catholic and the Orthodox Churches is due to the apostolic theology surviving longer in the East. It goes to establish that though the teachings of Jesus had two distinct streams, the core teachings meant for the select few were destroyed by the Pauline theology. As the Pauline theology took over the West much earlier, it did not give the apostolic traditions time to gain identification with the Apostles and, from a very early stage, identified them with persons who were declared heretics. In the East, as the Pauline theology came a couple of centuries later, several of the apostolic traditions had become so firmly grounded that they could not be uprooted.

The second element of the Vedic religion that is found in the teachings of Jesus is that the real substance of the core of the religion was kept a closely guarded secret. It was divulged only to the select few who had been adequately tested for being worthy of receiving it. This was normally not reduced to writing but was passed down as oral tradition. If at all it was written, a secret code was used and the crux of teachings were written in a coded language. In both situations, a teacher was necessary, without whom a person could not make a headway, as the teachings would not be understood by him even if he had access to the written text. In such a situation, the core teachings remained a mystery for the rest of the people.

It may be of interest to know why the crux of the core

teachings were kept as a closely guarded secret. One reason is evident. There were two sets of followers, whose requirements were different. One group was of the common believers who sought a benefactor in God and desired worldly things with divine intervention. The other was of the elect who sought God. In their belief God and the self were the same. There being no other entity, there could not be a benefactor. A common believer has his entire faith around a benefactor, which would get shattered on knowing this. The second reason was perhaps more important to them, though today it may be difficult to believe. A study of all mystic traditions, whether Christian, Islamic or Indian, shows that an Adept progressing on this path, at a stage, acquired supernatural powers. It was, thus, necessary to ensure that an undesirable person should not have access to these powers, as that could lead to untoward situations in society. A person to be admitted to the mysteries had to be such that he would either not use these powers at all or if he did so, he would do it only for the good of the people. There are a number of references where it has been reported that the Christian heretics often exhibited supernatural powers. The case of Simon Magus has already been mentioned. He is reported by his critics to have flown before the Roman senate. Reports about other heretics are mentioned here.

> But there is another among these heretics, Marcus by name. He is a perfect adept in magical impostures. It appears probable enough that this man possesses a demon as his familiar spirit, by means of whom he seems able to prophesy.
> (*The Writings of the Early Church Fathers*, Vol. 1, Irenaeus, Against Heresies, Book I, Chapter 13)

The mystic priests belonging to this sect lead profligate lives and practice magical arts.

Menander was a perfect adept in the practice of magic
> (*The Writings of the Early Church Fathers*, Vol. 1,
> Irenaeus, Against Heresies, Book I, Chapter 23)

And if they have in truth accomplished anything by means of magic, they strive deceitfully to lead foolish people astray, since they confer no real blessing on those over whom they declare that they exert supernatural powers.
> (*The Writings of the Early Church Fathers*, Vol. 1,
> Irenaeus, Against Heresies, Book II, Chapter 32)

He professes himself to be a Christian in such a way as the devil often feigns himself to be Christ.

For both to prophesy and to cast out devils, and to do great acts upon the earth is certainly a sublime and admirable thing, but one does not attain the kingdom of heaven although he is found in all those things, unless he walks in the observance of the right and just way.
> (*The Writings of the Early Church Fathers*, Vol. 5,
> Cyprian, On the Unity of the Church)

This Marcus alleged that there resided in him the mightiest power from invisible and unnameable places. Very often, taking the cup he would cause the appearance of a purple or red mixture, so that his dupes imagined that a certain Grace descended and communicated to the potion a blood-red potency.
> (*The Writings of the Early Church Fathers*, Vol. 5,
> Hippolytus, Refutation of All Heresies, Book VI, Chapter 34)

Montanus was carried away in spirit and suddenly being seized with a kind of frenzy and ecstasy began to speak strange things and to prophesy in a manner contrary to the customs of the Church.
> (*The Writings of the Early Church Fathers*, Vol. 7,
> Asterius Urbanus, The Exordium, Book I)

These reports of supernatural things having been done by the Christian heretics have not come from their followers and supporters. As they have come from the Pauline Church, which considered them to be rivals and heretics, they appear to be credible. The *Yog Sutra* of Patanjali has mentioned supernatural powers emerging in an Adept as he progresses in Yog. These are mentioned here.

> When peace has surfaced, there is a mystical knowledge of the moral character of all things and what follows from their fundamental character (14). Perfect constraint directed onto these three yields a deep comprehension of past and future events (16). By actively inspecting the latent tendency, knowledge of former births is revealed (18). Condition of other people's mind is revealed (19). When the body's form is grasped with ultimate discipline, there comes the power of suspending the body and rendering it imperceptible to others (21). By directing ultimate discipline towards elephants and other animals, one gains their strength (25). Ultimate discipline focused on the sun reveals knowledge of the entire world (27). When one masters one of the five vital airs, one can rise above water, mud, thorns and the like, without making contact with these, and levitate (40). One gains the power to journey through space (43). When the utter distinction between person and the natural quality of luminescence and buoyancy is discerned, there comes lordship over all things and omniscience (50).
>
> (*Yog Sutra,* Vibhuti Paad)

The *Yog Sutra* mentions all the powers that have been reported by the Christian fathers to have been exercised by the Christian heretics—the power to levitate, to see the past and future to prophesize, control over substances, etc. These powers, however, were required to be rejected by the Adept in the course of the journey, as the guiding principle has been stated in the following sutra.

> The emergence of these accomplishments are an obstacle to liberating states of absorption (Samadhi)
>
> (*Yog Sutra*, Vibhuti Paad, Sutra 38)

Whether we believe or not in the claim that supernatural powers were acquired by a person practising these percepts, the people who were doing so did believe in it and that would have been reason enough for them to keep the path a closely guarded secret. It appears that Paul was aware of these supernatural powers emerging because he is found to be aspiring for them and encouraging others, too, to try and acquire them. This emerges from the following passages.

> Having then gifts differing according to the grace that is given to us, whether prophecy, let us prophesy according to the proportion of faith.
>
> (Romans 12:6)

> Follow after charity, and desire spiritual gifts, but rather that ye may prophesy.
>
> I would that ye all spake with tongues, but rather that ye prophesied: for greater is he that prophesieth than he that speaketh with tongues.
>
> But if all prophesy, and there come in one that believeth not, or one unlearned, he is convinced of all, he is judged of all;
>
> And thus are the secrets of his heart made manifest; and so falling down on his face he will worship God, and report that God is in you of a truth.
>
> (1 Corinthians 14:1, 14:5 and 14:24–25))

Paul has, however, admitted that he did not have the ability to prophesy and that he had not reached perfection. This emerges from the following passages.

> Not as though I had already attained, either were already perfect: but I follow after, if that I may apprehend that for which also I am apprehended of Christ Jesus.
> Brethren, I count not myself to have apprehended: but this one thing I do, forgetting those things which are behind, and reaching forth unto those things which are before.
> (Philippians 3:12–13)
>
> For we know in part, and we prophesy in part.
> (1 Corinthians 13:9)

Paul was evidently violating the norms of the mystics in wanting to acquire supernatural powers and asking others also to do so. It appears likely that this was the real reason for which the Apostles did not admit him to the deeper secrets despite he having spent 14 years in their company. As this was the touchtone on which a person was judged to be admitted to the deeper secrets, if the Apostles had noticed Paul's inclination towards them, he would have been kept out. Though Paul was not aware that the supernatural powers have to be rejected and not used, Monk Antony and other Christian mystics were aware of it. The reference from Monk Antony are given here.

> Wherefore there is no need to set much value on these things, nor for the sake of them to practice a life of discipline and labour, but that living well we may please God. And we neither ought to pray to know the future, nor to ask for it as the reward of our discipline, but our prayer should be that the Lord may be our fellow-helper for victory over the devil.
> And it is not fitting to boost at the casting forth of the demons nor to be uplifted by the healing of diseases.
> (*The Writings of the Early Church Fathers*, Vol. 27, Athanasius, Life of Antony, Paras 34 and 38)

Apart from Monk Antony having been reported to have considered the supernatural powers to be worthless, Saint John of the Cross has expressed similar sentiments. These are given below.

> Such knowledge as this, whether it be of God or no, can be of very little assistance to the progress of the soul on its journey to God if the soul desire it and be attached to it; on the contrary, if it were not scrupulous in rejecting it, not only would it be hindered on its road, but it would even be greatly harmed and led far astray.
> He, then, that has supernatural gifts and graces ought to refrain from desiring to practice them.
> (St John of the Cross, Ascent of Mount Carmel, Chapters 27 and 31)

Evidence to establish that the core teachings of Jesus were not disclosed to the common believers but were to be kept as a closely guarded secret comes from several sources. Foremost is from Jesus himself. This emerges from the following passages.

> And the disciples came, and said unto him, Why speakest thou unto them in parables?
> He answered and said unto them, Because it is given unto you to know the mysteries of the kingdom of heaven, but to them it is not given.
> For whosoever hath, to him shall be given, and he shall have more abundance: but whosoever hath not, from him shall be taken away even that he hath.
> (Matthew 13:10–12)

> But without a parable spake he not unto then: and when they were alone, he expounded all things to his disciples.
> (Mark 4:34)

> For nothing is secret, that shall not be made manifest;

neither any thing hid, that shall not be known and come abroad.

    Take heed therefore how ye hear: for whosoever hath, to him shall be given; and whosoever hath not, from him shall be taken even that which he seemeth to have.

(Luke 8:17–18)

Both Mark and Luke have repeated Matthew's statement. All three have unequivocally reported that Jesus did not disclose to the multitudes all that he had to teach. This was revealed only to the disciples when they were alone. A few comments from Paul also indicate that a part of the teachings were kept concealed and the Apostles practised them in secrecy. These are given below.

    And have not fellowship with the unfruitful works of darkness, but rather reprove them.

    For it is a shame even to speak of those things which are done of them in secret.

(Ephesians 5:11–12)

    But have renounced the hidden things of dishonesty, not walking in craftiness, nor handling the word of God deceitfully; but manifestation of the truth commending ourselves to every man's conscience in the sight of God.

(2 Corinthians 4:2)

Paul is speaking of his rivals, the Apostles, and has stated that they did things in secret, attributing shame to something that could not be done in public. He has also called the hidden things to be dishonest and deceitful, which have been renounced by him, as everything stated by him was openly manifested to everyone.

    Along with the evidence that emerges from the Bible regarding the deeper truths being revealed by Jesus to only the Apostles and the disciples, there are a large number of statements by others saying the same and that the Apostles revealed them further only to the select. A few of them are given here.

> I send you a secret book which was revealed to me and Peter by the Lord. Endeavour earnestly and take care not to rehearse this text to many.
> (The Nag Hammadi Library, The Apocryphon of James)

> That is the gospel of him whom they seek, which he has revealed to the perfect through the mercies of the Father as the hidden mystery, Jesus the Christ.
> (The Nag Hammadi Library, The Gospel of Truth)

> The secret words that the saviour spoke to Judas Thomas which I, even I, Mathias, wrote down.
> (The Nag Hammadi Library, The Book of Thomas the Contender)

> They tell us, however, that this knowledge has not been openly divulged because all are not capable of receiving it, but has been mystically revealed by the Saviour through means of parables to those qualified for understanding it.
> (*The Writings of the Early Church Fathers*, Vol. 1, Irenaeus, Against Heresies, Book I, Chapter 3)

> They declare that Jesus spoke in a mystery to His disciples and apostles privately, and that they requested and obtained permission to hand down the things thus taught them, to others who should be worthy and believing.
> (*The Writings of the Early Church Fathers*, Vol. 1, Irenaeus, Against Heresies, Book I, Chapter 25)

> For they allege that the truth was not delivered by means of written documents but by voice.
> (*The Writings of the Early Church Fathers*, Vol. 1, Irenaeus, Against Heresies, Book III, Chapter 2)

The gnosis itself is that which has descended by transmission to a few, having been imparted unwritten by apostles.
(*The Writings of the Early Church Fathers*, Vol. 2, Clement of Alexandria, Stromata, Book VI, Chapter 7)

Since he frequently calls the Christian doctrine a secret system of belief we must confute him on this point also, since the world knows what Christians preach.
(*The Writings of the Early Church Fathers*, Vol. 4, Origen, Against Celsus, Book I, Chapter 7)

Basilides, therefore, and Isidorus say that Matthias communicated to them secret discourses, which, I being specially instructed, he heard from the Saviour.
(*The Writings of the Early Church Fathers*, Vol. 5, Hippolytus, The Refutation of All Heresies, Book VII, Chapter 8)

Some teachers who hold the law and the prophets of no importance, who decline to follow the Gospels, and who depreciate the epistles of the apostles, and who have made large promises regarding doctrine of this composition, as though it were some great and hidden mystery.
(*The Writings of the Early Church Fathers*, Vol. 6, Dionysius, Extant Fragments, From the Two Books on the Promises)

Meantime Peter thus said 'I also, for the most part by using a certain circumlocution, endeavour to avoid publishing the chief knowledge concerning the Supreme Divinity to unworthy ears.'
(*The Writings of the Early Church Fathers*, Vol. 8, Pseudo-Clementine Literature, Book III, Chapter 1)

The mysteries committed to them in secret and where few

could hear, hard to be known and obscure, He bids them, when enlightened and therefore said to be in the light, to make known to everyone who is made light.

(The Writings of the Early Church Fathers, Vol. 9, Origen, Commentary on John, Book II, Chapter 94)

These writers of antiquity have repeatedly stated that there was a deeper element in the teachings of Jesus that was not preached by him to the common followers but was imparted in secret only to his disciples, who in turn, repeated the same, of disclosing it only to the worthy. Apart from this, there are a large number of statements to the effect that the mystics and the Christians, termed heretics, kept their doctrine secret and disclosed them only to those considered worthy of receiving them. Some of these are given here.

The Valentinians, who are a large body of heretics, obscure their doctrine. The officiousness with which they guard their doctrine is an officiousness which betrays their guilt.

They beset all access to their body with tormenting conditions and require a long initiation before they enroll their members, instructing during five years for their perfect disciples. Then follows the duty of silence. All the divinity, however, lies in their secret recesses: there are revealed at last all the aspirations of the fully initiated, the entire mystery of the sealed tongue.

If you propose to them inquiries, they answer, 'The subject is profound.'

Not even to their own disciples do they commit a secret before they have made sure of them.

(The Writings of the Early Church Fathers, Vol. 3, Tertullion, Against the Valentinians, Chapter I)

Hence also, in the first book inscribed 'Baruch', has been written the oath, which they compel those to swear who are about to hear these mysteries and be initiated with Good One.

'I swear by that Good One who is above all, to guard these mysteries, and to divulge them to no one, and not to relapse from the Good One to the creature.'

(The Writings of the Early Church Fathers, Vol. 5, Hippolytus, Refutation of all Heresies, Book V, Chapter 22)

And subsequent to the first baptism, to these they promise another, which they call Redemption.

And when they consider that these have been tested, and are able to keep secret the mysteries committed to them, they then admit them to this baptism.

(The Writings of the Early Church Fathers, Vol. 5, Hippolytus, Refutation of all Heresies, Book VI, Chapter 36)

Peter to James, 'I beg you not to communicate to any one of the Gentiles the books of my preaching which I sent to you, nor to any one of our own tribe before trial.' Wherefore let him be proved not less than six years.

(The Writings of the Early Church Fathers, Vol. 8, Pseudo-Clementine Literature, Epistle of Peter to James)

And Peter said, 'We remember that our Lord and Teacher commanding us, said, 'Keep the mysteries for me and the sons of my house.' Wherefore also He explained to His disciples privately the mysteries of the kingdom of heaven.'

(The Writings of the Early Church Fathers, Vol. 8, Pseudo-Clementine Literature, Epistle of Peter to James)

For he thus commences this very book: 'For there are certain mystical rules which hold the key to the secret recesses of the whole law, and render visible the treasures

of truth that are to many invisible.
>   (*The Writings of the Early Church Fathers*, Vol. 2,
>   Augustine, On Christian Doctrine,
>   Book III, Chapter 30)

It is most agreeable to the revealing Oracles to conceal, through mystical and sacred enigmas, and to keep the holy and secret truth respecting the supermundane minds inaccessible to the multitude.
>   (Dionysius, Heavenly Hierarchy,
>   Caput II, Section 2)

Thus do all the godly-wise, and interpreters of the secret inspiration, separate the holy of holies from the uninitiated and the unholy, to keep undefiled, and prefer the dissimilar description of holy things, so that Divine things should not be reached by the profane
>   (Dionysius, Heavenly Hierarchy, Caput II, Section 5)

Nor did the inspired Hierarchs transmit these things in conceptions clear to the commonalty of worshippers, but in sacred symbols.
>   (Dionysius, Ecclesiastical Hierarchy,
>   Caput I, Section 4)

The imparting of the supremely Divine mysteries to the man initiated is the head and tail of every initiation.
>   (Dionysius, Ecclesiastical Hierarchy,
>   Caput III, Section 1)

The regulation of the Holy Hierarchy permits the catechumens to hear the sacred chanting of the Psalms, and the inspired reading of the Holy Scriptures, but it does not invite them to the next religious services and contemplations, but only to the eyes of the initiated.
>   (Dionysius, Ecclesiastical Hierarchy,
>   Caput III, Section 6)

But 'initiated' are those who are being conducted to a more perfect revelation of the symbols of the Law, in proportion to their capacity.

> (Dionysius, Ecclesiastical Hierarchy, Caput V, Section 2)

These reports about the traditions followed by the Christians, who were called heretics by the Pauline Church, empathetically establish that they kept their core teachings secret and divulged them only to those who had been duly tested and found worthy of receiving them. To the common followers, this remained a mystery. The tradition that the teachings of Jesus and, after him, of the Apostles had an element that was kept as a closely guarded secret, which appeared to be a mystery for the rest of the people, was evidently very strong in Paul's time, because of which he, too, declared that he had certain mysteries. This was followed up by the Pauline Church, which continued to declare what mysteries they had and kept adding to those that had been pronounced by Paul. The claims of Paul in this regard are in the following passages.

> Now to him that is of power to establish you according to my gospel, and the preaching of Jesus Christ, according to the revelation of the mystery, which was kept secret since the world began.
>
> (Romans 16:25)

> But we speak the wisdom of God in a mystery, even the hidden wisdom, which God ordained before the world unto our glory:
>
> Which none of the princes of this world knew: for had they known it, they would not have crucified the Lord of glory.
>
> But God hath revealed them unto us by his Spirit: for the Spirit searcheth all things, yea, the deep things of God.
>
> (1 Corinthians 2:7–8 and 2:10)

Behold, I shew you a mystery; We shall not all sleep, but we shall all be changed,

In a moment, in the twinkling of an eye, at the last trump: for the trumpet shall sound, and the dead shall be raised incorruptible, and we shall be changed.

For this corruptible must put an incorruption, and this mortal must put on immortality.

(1 Corinthians 15:51–53)

How that by revelation he made known unto me the mystery; (as I wrote afore in few words, whereby, when ye read, ye may understand my knowledge in the mystery of Christ)

(Ephesians 3:3–4)

And to make all men see what is the fellowship of the mystery, which from the beginning of the world hath been hid in God, who created all things by Jesus Christ.

(Ephesians 3:9)

This is a great mystery: but I speak concerning Christ and the Church.

(Ephesians 5:32)

Even the mystery which hath been hid from ages and from generations, but now is made manifest to his saints:

To whom God would make known what is the riches of the glory of this mystery among the Gentiles; which is Christ in you, the hope of glory

(Colossians 1:26–27)

That their hearts might be comforted, being knit together in love, and unto all riches of the full assurance of understanding, to the acknowledgement of the mystery of God, and of the Father, and of Christ.

(Colossians 2:2)

> And without controversy great is the mystery of godliness: God was manifest in flesh, justified in the Spirit, seen of angels, preached unto the Gentiles, believed on in the world, received up into glory.
>
> (1 Timothy 3:16)

Paul has claimed that the mystery was revealed to him by God through His Spirit. Like all other things that he preached, he has not stated that he had received it from the Apostles. He has also stated that the same was being revealed by him to all the believers. As per these statements, the mystery is in the godliness of Christ along with the Father and in the hope of resurrection. Another mystery he has declared is of the world coming to an end within the lifetime of the people he was addressing, as he has stated that 'we shall not all sleep, but we shall all be changed.' It is noteworthy that Paul has not declared the birth of Jesus from a virgin mother to be one of the mysteries. This confirms the view that the myth of Jesus having been born of a virgin mother had not emerged in his times. Later, when the Pauline Church developed the idea of having mysteries and declared several of their beliefs to be so, the concept of a virgin mother was also declared to be one of them. The declarations of the Church Fathers after Paul on what constituted the Christian mystery are given below.

> Now the virginity of Mary was hidden from the prince of this world, as was also her offspring, and the death of the Lord; three mysteries of renown, which were wrought in silence by God.
>
> (*The Writings of the Early Church Fathers*, Vol. 1, Ignatius, Epistle to the Ephesians, Chapter 19)

> Because if He came to man, that He might be the Mediator of God and men, it behoved Him to be with man, and the Word to be made flesh; so that reasonably the Son of

God might be made, by the assumption of flesh, the Son of man, and the Son of man by the reception of the Word of God the Son of God. This most profound and recondite mystery is found to be fulfilled in the Lord Jesus Christ.
    (*The Writings of the Early Church Fathers*, Vol. 5, Novation, Treatise Concerning the Trinity, Chapter 23)

Tremendous, verily, is the mystery connected with thee, O virgin mother, thou spiritual throne, glorified and made worthy of God.
    (*The Writings of the Early Church Fathers*, Vol. 6, Methodius, Oration Concerning Simeon and Anna)

For that God who is supreme and the maker of all things, who made man and conferred on him alone the gift of reason, that he might pay back honour to Him and by the exercise of this piety and obedience might gain the reward of immortality. This is true and divine mystery.
    (*The Writings of the Early Church Fathers*, Vol. 7, Lactantius, The Epitome of Divine Institutes, Chapter 41)

He who has not acknowledged the Son has been unable to acknowledge the Father. This is the mystery of the Supreme God.
    (*The Writings of the Early Church Fathers*, Vol. 7, Lactantius, The Epitome of Divine Institutes, Chapter 49)

I will now speak of the mystery of the cross, lest anyone say, if death must be endured by Him, it should have been not one that was manifestly infamous.
    (*The Writings of the Early Church Fathers*, Vol. 7, Lactantius, The Epitome of Divine Institutes, Chapter 51)

And whenever he invokes the Holy Spirit, and offers the most dread sacrifice, and constantly handles the common Lord of all, tell me what rank shall we give him?

And dost thou not yet tremble to introduce a soul into so sacred a mystery.
(*The Writings of the Early Church Fathers*, Vol. 18, John Chrysostom, On Priesthood, Book VI)

Wherefore it is necessary to understand the marvel of the mysteries, what it is, why it was given, and what is the profit of the action. We become one Body and the members of His flesh and of His bones.
(*The Writings of the Early Church Fathers*, Vol. 23, John Chrysostom, Homilies on John, Homily 46)

But the descent into the water, and the trine immersion of the person in it, involves another mystery.
(*The Writings of the Early Church Fathers*, Vol. 28, Gregary of Nyssa, The Great Catechism, Chapter 35)

The bread again is at the first common bread, but when the sacramental action consecrates it, it is called, and becomes, the body of Christ.
(*The Writings of the Early Church Fathers*, Vol. 28, Gregary of Nyssa, A Sermon for the Day of the Lights)

Water, certainly, but not water alone; you saw the deacons ministering there, and the bishop asking questions and hallowing.
Consider, however, how ancient is the mystery prefigured even in the origin of the world itself.
(*The Writings of the Early Church Fathers*, Vol. 33, Ambrose, The Book concerning the Mysteries, Chapter 3)

Paul had the compulsion of claiming that he knew the mysteries because the people of his time were aware that the teachings of Jesus and the Apostles had an element that was disclosed only to the select few. For the rest of the people, this was a mystery. He, therefore, claimed and declared certain things to be the mysteries of the belief system propounded by him. The Church later had a different compulsion in not limiting itself to only the mysteries declared by Paul because one of the mysteries declared by him had been proved to be false. He had declared it to be a mystery that the world would come to an end in the lifetime of the people he was addressing and had assured them they would not die but would be changed into the incorruptible and the immortal. In the gospel, Jesus had stated that the time of the Day of Judgement was known only to the Father. Even the Son was not in the know of it. Paul had, however, taken the liberty of fixing it within the lifetime of the people around him. As all of them as well as several generations that followed died without this promise of Paul coming true, the Church had to look for other things that could be declared to be the mysteries, as the tradition of having mysteries connected with the religion had become well established. The other mystery declared by Paul in the godliness of Christ was also elaborated in the process. The first passage above declares the virginity of Mary as one of the three mysteries. This is from a work ascribed to Ignatius. It has already been mentioned that all works ascribed to Ignatius are forged. This passage confirms this, because the myth of Jesus having been born of a virgin mother had not emerged as early as the times of Ignatius, who was the bishop of Antioch succeeding Peter. It had not emerged even in the times of Novation, whose statement is in the second passage. He is explaining the godliness of Jesus and explaining how he is both, the Son of man and the Son of God. For Jesus being the Son of God, he has not stated that he was so not because of his birth from God but because he received the Word of God. The next passage from Methodius declares the mystery connected with the virgin mother. Evidently, by his time the myth had come into the Christian Scriptures. The other mysteries stated are those related to the cross, to the Eucharist and to baptism. The powers of the cross to drive away demons and bad luck was a belief that had emerged by then. This was declared to be a mystery. The bread becoming the body of Christ and the wine mixed with water becoming his blood in the ritual of the Eucharist and the belief that by eating it the believers become a part of the body of Christ was the other mystery declared, as was also the removal of all sins by baptism. These were not mysteries in the sense in which the core teachings of Jesus and the Apostles were considered mysteries. In that case, there were certain teachings that were imparted only to the select few, while for the rest they remained a mystery. In this case, whatever could not be understood or explained and yet people were asked to believe were termed to be mysteries. The exercise on their part, however, goes to establish that the teachings of Jesus and the Apostles had a core element that was kept secret from the masses and appeared to be a mystery to the rest.

The third feature of the Upanishadic religion found in the belief system of the Christians termed heretics by the Pauline Church was the belief that the creation is a part of the Creator. Both are one and the same. This is significant because in the Pauline beliefs there is an unbridgeable chasm between God and man. Though all things promised are to be received after death, God still remains a benefactor and the king. Even after the Day of Judgement, it would be the kingdom of Christ where He would be the king and Christians His subjects. They would receive all the bounties from Him to live happily forever, but the distinction between Him and them would always remain. The belief of the Gnostic Christians and those declared heretics by the Pauline Church is, thus, diametrically opposite of what was propounded by the Pauline Church. The belief of Jesus on this point emerges from the following passage.

> And when he was demanded of the Pharisees, when the kingdom of God should come, he answered them and said, The kingdom of God cometh not with observation:

> Neither shall they say, Lo here! Or Lo there! for, behold, the kingdom of God is within you.
>
> (Luke 17:20–21)

On this point, the belief amongst the Gnostics emerges from the following passages.

> The All had been inside of Him, the illimitable, inconceivable one.
>
> He is the One who set the All in order and in whom the All existed and whom the All lacked.
>
> They were in the Father without knowing Him.
>
> They indeed are the truth, and the Father is in them, and they are in the Father, since they are perfect, inseparable from him who is truly good.
>
> (The Nag Hammadi Library, The Gospel of Truth)

> The Creator also sent down souls from his substance.
>
> (The Nag Hammadi Library, The Tripartite Tractate, Chapter II)

> You are from the fullness and you dwell in the place where the deficiency is.
>
> (The Nag Hammadi Library, The Dialogue of the Saviour)

> I am He who was within me.
>
> I am from the Pre-existent Father, and the son in the Pre-existent One.
>
> (The Nag Hammadi Library, The First Apocalypse of James)

> It is I who am in you, and you are in me, just as the Father is in you in innocence.
>
> They have come to know that perfect Blessed One, the external and incomprehensible Father, which is I.
>
> I am Christ, the Son of Man, the one from you who

is among you. I am despised for your sake, in order that you yourselves may forget the difference.

(The Nag Hammadi Library, The Second Treatise of the Great Seth)

It is the power that exists within you that often extended itself as word from the Triple-Powered One.
He who knows thee knows the Universal One.

(The Nag Hammadi Library, The Allogences)

For the Son of Man is within you.
Those who seek Him will find Him.

(The Nag Hammadi Library, The Gospel of Mary Magdalene)

These are the statements of Gnostic Christians whose works were fortunately found a few decades ago. As these were found in Egypt, they represent the views of the Christians of Egypt, Judea and the East. One can find complete expression of their views in these works, unlike the case of their Western counterparts whose works have not survived, because of which all that is known about them is from what has been quoted of them by their rivals and critics. Not only on this point wherein they unequivocally speak of the oneness of the Creator and the creation, but in all their beliefs they are very close to the Upanishads. The views of the heretic Christians of the West were very similar. Their views on this point emerge from the following passages.

Simon Magus represented himself as being the loftiest of all powers, that is, the Being who is the Father over all, and he allowed himself to be called by whatsoever title men were pleased to address him.

(*The Writings of the Early Church Fathers*, Vol. 1, Irenaeus, Against Heresies, Book I, Chapter 23)

According to their assertions, they have souls formed of the same substance as God Himself.
>(*The Writings of the Early Church Fathers*, Vol. 1,)
>Irenaeus, Against Heresies, Book II, Chapter 19)

They assert that they possess souls from the same sphere as Jesus, and that they are like him.
>(*The Writings of the Early Church Fathers*, Vol. 1,)
>Irenaeus, Against Heresies, Book II, Chapter 32)

But God has no natural relation to us, as the authors of the heresies will have it. We are totally distinct from God unless we shall dare to say that we are a part of Him, and of the same essence as God. And I know not how one, who knows God, can bear to hear this.
>(*The Writings of the Early Church Fathers*, Vol. 2,)
>Clement of Alexandria, Stromata, Book II, Chapter 16)

Carpocrates claims for himself such supernal qualities, that his disciples set their souls at once on an equality with Christ.
>(*The Writings of the Early Church Fathers*, Vol. 3,)
>Tertullian, Treatise on the Soul, Chapter 23)

He is in you, if you are willing to pay him homage, for the sake of appearances, that you may seem to honour God; for your fears he does not want. (Marcion's view)
>(*The Writings of the Early Church Fathers*, Vol. 3,)
>Tertullian, Against Marcion, Book I, Chapter 27)

From whom I am sent forth pure, being already part of the light of the Son and of the Father. (View of heretics)
>(*The Writings of the Early Church Fathers*, Vol. 4,)
>Origen, Against Celsus, Book VI, Chapter 31)

According to Simon there exists that which is blessed and

incorruptible in a latent condition in everyone.
(*The Writings of the Early Church Fathers*, Vol. 5,)
Hippolytus, Refutation of All Heresies, Book VI, Chapter 12)

Moreover, he maintains that every soul, yea, every living creature that moves, partakes of the substance of the Good Father.
(*The Writings of the Early Church Fathers*, Vol. 6,)
Archelaus, The Acts of the Disputation with the Heresiarch Manes)

'We must come to the true Prophet. He is everywhere near to them who seek Him. He is indeed within him, because He is everywhere, and is found within the minds of all men, but He is dormant to the unbelieving, and is held to be absent from those by whom His existence is not believed.' When Peter had said this and more, he dismissed the crowds.
(*The Writings of the Early Church Fathers*, Vol. 8,)
Pseudo-Clementine literature, Book VIII, Chapter 62)

Against Tatian who says 'I am God and besides me there is none else'.
(*The Writings of the Early Church Fathers*, Vol. 8,)
Theodotus, Excerpts of Theodotus, Para 38)

As nothing could exist without Thee, doth whatever exists contain Thee? Why, then, do I ask Thee to come into me, since I indeed exist, and could not exist if Thou wert not in me?

Or should I not rather say, that I could not exist unless I were in Thee from whom are all things, by whom are all things, in whom are all things?
(*The Writings of the Early Church Fathers*, Vol. 10,)
Augustine, Confessions of Augustine,
Book I, Chapter 2)

These are conclusions to which you are driven, because you say that the soul is a part of God.
(*The Writings of the Early Church Fathers*, Vol. 13,) Augustine, On the Morals of the Manicheans, Chapter 2)

But now when they speak of that part of the nature of God as everywhere mixed up in heaven, in earth, in all bodies dry and moist, in all sorts of flesh, in all seeds of trees, herbs, men and animals, not as present by the power of divinity which we say of God, but fettered, oppressed polluted, to be loosed and liberated, it is horrible to speak of.
(*The Writings of the Early Church Fathers*, Vol. 13,) Augustine, Concerning the Nature of Good, Chapter 44)

According to the brethren who prepared these objections understood him to have said that man's soul and God are of the same nature, and to have asserted that the soul is part of God.
(*The Writings of the Early Church Fathers*, Vol. 14,) Augustine, On the Proceedings of Pelagius, Chapter 65)

I have some apprehension lest you may fall in with this man's opinion, that 'God did not make the soul from nothing, but that the soul is so far out of Him as to have emanated from Him.'
(*The Writings of the Early Church Fathers*, Vol. 14,) Augustine, Anti Pelagian Writings, Book II, Chapter 5)

Where is supreme concord, supreme evidence, supreme steadfastness, supreme fullness and life supreme. Where nothing is lacking, nothing redundant. Where Begetter and begotten are one.
(*The Writings of the Early Church Fathers*, Vol. 16,) Augustine, Soliloquies, Book I, Para 4)

> The Divine Being, as our argument has shown, though distinctly something other than visible and material substances, nevertheless pervades each one amongst all existences, and by this penetration of the whole keeps the world in a state of being.
> (*The Writings of the Early Church Fathers*, Vol. 28,) Gregory of Nyssa, On the Soul and the Resurrection)

> They assert that there was an extension of God into man, not a decent; that He, who took our flesh to be Son of Man, had not been Son of God; that there was no divine birth in His case, but an identity of Begetter and begotten.
> (*The Writings of the Early Church Fathers*, Vol. 32,) Hilary of Poiters, On the Faith of the Easterns, Para 16, Book I)

All these passages bring out the belief that the Creator and the creation, especially the soul, are one and the same. Significant is the tenth passage, as this is a discourse of the Apostle Peter that has been recorded by someone and has survived. He has stated that God is everywhere and is within the person also. The twelfth and the seventeenth passages are also of interest. These are from Augustine, one from his autobiography and the other from the Soliloquies, wherein he has expressed the same view, the Begetter and the begotten are one. However, in the thirteenth, fourteenth, fifteenth and sixteenth passages, when others have said the same thing, Augustine has disapproved of the opinion and, in the text, has proceeded to argue at length against it. The last passage is very important as Hilary of Poiters has recorded the views of the Eastern Church. The other writers have recorded the views of people who had been dubbed as heretics, but this is the view of the Eastern Church, with which the Western Church was in conflict over certain issues of the Christian beliefs. They believed in the identity of the Begetter and the begotten. As has been mentioned earlier, the Pauline scriptures reached the Eastern Church, a few centuries later, because of which several elements of the apostolic theology had received a longer time to settle down and so survived. It is evident that, till the time of Hilary, this was the belief of the Eastern Church.

The fourth feature of the Vedic religion to be found in the teachings of Jesus and the Apostles is the belief in the transmigration of the soul. The belief is that the soul keeps taking births in various forms, based on the deeds performed. This is the theory of 'Karma'. There is no heaven or hell. The soul receives the rewards and punishments for its deeds in the form of its next birth. It is, however, possible for it to go out of this cycle of births and death, which is called 'moksha' or salvation. It is believed that the soul then merges with God. The beliefs of the Pauline Christianity are contradictory to this. The belief therein is that the soul, after death, waits for the Day of Judgement when the world would come to an end. Each soul would be judged by Jesus on behalf of God and would be awarded reward or punishment as per the deeds performed in the lifetime of the person. The reward would be an abode in heaven till eternity with all possible comforts, while the punishment would be sufferings in hell till eternity. There is nothing common in the two beliefs and one cannot be said to be a slight modification of the other. For Christianity, this is one of its fundamental beliefs, and Jesus saying something else has very serious implication.

The belief in the transmigration of the soul has two elements, one, that the soul is reborn with a new body after death, based on its deeds and, two, the soul can go out of this cycle of births and deaths, which is called salvation. The views of Jesus and the Christians who were termed Gnostics and Heretics can be seen on both these points. The understanding of what was meant by salvation is significant, as Paul has used this word in his epistles without defining it and the Church later developed a concept that was in tune with its belief in the Day of Judgement but has no support from the Scriptures.

A passage from the Bible has already been quoted that reflects the belief of Jesus in rebirth wherein he had stated that Elias had already been reborn as per the belief of the Jews that he would come before Christ and the disciples understood that he was referring to John the Baptist. The views of the Gnostics on rebirth can be seen from the following passages.

> Truth did not come into the world naked, but it came in types and images. The world will not receive truth in any other way. There is rebirth and an image of rebirth. It is certainly necessary to be born again through the image.
> (The Nag Hammadi Library,
> The Gospel of Philip)

> As long as she (the soul) was alone with the Father, she was virgin. But when she fell down into a body and came to this life, then she fell into the hands of many robbers. And the wanton creatures passed her from one to another.
> (The Nag Hammadi Library,
> The Exegesis on the Soul)

> Just as the mixtures (or qualities) that dwell in them hide the nature of the bodies and uninterruptedly have them pass from one to the other, likewise virtue and knowledge or evilness and ignorance hide the rational nature.
> (Evagrius, Kephalia Gnostika, 2.18)

> If it is true that living beings are susceptible of increment and diminution, it is clear that therefore this is the opposite of those who are dead, and they receive these things themselves. And if this is in this way, there will be again various bodies, and worlds/aeons will be created that are apt to them.
> (Evagrius, Kephalia Gnostika, 2.85)

> The change/succession of instruments is the transformation from (certain) bodies into (different) bodies, according to the measure of the orders of these that are joined with them.
> (Evagrius, Kephalia Gnostika, 3.20)

> For it is not the case that death is a change from (given) limbs into (other) limbs, but from a good or bad mixture to a good or bad transformation.
> (Evagrius, Kephalia Gnostika, 3.25)

These passages reflect a distinct belief in the transmigration of the soul on the part of the Gnostic Christians. Similar belief was there amongst those declared heretics by the Church. This can be seen in the following passages.

> They deem it necessary, that by means of transmigration from body to body, souls have the experience of every kind of life as well as every kind of action.
>
> They maintain that He delivers such souls to another angel that he may shut them up in other bodies for they declare that the body is the prison.
> (*The Writings of the Early Church Fathers*, Vol. 1, Irenaeus, Against Heresies, Book I, Chapter 25)

> They maintain that souls pass on account of the deeds done in the body.
> (*The Writings of the Early Church Fathers*, Vol. 1, Irenaeus, Against Heresies, Book II, Chapter 29)

> But the hypothesis of Basilides says that souls having sinned before in another life endure punishment in this.
> (*The Writings of the Early Church Fathers*, Vol. 2, Clement of Alexandria, Stromata, Book IV, Chapter 12)

Laberius holds, following an opinion of Pythagoras, that man may have his origin from a mule, a serpent from a woman.
(*The Writings of the Early Church Fathers*, Vol. 3, Tertullian, The Apology, Chapter 48)

He says that when you go forth from the body, do not crave for this because then the passions will once more confine you within the body. For these suppose that there is a transition of souls from one body to another, adopting the principles of Pythagoras.
(*The Writings of the Early Church Fathers*, Vol. 5, Hippolytus, Refutation of all Heresies, Book VI, Chapter 21)

The followers of Carpocrates allege that the souls are transferred from body to body, so far as that may fill up the measure of all their sins. When no sin is left the soul is then emancipated and departs unto God.
(*The Writings of the Early Church Fathers*, Vol. 5, Hippolytus, Refutation of all Heresies, Book VII, Chapter 20)

The rejected opinion is that souls which once sinned descend by stages and degrees to bodies suited to their deserts and as a penalty for their previous life.
(*The Writings of the Early Church Fathers*, Vol. 14, Augustine, Anti-Pelagian Writings, Book I, Chapter 31)

They tell us that one of their sages said that he, being one and the same person, was born a man, and afterwards assumed the form of a woman, and flew about with birds, and grew as a bush, saying that one soul passed through so many changes.
(*The Writings of the Early Church Fathers*, Vol. 28, Gregory of Nyssa, On the Making of Man, Chapter 28)

> But is their opinion preferable, who say that our soul, when they have passed out of these bodies, migrate into the bodies of beasts, or of various living creatures?
> (*The Writings of the Early Church Fathers*, Vol. 33, Ambrose, On the Belief in the Resurrection, Book II, Para 127)

> And hence that which was deservedly condemned in Origen must be punished in Eutyches also, unless he prefers to give up his opinion, viz. the assertion that souls have had not only a life but also different actions before they were inserted in men's bodies.
> (*The Writings of the Early Church Fathers*, Vol. 35, Leo the Great, Letter 35, To Julian, Bishop of Cos)

All these passages show that the Christians who were declared heretics by the Church not only believed in the transmigration of the soul but that their belief was identical to the Vedic belief on the subject. It is brought out very clearly in the sixth passage wherein it is stated that the souls are transferred from body to body as per their sins and when no sin is left the soul is emancipated and departs unto God. This is the theory of 'Karma'. It appears that this belief was there amongst the Christians for several centuries and was finally anathematized in an ecumenical council. The said anathematization is in the passage below.

> If anyone asserts the fabulous pre-existence of souls, and shall assert the monstrous restoration which follows from it: let him be anathema.
> (*The Writings of the Early Church Fathers*, Vol. 37, The Seven Ecumenical Councils, The Second Council of Constantinople)

The concept of 'moksha' or salvation is an integral part of the theory of transmigration of the soul. It is the ultimate objective set forth for a person. The belief in this is that the soul goes out of the cycle of births and death to become one with God. That is its emancipation and final beatitude. Though the Church stamped out the belief in rebirth by anathematising it, the belief in salvation was evidently so strong that it could not be wiped out despite it having contradictions with the theory of the Day of Judgement. Before examining how different churches accommodated this belief without accepting rebirth of the soul, the belief of Jesus, the Gnostics and the heretics on this point may be seen. The views of Jesus emerge from the following passage.

> Then Jesus said to those Jews which believed in him, If ye continue in my word, then are ye my disciples indeed;
> And ye shall know the truth, and the truth shall make you free.
>
> (John 8:31–32)

In this passage, Jesus has also spoken of how salvation is to be achieved. This would come up for examination ahead. The point to note here is what he thought of salvation, and for this he has stated 'the truth shall make you free'. It is, thus, freedom that has to be attained by the soul. The Sanskrit word 'moksha' means emancipation or freedom. Jesus is speaking of the same concept, freedom of the soul from the cycle of births and deaths, and becoming one with God. The views of the Gnostics emerge from the following passages.

> Blessed will they be who ascend to the Father.
> (The Nag Hammadi Library,
> The Apocryphon of James)

> Since the perfection of all is in the Father, it is necessary for all to ascend to Him.
> By means of unity each one will understand itself. By means of knowledge it will purify itself of diversity with a view towards unity, devouring matter within itself like fire and darkness by light, death by life.

The end, you see, is the recognition of Him who is hidden, that is, the Father, from whom the beginning came forth and to whom will return all who have come from Him.
(The Nag Hammadi Library, The Gospel of Truth)

Freedom is the knowledge of the truth which existed before ignorance was ruling, forever without beginning and without end, being something good, and a salvation of things, and a release from servile nature in which they have suffered.
(The Nag Hammadi Library, The Tripartite Tractate)

Whoever, then, knows the Father in pure knowledge will depart to the Father and repose in the Unbegotten Father.
(The Nag Hammadi Library, The Sophia of Jesus)

Since the body is a temporary dwelling which the rulers and authorities have as an abode, the man within, after being imprisoned in the fabrication, fell into suffering.
(The Nag Hammadi Library, The Interpretation of Knowledge)

Every procession of illuminating light turns us to the oneness of our conducting Father, and to a deifying simplicity.
(Dionysius, Heavenly Hierarchy, Caput I, Section I)

Now the assimilation to, and union with, God, as far as attainable, is deification. And this is the common goal of every Hierarchy.
(Dionysius, Ecclesiastical Hierarchy, Caput I, Section III)

He will see his proper self in what he was originally and will depart from the gloomy recess of ignorance, but being imperfect, he will not at once derive the most perfect union

and participation of God, but little by little will be carried forward, and when perfected reach the supremely divine summit. The Divine Blessedness receives the man, thus conducted, into communion with Itself.
(Dionysius, Ecclesiastical Hierarchy, Caput II, Contemplation, Section IV)

When we are in that which is, we shall see that which is. But when those in which we are will be removed, that which is not will no more exist.
(Evagrius, Kephalaia Gnostika, First Discourse, 1.3)

The knowledge of the One is the knowledge of that one who only is.
When only the intellections of all those things that have come to existence by accident will remain in us, then only the One who is known will be known, only he, by the subject who knows.
(Evagrius, Kephalaia Gnostika, First Discourse, 1.19–1.20)

The end of natural knowledge is the holy Unity, whereas the end of ignorance does not exist.
(Evagrius, Kephalaia Gnostika, First Discourse, 1.71)

The coheir of Christ is the one who comes to be in Unity and delights in contemplation together with Christ.
(Evagrius, Kephalaia Gnostika, Fourth Discourse, 4.8)

Who will investigate the logoi of Providence, and how Christ leads the rational nature through various aeons, towards union in the holy Unity?
(Evagrius, Kephalaia Gnostika, Fourth Discourse, 4.89)

All these passages ring a clear message that salvation is the union with God. The third passage says that with this there is 'a release from the servile nature in which they have suffered'. The concept of salvation of the Gnostic Christians was, thus, identical with the Vedic concept of salvation wherein the soul is freed from the cycle of births and deaths and becomes one with God. The Christians who were branded as heretics, too, had a similar view. This emerges from the following passages.

> All these have for their object the attaining of the unity of God.
> (*The Writings of the Early Church Fathers*, Vol. 1, Ignatius, Epistle to the Philadelphians, Chapter 2)

> They maintain that those who have attained to perfect knowledge must of necessity be regenerated into that power which is above all.
> (*The Writings of the Early Church Fathers*, Vol. 1, Irenaeus, Against Heresies, Book I, Chapter 21)

> He, then, who has first moderated his passions and trained himself for impassability, and developed to the beneficence of gnostic perfection, speeds by righteous knowledge through the love of God to the sacred abode.
> Thus receiving the Lord's power, the soul studies to be God.
> (*The Writings of the Early Church Fathers*, Vol. 2, Clement of Alexandria, Stromata, Book VI, Chapter 13)

> The Gnostic at last imitates the Lord, having received a sort of quality akin to the Lord Himself, in order to assimilation of God.
> (*The Writings of the Early Church Fathers*, Vol. 2, Clement of Alexandria, Stromata, Book VI, Chapter 17)

There are a great many also, who, claiming to hold a resurrection after the soul's departure, maintain that going out of the sepulchre means escaping out of the world, since in their view the world is the habitation of the dead, that is, of these who know not God.
> (*The Writings of the Early Church Fathers*, Vol. 3, Tertullion, On the Resurrection of the Flesh, Chapter 19)

Those, who, mortifying their members and the earth, and, rising above not only their corporeal nature, but even the uncertain and fragile movement of the soul itself, have united themselves to the Lord, being made spiritual, that they may be forever one spirit with Him.
> (*The Writings of the Early Church Fathers*, Vol. 4, Origen, Contra Celsus, Book I, Chapter 8)

There are some who think themselves capable of being cleansed by their own righteousness, so as to contemplate God, and to dwell in God.

For these persons promise themselves cleansing by their own righteousness for this reason, because some of them have been able to penetrate with the eye of the mind beyond the whole creature, and to touch, though it be in ever so small a part, the light of the unchangeable truth, a thing which they deride many Christians for being not yet able to do.
> (*The Writings of the Early Church Fathers*, Vol. 12, Augustine, On the Trinity, Book IV, Chapter 15)

The concept of salvation of the Christians termed heretics by the Church was, thus, identical with that of the Gnostics and the Vedas. The object was to go out of this world and become one with God. This concept was so strong that despite its contradictions with the belief in the Day of Judgement, the

Church could not completely erase it, even after it anathematized the belief in rebirth. The concept has, however, been handled by different Churches in their own way by trying to assimilate it with their other beliefs. Several Church Fathers who are held in high esteem by the Roman Catholic Church have expressed a belief in the concept of salvation that is identical to that of the aforementioned heretics. This emerges from the following passages.

> The union of the soul with the incorruptible Deity can be accomplished in no other way but by herself attaining by her virgin state to the utmost purity possible, a state which, being like God, will enable her to grasp that to which it is like.
> (*The Writings of the Early Church Fathers*, Vol. 28, Gregory of Nyssa, On Virginity, Chapter 2)

> Then that godly beauty of the soul which was an imitation of the Archetypal Beauty, like fine steel blackened with the vicious rust, preserved on longer the glory of its familiar essence, but was disfigured with the ugliness of sin.
> The earthly envelopment once removed, the soul's beauty will again appear.
> In fact this likeness to the divine is not our work at all, it is the great gift of God. Human efforts can only go so far as to clear away the filth of sin, and so cause the buried beauty of the soul to shine forth again.
> (*The Writings of the Early Church Fathers*, Vol. 28,) Gregory of Nyssa, On Virginity, Chapter 12)

> The soul should be free from such emotions, and turning back upon herself should behold the original Beauty reflected in the mirror and in the figure of her own beauty. For truly herein consists the real assimilation to the Divine.
> When it looks within itself, it wishes for what it contains

and contains that which it wishes and admits nothing external.

Whenever the soul, having divested itself of its multifarious emotions incident to its nature, gets its Divine form and mounting above desire, enters within that towards which it was once incited by the desire, it offers no harbor within itself for hope or for memory.

(*The Writings of the Early Church Fathers*, Vol. 28, Gregory of Nyssa, On the Soul and the Resurrection)

In order to expound and describe this dark night, through which the soul passes in order to attain to the Divine light of the perfect union of the love of God, as far as possible in this life.

And if aught I stray, it is not my intention to depart from the sound sense and doctrine of our Holy Mother, the Catholic Church.

(John of the Cross, Ascent of Mount Carmel, Prologue)

It must be known that God dwells and is present substantially in every soul.

When we speak of union of the soul with God, we speak not of this substantial union which is continually being wrought, but of the union and transformation of the soul with God.

(John of the Cross, Ascent of Mount Carmel, Chapter 5)

For to seek oneself in God is to seek the favour and refreshments of God; but to seek God in oneself is not only to desire to be without both of these.

The truly spiritual man may understand the mystery of the gate and of the way of Christ, and so become united with God, and may know that, the more completely he is annihilated for God's sake, the more completely is he united to God.

(John of the Cross, Ascent of Mount Carmel, Chapter 7)

I mean that the King of glory will not come to our souls - that is, so as to be united with them-unless we strive to gain the greatest virtues.

(Teresa of Avila, The Way of Perfection, Chapter 16)

Remember how Saint Augustine tells us about his seeking God in many places and eventually finding Him within himself.

(Teresa of Avila, The Way of Perfection, Chapter 28)

The ultimate end of an intellectual creature is the vision of God in His essence.

(Thomas Aquinas, Shorter Summa, 104)

He endows with these effects of His love by which they are enabled to reach their last end, which is He Himself, the fountainhead of all goodness.

(Thomas Aquinas, Shorter Summa, 143)

Man's consummation consists in the attainment of his last end, which is perfect beatitude or happiness, and this consists in the vision of God.

(Thomas Aquinas, Shorter Summa, 149)

Yet some gifts do render man pleasing to God and join man to Him.

(Thomas Aquinas, Shorter Summa, 214)

It was also appropriate that that soul which was united to God more closely than all others should be beatified by the vision of God.

(Thomas Aquinas, Shorter Summa, 216)

Accordingly, resurrection is also twofold: one is a bodily resurrection, in which the soul is united to the body for the second time; the other is spiritual resurrection, in

which the soul is again united to God.
(Thomas Aquinas, Shorter Summa, 239)

Consequently man's ultimate perfection and final good consists in union with God.

We conclude, therefore, that perfect beatitude consists in the direct union of the spirit with God in knowledge and love.
(Thomas Aquinas, Shorter Summa,
Second Part, Hope and Prayer, 9)

All these passages are from theologians of the Roman Catholic Church. Thomas Aquinas, in particular, is considered to be an important theologian of this Church. All of them defining salvation to be a union of the soul with God is an evidence of this deep-rooted belief amongst the Christians that could not be erased despite its contradictions with the belief in the Day of Judgement. The difficulties of these writers in trying to synthesize this with the accepted beliefs of the Church is visible in these passages. At times 'as far as possible' is added to the union with God, while in the fourteenth passage two resurrections have been propounded. In this a major contradiction has crept in. The belief in the resurrection of the body claims that the body is united to the soul and remains so till eternity. If this union of body and soul has to remain till eternity, where is the scope left for the union of the soul and God, as has been stated further ahead in the passage. It is evident that Thomas Aquinas was caught between the two beliefs and tried to find a way to synthesize them. Between all these difficulties, the Roman Catholic Church developed the concept of a purgatory for penance for the sins. The sins could also be remitted by the clergy often on payment of a certain sum. A level just below God was also brought in, where the saintly dwelt till they waited for the Day of Judgement. There is, however, no scriptural basis for any of these beliefs.

The Orthodox Church, which carries the heritage of the Eastern Church, presents a very interesting picture on this point. The original concept of salvation has survived in it till now. This emerges from the following passages.

> In order to live within Tradition, it is not enough simply to give intellectual assent to a system of doctrines; for Tradition is far more than a set of abstract propositions—it is a life, a personal encounter with Christ in the Holy Spirit.
> (Timothy Ware, The Orthodox Church, Chapter 10)

> The incorporation of humans into Christ and our union with God requires the cooperation of two unequal, but equally necessary forces: divine grace and human will.
> (Timothy Ware, The Orthodox Church, Chapter 2)

> Such, according to the teachings of the Orthodox Church, is the final goal at which every Christian must aim: to become god, to attain theosis, deification or divinization. For Orthodoxy our salvation and redemption mean our deification.
> The Orthodox doctrine of deification, so far from being unscriptural (as is sometimes thought) has a solid Biblical basis.
> Unlike the eastern religions which teach that humans are swallowed up in the Deity, Orthodox mystical theology has always insisted that we humans, however closely linked to God, retain our full personal integrity.
> (Timothy Ware, The Orthodox Church, Chapter 2)

As has been mentioned earlier, the Pauline theology reached the Eastern Church a few centuries later as compared to Rome. The effect of this late takeover is reflected in the difference in the belief of salvation surviving in the two Churches. The Orthodox Church believes that salvation means their deification, their becoming God. Timothy Ware has pointed out that it is thought by some that there is no scriptural basis for it and has mentioned some passages of the Bible. What has been mentioned by him therein is certainly very weak to support the belief. This is evidently because the scriptures are Pauline and the teachings of Jesus and the Apostles were declared to be heresies in the past. Ware has also tried to draw a distinction from the beliefs of the Eastern religions wherein the soul merges in God, by stating that in their case full personal integrity of the soul is maintained. This is because he is burdened with the Pauline theology wherein there is an unbridgeable chasm between the Creator and the creation. In such a situation, the soul, being a creation, would have its independent existence, which, Ware is saying, is retained. Since the belief of the Eastern Church was the same as the Vedic religion, that the Creator and the creation are one and the same, the soul does not have an independent existence. God and the soul are one and the same, and the separate identity of the soul is only an illusion. As the soul does not have a real existence, it cannot maintain its personal identity and only God can remain.

The fifth element of the Vedic religion, to be found in the teachings of Jesus and the Apostles, is what has been prescribed as the way for salvation. It has been propounded in the Upanishads that to achieve salvation a person has to realize his true self because when he does so, he sees that he and God are one and the same. He has the vision of God and with this he ceases to be what he was and becomes one with God. It is the path of knowledge. The knowledge of your true self is what leads to salvation. Several passages that have already been quoted to bring out the concept of salvation have also stated this to be the path. In a passage from the Bible Jesus has said 'And ye shall know the truth, and the truth shall make you free'. It is the knowledge of the truth that is leading to emancipation. Evidently, he has prescribed the path of knowledge. Other passages from the Bible which show the same belief are given below.

> Be ye therefore perfect, even as your Father which is in heaven is perfect.
>
> (Matthew 5:48)

> The disciple is not above his master: but everyone that is perfect shall be as his master.
>
> (Luke 6:40)

Jesus has spoken of achieving perfection equal to the perfection of God in these passages. Perfection of God can be achieved only by becoming God and ceasing to be human. He is requiring his disciples to realize their true self and, by that, realize that they are God and become perfect like Him. This was the belief of the Apostles also, as emerges from the following passages.

> Let no man deceive you by any means: for that day shall not come, except there come a falling away first, and that man of sin be revealed, the son of perdition;
>
> Who opposeth and exalteth himself above all that is called God, or that is worshipped; so that he as God sitteth in the temple of God, shewing himself that he is God.
>
> (2 Thessalonians 2:3–4)

> They profess that they know God; but in works they deny him, being abominable, and disobedient, and unto every good work reprobate.
>
> (Titus 1:16)

In these passages, Paul is speaking of his adversaries, the Apostles. He has stated that they exalt themselves as God and claim to be God. They also profess to know God. The Apostles, as they were the chosen disciples of Jesus, would have been self-realized souls. They would have reached the stage where they had ceased to exist and only God existed in them. Paul, as an opponent, has derided them for making these claims.

The Gnostic Christians had the same belief. Their views emerge from the following passages.

> For He revealed Himself to him within him, is a fellow sufferer with him, gives him rest little by little, makes him grow, lifts him up, gives Himself to him completely for enjoyment from a vision.
>
> He should receive of the greatest good, which is life eternal, that is a firm knowledge of the Totalities.
>
> (The Nag Hammadi Library,
> The Tripartite Tractate)

> When you know yourself, then you will be known, and you will understand that you are the children of living Father.
>
> If you bring forth what is within you, what you have will save you.
>
> (The Nag Hammadi Library,
> The Gospel of Thomas)

> You saw the Spirit, you became Spirit. You saw Christ, you become Christ. You saw the Father, you shall become Father.
>
> For this person is no longer a Christian but a Christ.
>
> 'I came to make the things below like the things above, and the things outside as the things inside. I came to unite them in the place.'
>
> But those who have come to know themselves will enjoy their possessions.
>
> He who has the knowledge of the truth is a free man.
>
> (The Nag Hammadi Library, The Gospel of Philip)

> He who has known himself has at the same time already achieved knowledge about the depths of the All.
>
> (The Nag Hammadi Library,
> The Book of Thomas the Contender)

Everyone who has known himself has seen it in everything given to him to do.

(The Nag Hammadi Library,
The Dialogue of the Saviour)

The soul learned about God. She came to rest in Him who is at rest.

(The Nag Hammadi Library,
Authoritative Teaching)

You have shown us Yourself. We rejoice because while we were in the body, You have made us divine through Your knowledge.

(The Nag Hammadi Library,
The Prayer of Thanksgiving)

I turned to myself and saw the light that surrounded me and the Good that was in me, I became divine.

If you seek with a perfect seeking, then you shall know the Good that is in you, then you will know yourself as well as the one who derives from the God who truly pre-exists.

There was within me a stillness of silence, and I heard the Blessedness whereby I knew my proper self.

I knew the One who exists in me.

(The Nag Hammadi Library, Allogenes)

The reception of the supremely Divine Science is, both purification and enlightenment, and perfecting, enlightening by the self-same Divine knowledge.

(Dionysius, Heavenly Hierarchy,
Caput VII, Section 3)

All men should be saved by their assimilation towards God and come to the recognition of the Truth.

(Dionysius, Ecclesiastical Hierarchy,
Caput II, Section 1)

The Divine Being is the source of the sacred order. He who recurs to the proper view of Nature, will see his proper self in what he was originally.

The Divine Blessedness receives the man, thus conducted, into communion with Itself.

(Dionysius, Ecclesiastical Hierarchy, C,ontemplation, Section 4)

The secondary nature is the species of the mortal body, while the primary one is that of the soul; the intellect, then, is Christ, the one who is united to the knowledge of the Unity.

(Evagrius, Kephalaia Gnostika, 1.77)

And whoever knows that soul is called the soul of the One who is.

(Evagrius, Kephalaia Gnostika, 2.5)

The intellect is the seer of the Holy Trinity.

(Evagrius, Kephalaia Gnostika, 3.30)

Contemplation is the spiritual knowledge of those realities that were and will be, which lifts the intellect toward its original order.

(Evagrius, Kephalaia Gnostika, 3.42)

These passages justify the belief that the path to salvation is by knowing your own self because when the true self is known and seen, God is known and seen. The vision of God results in salvation. The beliefs of the Christians, who were declared heretics by the Church, were also identical. There are a very large number of references that bring this out but only a few are quoted below.

They further hold that the consummation of all things will take place when all that is spiritual has been formed and perfected by Gnosis and by this they mean spiritual men

who have attained to the perfect knowledge of God.
> (*The Writings of the Early Church Fathers*, Vol. 1,
> Irenaeus, Against Heresies,
> Book I, Chapter 6)

They assert that they themselves know more than all others and that they alone have imbibed the greatness of the knowledge of that power which is unspeakable.
> (*The Writings of the Early Church Fathers*, Vol. 1,
> Irenaeus, Against Heresies,
> Book I, Chapter 13)

They interpret as spoken with this view, that they should discover themselves to be above the Creator, styling themselves greater and better than God.
> (*The Writings of the Early Church Fathers*, Vol. 1,
> Irenaeus, Against Heresies,
> Book II, Chapter 30)

They hold that the resurrection of the dead is simply an acquaintance with the truth.
> (*The Writings of the Early Church Fathers*,
> Vol. 1, Irenaeus, Against Heresies,
> Book II, Chapter 31)

The greatest of all lessons is to know one's self. For if one knows himself, he will know God, and knowing God he will be made like God.
> (*The Writings of the Early Church Fathers*, Vol. 2,
> Clement of Alexandria, Stromata,
> Book III, Chapter 1)

We must after all this turn our attention to those scriptures also which forbid our belief in such a resurrection as is held by your Animalists (for I will not call them Spiritualists), that it is either to be assumed as taking place now as soon

as men come to the knowledge of the truth, or else that
it is accomplished immediately after their departure from
this life.
(*The Writings of the Early Church Fathers*, Vol. 3,
Tertullion, On the Resurrection of the Flesh,
Chapter 22)

These who are perfect shall behold face to face the glory
of the Lord.
(*The Writings of the Early Church Fathers*,
Vol. 4, Origen, True Discourse,
Book I, Chapter 4)

Beholding with open face the glory of the Lord, we are
changed into the same image, from glory to glory.
(*The Writings of the Early Church Fathers*, Vol. 4,
Origen, True Discourse, Book VII, Chapter 38)

And they suppose that the knowledge of him is the
originating principle of the capacity for a knowledge of
God, expressing themselves thus, 'The originating principle
of perfection is the knowledge of man, while the knowledge
of God is absolute perfection.'
(*The Writings of the Early Church Fathers*, Vol. 5,
Hippolytus, Refutation of all Heresies,
Book V, Chapter 1)

They style themselves Gnostics in this peculiar sense,
that they alone themselves have imbibed the marvelous
knowledge of the Perfect and Good Being.
(*The Writings of the Early Church Fathers*, Vol. 5,
Hippolytus, Refutation of All Heresies,
Book V, Chapter 18)

Monoimus makes this statement, 'Omitting to seek after
God and creation and things similar to these, seek for Him

from out of thyself, and learn who it is that absolutely appropriates unto Himself all things in thee.'
(*The Writings of the Early Church Fathers*, Vol. 5, Hippolytus, Refutation of all Heresies, Book VIII, Chapter 8)

Wherefore I counsel thee to now thyself, and to know God.
(*The Writings of the Early Church Fathers*, Vol. 8, Melito, the Philosopher, Discourse with Antonius Ceasar)

Each one, according to his own stage of advancement possesses the knowledge of God and in this knowledge God reposes and those who possess knowledge being made immortal by knowledge.
(*The Writings of the Early Church Fathers*, Vol. 8, Theodotus, Excerpts of Theodotus, Para 57)

One activity that will be left for those who have come to God on account of His word, is of knowing God, so that, being found by the knowledge of the Father, they may all be His Son.
(*The Writings of the Early Church Fathers*, Vol. 9, Origen, Commentary on John, Book I, Chapter 16)

He is to be sought not outside the seeker, and that these find Him in themselves who set their heart on doing so.
(*The Writings of the Early Church Fathers*, Vol. 9, Origen, Commentary on John, Book I, Chapter 42)

Since He has displayed so great mercy towards us, we should attain through Him to the knowledge of the true Father.
(*The Writings of the Early Church Fathers*, Vol. 9, Clement, Second Epistle of Clement, Chapter 3)

The Manichees would lead within to God, and set free from all errors those who are willing to be their hearers.
(*The Writings of the Early Church Fathers*, Vol. 12, Augustine, On the Profit of Believing, Para 2)

If he loved with spiritual love him whom he sees with human sight, he would see God, who is love itself, with the inner sight by which He can be seen.
(*The Writings of the Early Church Fathers*, Vol. 12, Augustine, On the Trinity, Book VIII, Chapter 8)

With regard to the Creator of the world, we know that He exists, but of His essential nature we cannot deny that we are ignorant. But, boosting as they do that they know these things.

If, then the lower creation which comes under our organs of sense, transcends human knowledge, how can He, who by His mere will made the world, be within the range of our apprehension.
(*The Writings of the Early Church Fathers*, Vol. 28, Gregory of Nyssa, Answer to Eunomius' Second Book)

All of whom hold that it is possible for human virtue and human knowledge to attain perfection and arrive, I will not say merely at a likeness to, but an equality with God.
(*The Writings of the Early Church Fathers*, Vol. 29, Jerome, Against the Pelagians, Prologue)

They claimed, not only that they had ascended to an infinite knowledge of infinite things, but that they had reduced all knowledge, undefined before, within the scope of ordinary reason.
(*The Writings of the Early Church Fathers*, Vol. 93, Hilary of Poiters, The Faith of the Easterns, Book I, Para 15)

They declared that men could by their own lives obtain just that which God had wrought by dying for man's salvation.
(The Writings of the Early Church Fathers, Vol. 34, John Cassian, Seven Books of John Cassian, Book I, Chapter 3)

These passages, which bring out the belief of the heretic Christians, show that the path for attaining salvation was by knowing oneself and thereby knowing and seeing God as identical with oneself. This is identical with the beliefs of the Gnostics and the Vedas. Of interest is the twenty-first passage wherein Hilary of Poitiers has recorded the belief of the Eastern Church. It shows that the Eastern Church believed that an individual could attain the knowledge of God.

This belief was evidently so strong amongst all Christians that it is found recorded even by writers who are considered to be very important theologians by the Roman Catholic Church. This emerges from the following passages.

> It appears that the full likeness of God is to take place in that image of God at that time when it shall receive the full sight of God.
> (*The Writings of the Early Church Fathers*, Vol. 12, Augustine, On the Trinity, Book 14, Chapter 18)

> Though He is everywhere present to the inner eye when it is sound and clear.
> (*The Writings of the Early Church Fathers*, Vol. 2, Augustine, On Christian Doctrine, Book I, Chapter 12)

> The sixth step, in which he purifies the eye itself which can see God, so far as God can be seen by those who as far as possible die to this world. For men see Him just so far as they die to this world, and so far as they live to it they see Him not.
> (*The Writings of the Early Church Fathers*, Vol. 2, Augustine, On Christian Doctrine, Book II, Chapter 7)

Our whole business in this life is to heal the eye of the heart whereby God may be seen.
> (*The Writings of the Early Church Fathers*, Vol. 15,
> Augustine, Sermons on the Gospel, Sermon 38,
> Para 5)

The eye, therefore, being cleansed and rendered single, will be adapted and suited to behold and contemplate its own inner light. For the eye in question is the eye of the heart.
> (*The Writings of the Early Church Fathers*, Vol. 15,
> Augustine, Sermon on the Mount, Book II,
> Chapter 11, Para 76)

Let us rejoice, then, and give thanks that we are made not only Christians, but Christ.
> (*The Writings of the Early Church Fathers*, Vol. 16,
> Augustine, On John, Tractate 21, Para 8)

Let me know myself, let me know Thee.
> (*The Writings of the Early Church Fathers*, Vol. 16,
> Augustine, Soliloquies, Book II, Para 1)

The speculative and critical faculty is the property of the soul's godlike part by which we grasp the Deity.

If the soul is purified of every vice it will be in the sphere of Beauty. The Deity is in very substance Beautiful and to the Deity the soul will in its state of purity have affinity and will embrace it like itself.

For truly herein consists the real assimilation to the Divine.
> (*The Writings of the Early Church Fathers*, Vol. 28,
> Gregory of Nyssa, On the Soul and the Resurrection)

In my opinion God will be discovered when that within us which is godlike and divine shall have mingled with its like, and the image shall have ascended to the Archetype.
> (*The Writings of the Early Church Fathers*, Vol. 30,
> Gregory of Nazianzen, Oration 28, Para 17)

A soul that has been brought low by these, and so obtained purity of heart and body will be the more easily united to God.

(*The Writings of the Early Church Fathers*, Vol. 34, John Cassian, Second Conference of Abbot Moses, Chapter 2)

I assure you, however, that before long you will have the great comfort of finding it unnecessary to tire yourself with seeking this holy Father to Whom you pray, for you will discover Him within you.

(Teresa of Avila, The Way of Perfection, Chapter 29)

It cannot fail to draw the Almighty to become one with our lowliness and to transform us into Himself and to effect a union between the Creator and the creature.

(Teresa of Avila, The Way of Perfection, Chapter 32)

The created intellect will see God in His essence and not in any mere likeness.

(Thomas Aquinas, Shorter Summa, 164)

The divine essence must be perceived directly in Itself and not through the medium of some likeness. Such vision requires a certain union of the created intellect with God.

In the vision of the divine essence the created spirit possesses God as present.

(Thomas Aquinas, Shorter Summa, Hope and Prayer, 9)

These writers, particularly Augustine and Thomas Aquinas, are very significant theologians even for the Roman Catholic Church. They expressing these views show the dilemma in which they were between the teachings of Jesus as had come down by way of tradition and the precepts laid down by Paul in the form of written scriptures. While trying to remain loyal to the Pauline theology, these elements have come in their writings, which have no support from Paul in any way and are in contradiction to the unbridgeable chasm he laid down between the Creator and the creation.

The Orthodox Church retains this concept in its beliefs till now. This emerges from the following passage.

> Humans were made for fellowship with God: this is the first and primary affirmation in the Christian doctrine of the human person.
>
> It means that we are God's offspring, His kin; it means that between us and Him there is a point of contact and similarity. The gulf between creature and Creator is not impassable.
>
> To acquire the likeness it is to be deified, it is to become a second god, a god of grace.
>
> 'Know yourselves' said St Antony of Egypt. He who knows himself, knows God.
>
> (Timothy Ware, The Orthodox Church, Chapter 11, The Human Person)

The sixth feature of the Vedic religion to be found associated with the Gnostic Christians and those declared to be heretics is the presence of two philosophies on the creation of the universe—the dualism of 'Sankhya' and the non-dualism of 'Vedanta'. Dualism of 'Sankhya' believes that there are two eternal, co-existent entities of Consciousness and Matter. There is no creation when the two are separated from each other. Creation begins when they mingle and ends when they separate again. The non-dualism of 'Vedanta' believes that there is only one eternal entity—'Brahm' or the Supreme God. When at rest, it has no qualities and exists only as consciousness and bliss. When It decides to create the universe, It acquires qualities and becomes 'Ishwar' or the Inferior God. Everything is created by this Inferior God, who creates material out of Itself, which is called 'Maya'. When creation has to end, 'Maya' separates itself from 'Ishwar' and dissolves into non-existence, while 'Iswhar' sheds His qualities and becomes 'Brahm' again. These two philosophies are contradictory, so a question could be raised as to how both existed together in the same people. They appear to be contradictory if they are compared on the basis of logic, but the contradiction melts away if they are seen from the viewpoint of the people who propounded them. Philosophy based on deductive logic is a later development. It starts from Socrates. Before him, even in Greece, Pythagoras just propounded his views without giving any reason for anything. These philosophies have been propounded by people who were Seers. They could see the past and the future. In the non-dualism of 'Vedanta', there is a stage when 'Maya' and 'Ishwar' have separated from each other, but 'Maya' has not dissolved into non-existence and 'Ishwar' has not shed His qualities to become 'Brahm'. The Seers who could see up to this point only would have seen these two entities, one Consciousness and the other Matter, and as they could not see beyond that, they would have propounded the dualism of 'Sankhya', believing both entities to be eternal. Those who could see beyond would have seen that ultimately only 'Brahm' remains and so propounded the non-dualism of 'Vedanta'. The presence of these two beliefs is, thus, not because of application of logic in two different ways but because of the extent to which certain Seers could see. The presence of both these beliefs amongst the Gnostics and Heretic Christians shows that both these beliefs had been with the Aryans from very early times, though the non-dualism of 'Vedanta' appears to have been the more acceptable opinion, as even amongst these Christians it seems to have been more widely believed.

The passages which bring out the belief in the dualism of 'Sankhya' are given below.

The followers of Marcion do directly blaspheme the Creator, alleging him to be the creator of evils also, but holding a more tolerable theory as to his origin and maintaining that there are two beings, gods by nature, differing from each other, the one being good, but the other evil.
(*The Writings of the Early Church Fathers*, Vol. 1, Irenaeus, Against Heresies, Book III, Chapter 12)

Moreover, we shall also examine the doctrine of Marcion, inquiring how he holds that there are two gods, separated from each other by an infinite distance.
(*The Writings of the Early Church Fathers*, Vol. 1, Irenaeus, Against Heresies, Book IV, Chapter 33)

Hermogenes introduces matter as having no beginning and then compares it with God who has no beginning. By thus making the matter of the elements a goddess.
(*The Writings of the Early Church Fathers*, Vol. 3, Tertullion, Prescription against Heretics, Chapter 32)

So he concludes that God always had Matter co-existent with Himself as the Lord thereof.

Hermogenes supposes that Matter was eternal, on the ground that the Lord was eternal.
(*The Writings of the Early Church Fathers*, Vol. 3, Tertullion, Against Hermogenes, Chapter 3)

I shall begin to treat of Matter, how according to Hermogenes God compares it with Himself as equally unborn, equally unmade, equally eternal, set forth as being without a beginning, without an end.

Hermogenes therefore introduces two Gods, he introduces Matter as God's equal.
(*The Writings of the Early Church Fathers*, Vol. 3, Tertullion, Against Hermogenes, Chapter 4)

You, however, affirm that it is by pervading Matter that God makes the world, by simply approaching it, just as beauty affects a thing by simply appearing.

How immense the place, where God kept Himself so far aloof from Matter, as to have neither appeared nor approached it before the creation of the world.

(*The Writings of the Early Church Fathers*, Vol. 3, Tertullion, Against Hermogenes, Chapter 44)

Marcion supposed the existence of two originating causes of the universe, alleging one of them to be good but the other an evil one.

Discord and friendship are the principles artistically fabricating the universe. Friendship is a certain peace whose entire effort is that there should be one finished and complete world. Discord, however, invariably separates. Therefore discord is of the entire creation a cause, which he styles destructive.

(*The Writings of the Early Church Fathers*, Vol. 5, Hippolytus, Refutation of All Heresies, Book VII, Chapter 17)

For those inventors of stupid fables say, that there are two Unbegottens.

(*The Writings of the Early Church Fathers*, Vol. 6, Alexander of Alexandria, Epistles on the Arian Hersy, Epistle 1)

Manichaeus laid down two principles, God and Matter. God he called good and matter he affirmed to be evil.

(*The Writings of the Early Church Fathers*, Vol. 6, Alexander of Alexandria, Of the Manicheans, Chapter 2)

Manes worships two deities, unoriginated, self-existent, eternal, opposed the one to the other. Of these he represents the one as good, and the other as evil.

He maintains that a certain commingling or blending has been affected between the two.

> (*The Writings of the Early Church Fathers*, Vol. 6, Archelaus, Acts of the Disputation with the Heresiarch Manes, Para 6)

Origen says that what he calls the Centaus is the universe which is co-eternal with the only wise and independent God.

> (*The Writings of the Early Church Fathers*, Vol. 6, Methodius, Extracts from the Work on Things Created)

What could that reputed nation of darkness, which the Manicheans are in the habit of setting up as a mass opposed to Thee, have done unto Thee?

Shouldest Thou be subject to violence and corruption. Thy very substance should be blended with adverse powers and natures not of Thy creation, and be by them corrupted. Thy substance being enslaved, contaminated and corrupted.

> (*The Writings of the Early Church Fathers*, Vol. 10, Augustine, Confessions of Augustine, Book VII, Chapter 2)

These passages bring out the belief in two eternal, co-existent entities, styled by different writers differently. Some have called them God and Matter, some as two gods and some as good and evil. They also bring out the belief that creation takes place when there is a commingling of the two and ends when they are separated from each other. The belief is identical with the Vedic belief of 'Sankhya'. In elaborating this theory further in their writings, some writers have mentioned the process of creation after the mingling of the two eternal entities and have talked of the creation by numbers. 'Sankhya' also proceeds to talk of creation by number. In fact, the word 'Sankhya' means 'Of Numbers'. The two beliefs are identical, though what has been reported of the Christian beliefs has come from its critics and adversaries, who have not presented it in its complete sequence and have quoted only things that they were rejecting or proving to be incorrect.

Alongside the dualism identical with dualism of 'Sankhya', the presence of non-dualism is evident from the following passages.

> For who is it who exists if it is not the Father himself?
> Each space which, on its part, is in the Father comes from the existent Father, who, on his part, has established it from the nonexistent.
> Thus the Logos of the Father goes forth into the all, being the fruit of His heart and expression of His will.
> The Logos, who was first to come forth.
> (The Nag Hammadi Library, The Gospel of Truth)

The mirror of God's goodness, and power, and wisdom, is those that in origin were brought into being, something from nothing.

In the secondary natural contemplation we see Christ's Wisdom, full of varieties, that which he used and in which he created the worlds.

(Evagrius, Kephalaia Gnostika, 2.1–2)

Cerinthus taught that the world was not made by the primary God, but by a certain Power far separated from Him.
(*The Writings of the Early Church Fathers*, Vol. 1, Irenaeus, Against Heresies, Book I, Chapter 26)

I proved also that there is one God, the Creator, and that He is not the fruit of any defect, nor is there anything either above Him or after Him.
(*The Writings of the Early Church Fathers*, Vol. 1, Irenaeus, Against Heresies, Book II, Preface)

For how can there be any other Fullness, or Principle, or Power, or God, above the Creator.
> (*The Writings of the Early Church Fathers*, Vol. 1, Irenaeus, Against Heresies, Book II, Chapter 1)

The Framer of the world sprang from the Supreme Father as Basilides asserts.
> (*The Writings of the Early Church Fathers*, Vol. 1, Irenaeus, Against Heresies, Book II, Chapter 2)

Let them cease to affirm that the world was made by any other, for as soon as God formed a conception in His mind, that was also done which He had thus mentally conceived. For it is not possible that one Being should mentally form the conception and another actually produce the things.
> (*The Writings of the Early Church Fathers*, Vol. 1, Irenaeus, Against Heresies, Book II, Chapter 3)

They maintain that the Father of all no doubt contains all things, but that the creation to which we belong was not formed by Him, but by a certain other power.
> (*The Writings of the Early Church Fathers*, Vol. 1, Irenaeus, Against Heresies, Book II, Chapter 31)

They represent that the Maker and Framer, who is one God was produced from a defect or apostasy.
> (*The Writings of the Early Church Fathers*, Vol. 1, Irenaeus, Against Heresies, Book IV, Preface)

Apelles made the Creator of some nondescript glorious angel, who belonged to the superior God.
> (*The Writings of the Early Church Fathers*, Vol. 3, Tertullion, Prescription Against Heretics, Chapter 36)

Whether God ought to be regarded as a Being of simple goodness, to the exclusion of other attributes, sensations and affections, which the Marcionites indeed transfer from

their God to the Creator.
> (*The Writings of the Early Church Fathers*,
> Vol. 3, Tertullion, Five Books Against
> Marcion, Book I, Chapter 25)

Cerinthus asserted that the world was not made by the primal Deity, but by some virtue which was an offshoot from the Power which is above all things.
> (*The Writings of the Early Church Fathers*,
> Vol. 5, Hippolytus, Refutation of All Heresies,
> Book VII, Chapter 21)

Appelles expresses himself saying that there is a certain good Deity and that He who created all things is just.
> (*The Writings of the Early Church Fathers*, Vol. 5,
> Hippolytus, Refutation of All Heresies,
> Book VII, Chapter 26)

Simon shows that He who made the heaven and the earth is not the Supreme God, but that there is another, unknown and supreme.
> (*The Writings of the Early Church Fathers*,
> Vol. 8, Pseudo-Clementine Literature,
> Homily 3, Chapter 2)

This we have treated of elsewhere especially in dealing with the question of the greater than the Demiurge; Christ we have taken to be the Demiurge and the Father the greater than He.
> (*The Writings of the Early Church Fathers*,
> Vol. 9, Origen, The Commentary on John,
> Book I, Chapter 40)

How void of reason, they say concerning Him that, 'God willing to create originate nature, when He saw that it could not endure the untempered hand of the Father and

to be created by Him, makes and creates first and alone one only, and calls Him Son and Word, that through Him as a medium all things might thereupon be brought to be.
(*The Writings of the Early Church Fathers*, Vol. 27, Athanius, Discourse II, Chapter 17)

Such is the result of the teaching of this theologian who affirms of the Lord Artificer of heaven and earth and of all creation, the Word of God who was in the beginning, through Whom are all things, that He owes His existence to such a baseless entity or conception as that unnameable energy.
(*The Writings of the Early Church Fathers*, Vol. 28, Gregory of Nyssa, Against Eunomius, Book I, Chapter 20)

'We believe in God', he tells us, 'not separated as regards the essence wherein He is one, into more than one, or becoming sometimes one and sometimes another, or changing from being what He is, or passing from one essence to assume the guise of a threefold personality for He is always and absolutely one, remaining uniformly and unchangeably the only God'.
(*The Writings of the Early Church Fathers*, Vol. 28, Gregory of Nyssa, Against Eunomius, Book II, Chapter 5)

Polytheism has prevailed. Our opponents own a great God and a small God.
(*The Writings of the Early Church Fathers*, Vol. 31, Basil, Letter 243, Para 4)

How is Arius wise, who prefers an imperfect and inferior creator to one who is a true and perfect one?
(*The Writings of the Early Church Fathers*, Vol. 33, Ambrose, On the Duties of the Clergy, Book I, Chapter 25)

These passages bring out the belief in a Creator who was not the Supreme God. He has been called the Logos, the Son, the Demiurge, Word, Power, etc. The Supreme God remains above Him. As these statements have come from people who were opposed to these views, the presentation is distorted, but it does emerge that the Creator is the same Supreme God after He has acquired qualities. The fourth, ninth and eleventh passages bring out the belief that the Creator has emerged on acquiring qualities. The writers have, however, called them defects, apostasy and other such names. This belief of the Christians, declared heretics by the Pauline Church, was, thus, identical with the Vedic belief of non-dualism of 'Vedanta'.

Philosophy being irrelevant to a seeker of truth, Jesus, like Buddha, seems to have ignored it. He is not found to have spoken on the subject in the Bible. However, the belief in the non-dualism, identical with the Vedantic belief, seems to have been the prevalent belief amongst all Christians in the early years of Christianity. This emerges from the following passage.

> In the beginning was the Word, and the Word was with God, and the Word was God.
> The same was in the beginning with God.
> All things were made by him; and without him was not any thing made that was made.
> (John 1:1–3)

John speaks of two identities, God and the Word. The Word was in the beginning. It was with God. It was God. The two are different yet the same. The Word has its separate identity yet It is also God Himself. It is, thus, a situation of one entity having two identities. Both are one, and yet they are two. The Word remains subordinate to God as it was with God. All things were made by it and not by God. John, thus, speaks of a Creator and a Supreme God above Him.

It is, thus, evident that all essential elements of the Upanishadic religion were present in the core teachings of Jesus.

The religion that he was preaching also had the same pattern as the Vedic religion, in which a different set of teachings were there for the common believers and something much deeper for the select few. These teachings for the select few were kept as a closely guarded secret. It is true that for the common believers Jesus was not preaching the adherence to the Vedic religion but was asking them to follow the tenets of Judaism in their true spirit, but his core teachings which were for the select few were the same as the core teachings of the Vedic religion. They are identical to an extent that no distinction can be drawn between the two. Unfortunately, these have been lost to a very large extent to Christians, as, over the centuries, they were declared to be heretical because they were not in line with the Pauline theology, which had written scriptures to support it. It is also unfortunate that Jews were persecuted over the centuries, though it was their religion that the Apostles wanted Christians to follow.

6

THE FURTHER QUESTION

Should the core of the religion preached by Jesus be identical with that of the Vedic religion, a question does arise whether Jesus was influenced by this Aryan religion and had adopted its beliefs. Though it is possible because by the time of Jesus, the Vedic people were all over west Asia, Egypt and beyond, it does not fit the personality of Jesus as it emerges from the Bible wherein he comes across as a staunch believer of Judaism, wishing to propagate his teachings amongst the Jews alone. For the common believers, his message was to follow the tenets of Judaism in true spirit instead of making only an appearance of doing so. A person having such deep feelings for his own religion and wishing to confine his teachings only to his own people could not have adopted the core teachings of another religion and continued to have the same approach to his own religion. It is not necessary either, as Judaism of his time seems to be having the same features as the Vedic religion. The Jews had three divisions amongst them, the Sadducees, the Pharisees and the Essenes. Of these, the Sadducees and the Pharisees fell in the category of common believers, while the Essenes were monks and had their beliefs and practices that were identical with the core of the Vedic religion. Some of their writings have been recovered in the last century in the Dead Sea area, for which they are called the Dead Sea Scrolls. They reveal their close identity with the Vedic beliefs and a clear departure from the beliefs of the other Jews as emerge from the Tanakh. The Dead Sea area had a lot of their monasteries, though, apparently, they were persecuted by the other Jews who must have considered them to be apostates, as their beliefs were not in line with the beliefs of their scriptures. Jesus was in Galilee, which is very close to the north of this area, and could have been a part of the Essene tradition.

The belief of the Essenes in the transmigration of the soul emerges from the views of Jesus on the subject, which have already come up for mention. Their other beliefs that were identical with Vedic beliefs emerge from the following passages.

> I will impart/conceal knowledge with discretion and will prudently hedge it within firm bound to preserve faith and strong judgement in accordance with the justice of God.
> (The Dead Sea Scrolls, The Community Rule, IQS, Rules of Conduct for the Master)

> The members of my covenant have rebelled and have murmured round about me. They have gone as tale bearers before the children of mischief concerning the mysteries which Thou hast hidden in me.
> (The Dead Sea Scrolls, Remonstrances, 4Q471, Hymn 14 [Formerly 9])

> Contemplating the mysteries of Thy wisdom I have sought Thee.
> That Thou mightiest show Thyself great to him in the multitude of Thy mercies and enlarge his strained soul to eternal salvation.
> (The Dead Sea Scrolls, The Thanksgiving Hymns, 1QH ,1Q36, Hymn 5 [Formerly 22])

> Through me Thou has illumined the face of the congregation and has shown Thine infinite power. For Thou has given

me knowledge through Thy marvelous mysteries and hast shown Thyself mighty within me.
>(The Dead Sea Scrolls, Remonstrances, 4Q471, Hymn 12 [Formerly 7])

I thank Thee for Thou has enlightened me through Thy truth.
Thou has granted me knowledge.
>(The Dead Sea Scrolls, Remonstrances, 4Q471, Hymn 16 [Formerly 12])

I am reckoned with the gods and my dwelling place is in the congregation of holiness.
>(The Dead Sea Scrolls, Hymn of Glorification, 4Q471b, Hymn B)

Blessed is the man who has attained wisdom.
>(The Dead Sea Scrolls, Beatitudes, 4Q525, Fr 2)

These passages outline the similarities of the beliefs and practices of the Essenes with those of the Vedic religion. The first two passages show that Judaism, too, had two distinct streams of beliefs meant for the common believers and the select few. The other Jews fell in the category of common believers who followed the usual customs and practices laid down by their religion, while the Essenes followed the path meant for the select few. The doctrines and practices of these were kept as a closely guarded secret to be disclosed only to a worthy disciple after he had been thoroughly examined and deemed worthy of receiving it. The first passage is a pledge of a master to 'impart/conceal knowledge with discretion' and to keep it within a firm bound. The second passage reports that some disciples have rebelled against the master. These would have been disciples who were not considered to be worthy of receiving the core teachings and were left to practice what was of peripheral value only. They are reported to have gone to people who have been called 'the children of mischief' to reveal the mysteries that were concealed by the master. The Essenes suffered persecution at the hands of the other Jews who considered them to be apostates, as their beliefs and practices were not as were laid down in the Tanakh, and this is understood from the manner in which the Dead Sea Scrolls have been found. Unlike the Nag Hammadi Library that was found properly packed and sealed before it was buried under the surface, the Dead Sea Scrolls have been found randomly placed in open pitchers in caves. Apparently, they had been left there for safekeeping by people who were looked for in their monasteries. They appear to have expected to take the scrolls back once the danger had passed; unfortunately, this did not happen, perhaps because they were killed. This reference to 'the children of mischief' is an evident reference to these other Jews who thought the Essenes to be apostates. The crucifixion of Jesus could have been a part of the persecution of the Essenes by the other Jews.

The remaining passages show that the Essenes practised meditation to know God through it. It was the same path of knowledge of the Vedic traditions. The fourth passage shows that in trying to know God, they found Him within themselves.

A few Christian writers have also mentioned the Essenes and have given an idea of their beliefs and practices, as evident in the following passages.

> These practice a more devotional life. They turn away from every act of inordinate desire. And they renounce matrimony, but they take the boys of others and thus have an offspring begotten for them. And they lead these adopted children into an observance of their own peculiar customs. Women, however, even though they may be disposed to adhere to the same course of life, they do not admit.
> (*The Writings of the Early Church Fathers*, Vol. 5, Hippolytus, Refutation of All Heresies, Book IX, Chapter 13)

But to those who wish to become disciples of the sect, they do not immediately deliver their rules, unless they have previously tried them.

When at the expiration of this period, one affords proof of self control, he approaches nearer to the sect's method of living, and he is washed more purely than before.

For two years the habit of a person of this description is on trial, and when he has appeared deserving, he is thus reckoned amongst the members of the Sect. Previous, however, to his being allowed to partake of a repast along with them, he is bound under fearful oaths.

In addition to the other promises, he swears to impart to no one a knowledge of the doctrines in a different manner from that in which he has received them himself.

(*The Writings of the Early Church Fathers*, Vol. 5, Hippolytus, Refutation of All Heresies, Book IX, Chapter 18)

These passages depict the Essenes as monks who lived a very disciplined life in monasteries. They took disciples and trained them as they would their own children, yet the real secrets were not delivered to anyone who was not found worthy of receiving them. They were put through a proper trial spread over several years and only after that a decision was taken whether the disciple was worthy of being admitted into their secrets. He was also bound under oath not to impart the knowledge of these doctrines unless the person has been duly tested in the manner in which they themselves had been tested. Though the information emerging from the Christian sources and the Dead Sea Scrolls is sketchy about the Essenes, whatever emerges shows a complete similarity with the Vedic beliefs. A question then emerges as to whether the Essenes were influenced by the Vedic people and received these beliefs and practices from them. Though, again, it is possible, as the Vedic people had been there for a very long time, the Jews claim that they received these concepts from Abraham. Other information available also shows that the Essenes existed from very early times and these practices were with them from the beginning. A remark made by Pliny in the first century suggests their antiquity.

> Thus through thousands of ages (incredible to relate) a race in which no one is born lives on for ever, so prolific for their advantage is other men's weariness of life.
> (Pliny the Elder, Natural History, Book V, Para 15)

Pliny has stated that they had existed for 'thousands of ages', which shows that they were a part of the Jewish community from the earliest times. The case of the Carmelites or White Friars also leads to the same conclusion. These were Christian monks who migrated to the West after Palestine had gone under Muslim rule. They were hermits from Mount Carmel who claimed to have had a continuous tradition from the times of Elijah. As the Jews had religious traditions identical with the Vedic religion and they appear to have had them from the very beginning, a bigger question arises, whether Abraham and all the Abrahamic races, including the Jews, were Aryans, and if so, whether they were Devs or Asurs. Based on the evidence emerging from the literary sources, the answer is a definite yes. These show that the Jews were Aryans and that they were Devs. There are several instances in the scriptures and other writings which point to this.

The first is the manner of Abraham's migration out of Babylon, as seen in the Bible:

> Now these are the generations of Terah: Terah begat Abram, Nahor and Haran; Haran begot Lot.
> And Haran died before his father Terah in the land of his nativity, in Ur of the Chaldees.
> (Genesis 2:27–28)

And Terah took Abram his son, and Lot the son of Haran

his son's son, and Sarai his daughter in law, his son Abram's wife; and they went forth with them from Ur of the Chaldees, to go into the land of Canaan; and they came unto Haran, and dwelt there.

And the days of Terah were two hundred and five years: and Terah died in Haran.

(Genesis 2:31–32)

Now the Lord had said unto Abram, Get thee out of thy country, and from thy kindred, and from thy father's house, unto a land that I will shew thee:

And I will make thee a great nation, and I will bless thee, and make thy name great; and that shalt be a blessing.

(Genesis 12:1–2)

So Abram departed, as the Lord had spoken unto him; and Lot went with him: and Abram was seventy and five years old when he departed out of Haran.

And Abram took Sarai his wife, and Lot his brother's son, and all their substance that they had gathered, and the souls that they had gotten in Haran; and they went forth to go into the land of Canaan; and into the land of Canaan they came.

(Genesis 12:4–5)

When Abram was ninety years old and nine, the Lord appeared to Abram, and said unto him, I am the Almighty God; walk before me, and be thou perfect.

And I will make my covenant between me and thee, and will multiply thee exceedingly.

(Genesis 17:1–2)

Neither shall thy name any more be called Abram, but thy name shall be Abraham; for a father of many nations have I made thee.

(Genesis 17:5)

And I will give unto thee, and to thy seed after thee, the land wherein thou art a stranger, all the land of Canaan, for an everlasting possession; and I will be their God.
(Genesis 17:8)

And Joshua said unto all the people, Thus said the Lord God of Israel, Your fathers dwelt on the other side of the flood in old time, even Terah, the father of Abraham, and the father of Nachor: and they served other gods
   And I took your father Abraham from the other side of the flood, and led him throughout all the land of Canaan, and multiplied his seed, and gave him Isaac.
(Joshua 24:2–3)

This account of Abraham's migration reveals certain facts about him. First, that he was from Ur in Babylon and that the Chaldeans were his kindred. This would make him a Chaldean as well. The Assyrians and the Chaldeans had empires at different times with their capitals somewhat distant from each other, but ethnically they were the same people. The next point that emerges is that while living with their kindred, there appears to have been some event or situation that forced them to migrate. This did not start with Abraham, as his father Terah left Ur and moved to Haran, where he died. Abraham moved out of Haran and the Chaldean country to go beyond the river Jordan. The movements of Abraham show that he did not have a destination in mind. He is reported to have gone West into the land of the Canaan and from there to Egypt because of a famine. Later, he returned from Egypt to the area that was later called Judea. As he had no place in mind when he migrated out of Babylon, it is evident that he moved away from his homeland because the conditions there were difficult for him. Evidently, he was being persecuted in Babylon by his kinsmen. The reason for this persecution appears to be a difference in the religious beliefs between him and his kinsmen, because God is reported to have asked him to move out from his homeland and asked him to 'walk before me, and be thou perfect'. The passage from Joshua also shows that while living in Babylon, they served other gods. This proves that the group of people led by Abraham had different religious beliefs from the majority of their kinsmen and that, while living with them, they could not follow their own religious practices and were under compulsion to follow the religious practices of the rest of the people.

This account further shows that when Abraham moved out of Babylon, the Assyrians experienced a deep religious rift amongst themselves, in which the majority was persecuting the minority to the extent of not allowing them even to practice their rituals as per their beliefs, leading, finally, to their migration. They seem to have been moving aimlessly in search of a place where they could practice their religion without any hindrance. Though there are numerous indications that the Assyrians were Aryans and that they were the Asurs of the Vedas, this is yet to be established by a proper study. However, the deep religious rift appears to point in this direction, as it is very unlikely for another ethnic group in such remote times to have it in the way the 'Devs' and 'Asurs' had it, as has been brought out in *An Aryan Journey*. Abraham and the Abrahamic races appear to be the same people who have been called 'Devs' in the Vedas and the Zoroastrian scriptures. They migrated away from Arjika and later from the delta of Amu Dariya when they moved with the Asurs, trusting kinship, just as the Kimmerians stayed back with the Devs despite being Asurs. Religion had just emerged as a force and they could not have believed that it could be a divisive force strong enough to submerge kinship and centuries of peaceful life together. Just as the Kimmerians had moved out from the land where their kinsmen, the Devs, were dominant, as their persecution had become intolerable, so did the Abrahamic races move away from their kinsmen, the Asurs. Just as the

Kimmerians moved away without any destination in mind and went aimlessly only to escape the persecution back home, so did the Abrahamic races migrate to flee the persecution and to follow their religious practices in peace.

The second fact that points to the Aryan-Jew connection is the similarities in their rituals of sacrifice. The following passage speaks of the manner in which the Jews offered sacrifices.

> He shall kill the bullock before the Lord: and the priests, Aaron's sons, shall bring the blood, and sprinkle the blood round about upon the altar that is by the door of the tabernacle of the congregation.
>
> And he shall flay the burnt offering, and cut it into his pieces.
>
> And the sons of Aaron the priest shall put fire upon the altar, and lay the wood in order upon the fire:
>
> And the priests, Aaron's sons, shall lay the parts, the head, and the fat, in order upon the wood that is on the fire which is upon the alter:
>
> But his inwards and his legs shall he wash in water: and the priest shall burn all on the altar, to be a burnt sacrifice, an offering made by fire, of a sweet savour unto the Lord.
>
> (Leviticus 1:5–9)

This shows several similarities with the Vedic practices of sacrifice. First, the sacrificial animal was immolated, skinned and dismembered at the site of the offering itself. Second, the blood of the animal was sprinkled around the altar. Third, specific body parts were placed in the fire in a sequence, to be completely burnt. Last, it was believed that fire took the sacrifice to God. Though the Jews appear to have forgotten the reasons for some of these rituals, what they were doing was identical to the Vedic practices. The sacrificial animal was dismembered in the Vedic sacrifices because each body part was specifically required to be offered to a particular god, and as the Vedic gods had a fixed hierarchy, these parts were offered in a particular sequence. The stress on completely burning the sacrifice and the belief that by doing so fire carried it to the gods was the fundamental issue over which the Devs and the Asurs had split from each other in Arjika. The sprinkling of blood around the altar before the sacrifice is significant as the Abrahamic races had another belief linked with the blood of animals, which was of not eating it as food. At several places in the Old Testament there is a complete prohibition on the consumption of blood. Because of this, a specific method has been prescribed for the slaughter of the animal for food, in which the blood is drained out to make the meat kosher. No cogent reason has been given for it. At one place it has been stated that blood is life and life must not be eaten. The inadequacy of this explanation must have been apparent to the people then also because there are situations wherein death occurs but the body is uninjured, for which the blood remains intact, while life has ended. The reason appears to be the Vedic belief that must have been lost to the Jews. Though this did not lead the Vedic people to eat kosher meat only, they believed that in a sacrifice blood was the share of the evil spirits. Because of this, blood was offered to them before offering the sacrifice to the gods, and as fire was the messenger of the gods, the share of the evil spirits could not be consigned to the fire but was sprinkled around the alter to keep them from disturbing the sacrifice. The Jews, too, used to sprinkle the blood of the animal around the altar, though no reason for it was remembered by them, because of which it has not been mentioned in the Old Testament. However, apparently, they had it in their memory up to a certain stage that blood was the share of the evil spirits, and it is probably because of this that they began to avoid it even in their food.

The next instance that shows the connection of the Jews with the Aryans is the survival of certain words and words linked to certain Aryan beliefs in their language and scriptures. The first is the word psalm, spoken as saam. The hymns in the Old Testament are called psalms. The word is not used for the hymns that were composed later. In the Vedic literature, the hymns that were lyrical were called saams. There is a complete Veda, called the Sama Veda, containing them. The psalms of the Old Testament were sung just as the saams of the Vedas were sung. The Aryans evidently had a tradition of composing and singing saams from times much before the split between Devs and Asurs, because although the Avesta does not have saams, it has the name saman, used for a singer of saams. The Jews appear to have carried this word that has found place in their scriptures in the same manner in which it was used by the Vedic people.

The second such word is 'vacat'. This is found in the Dead Sea Scrolls at several places at the end of the sentences. Evidently, no meaning was assigned to it, because of which the translators have not translated it but have recorded it as it was found. The exclamation of 'vashat' is found in the Rig Veda and was later replaced by 'swaha'. There is no meaning assigned to either of the two words, but these were exclamations made at the end of the 'mantra' with which the sacrificial material was offered. Apparently, the exclamation 'Vashat' was in use when the offering was not consigned to fire but was only lifted up as an offering to God and was eaten thereafter by the worshippers. It got replaced by the exclamation 'swaha' when the Devs started consigning the offering to fire. Up to a certain stage, the exclamation 'vashat' is found used in the Rig Veda along with 'Swaha', after which the former seems to have been given up. In the Zoroastrian scriptures, the exclamation 'vashat' has been corrupted to 'ushta', as the language of the Avesta got corrupted from chaste Sanskrit. The presence of this word at the end of sentences in the Dead Sea Scrolls shows that the memory of this word and of its use at the end of a sentence had survived with the Jews, though perhaps nobody knew what it was and where it was to be used because it does not find mention in the Old Testament, even where the rules of sacrifice have been laid down. In the Old Testament, the exclamation 'saleh' is found used at a few places in the psalms in the same manner in which 'vacat' is found in the Dead Sea Scrolls.

Another significant word to be found in usage at a remote time amongst the Jews is 'Deus' for God. In the Rig Veda, the earliest word used for God is 'Tvasta'. This, however, had gone out of use when the Aryans were in Arjika when the Devs and Asurs split. By that time, the word used for the Supreme God was 'Dyau', which is written by the Greeks as 'Dyas'. The use of the word 'Deus' by the Jews, thus, appears to have been a part of this memory. The passages which tell of the use of this word for God are given below.

> For God is not the two short syllables 'Deus', and it is not the two short syllables that we worship
> (*The Writings of the Early Church Fathers*, Vol. 16, Augustine, On John, Tractate 29, Para 4)

> For, since this name God (Deus), is apparently derived from the Greek name Theos, which comes from theasthai, meaning 'to see or to consider', the very name of God makes it clear that He is intelligent and consequently He wills.
> (Thomas Aquinas, Shorter Summa, The Divine Trinity 35)

The Bible does not contain this word. In the Old Testament, 'Yahweh' has been given as the name of God. However, the mention of 'Deus' by these Christian writers shows that this word was in use in the past and had survived until then. It has been used by the Romans also for Simon Magus.

It is interesting also to note the Aryan connection of the

word 'Amen'. It is usually uttered at the end of a prayer. The Aryans held the number nine and its repetition to be significant. It is not very clear what was meant by it, but it appears to have meant 'all'. This has been detailed in *An Aryan Journey*. The usage of the number nine with its repetition was evidently very old, as it is found in the Zoroastrian scriptures also. It emerges from the following passage that the word 'Amen' represents the repetition of the number nine.

> Thus, therefore, the numbers that were left, viz, nine, as respects the pieces of money, and eleven in regard to the sheep, which multiplied together, give birth to the number ninety nine. Wherefore also they maintain the word 'Amen' contains this number.
> (*The Writings of the Early Church Fathers*, Vol. 1, Irenaeus, Against Heresies, Book I, Chapter 16)

Apart from some of these words that had religious significance and survived with the Jews, it appears that the memory of Arjika and the war between the Devs and the Asurs had also survived with them. This emerges from the following passages.

> These are the seven forces of the seven heavens of chaos.
> And when they had become disturbed, they made a great war in the seven heavens.
> (The Nag Hammadi Library, On the Origin of the World)

> They say also that there are seven zones of the heaven, one higher than the other.
> (*The Writings of the Early Church Fathers*, Vol. 32, John of Damascus, Concerning the Orthodox Faith, Book II, Chapter 6)

Arjika was in the delta of the river Ili in Kazakhstan and has been discussed in *An Aryan Journey*. This delta had seven riverine islands that have been called 'the seven kashwares' in the Avesta. Arjika is remembered in the Vedas with a lot of nostalgia and reverence, indicating it to be a divine place. At several places, the word becomes interchangeable with heaven. The Jews seem to have carried a similar sentiment for it and treated it as the heaven. The memory of these seven riverine islands led to the belief that there were seven zones in heaven or there were seven heavens. They have also remembered that there was a lot of chaos in this heaven that finally led to a great war. The 'Dev Asur Sangram' or the war between the Devs and Asurs appears to have been remembered by them, which has found expression in this passage. Some of the Christian writers have tried to argue that the concept of seven heavens is not a part of the Christian tradition, but it seems that this belief was so strong amongst the Jews that it continued to echo amongst the Christians. Origen wrote against this concept, noting,

> The scriptures which are current in the Churches of God do not speak of seven heavens, or of any definite number at all, but they do appear to teach the existence of 'heavens', whether that means the 'spheres' of those bodies which the Greeks call 'planets', or something more mysterious.
> (*The Writings of the Early Church Fathers*, Vol. 4, Origen, Contra Celsum, Book VI, Chapter 21)

Though these elements in the Jewish scriptures and beliefs point to their Aryan connections, there are certain strong factors that point to the contrary. First, that the Hebrew language does not have Sanskrit as its root. Second is the absence of the cremation of the dead amongst the Jews. Third, the concept of the Day of Judgement in their beliefs. Fourth, the monotheism of the Bible compared to Vedic polytheism. And, finally, the concept of the Devil. However, if these factors are closely examined, they do not appear to be contrary to the hypothesis that the Jews were Aryans and that they were Devs.

The first factor is that the Hebrew language does not have its roots in the Sanskrit language and has not originated from it. For this, the history of the Jews in the early days has to be taken into account. The Jews lived in slavery for 400 years in Egypt. This is a period long enough for a race to lose its language, if it is scattered and is living in an alien land where the language is different. The Jews appear to have lost their original language during this time. The following passage describes how Hebrew was developed by the Jews after leaving Egypt.

> But some who have carefully studied the scriptures tell us that the Hebrew tongue is not even ancient like the others, but that along with other miracles this miracle was wrought on behalf of the Israelites, that after the exodus from Egypt, the language was hastily improvised for the use of the nation. And there is a passage in the Prophet which confirms this. For he says, 'when he came out of the land of Egypt he heard a strange language'.
> (*The Writings of the Early Church Fathers*, Vol. 28, Gregory of Nyssa, Answer to Eunomius' Second Book)

It is evident that the Jews had lost their original language over the 400 years in Egypt. It is likely that at that stage, Egyptian would have been the language spoken by them, but since this was associated with their slavery, it can be argued that they wished to shed it to maintain a separate identity for themselves, and, thus, improvised a new language for themselves. As they had moved to the land of the Phoenicians, they seem to have leaned on their language to do so. Several writers have reported that many words of Hebrew were akin to words in the Phoenician language. What really happened in the formation of this new language cannot be said, but it can be said with certainty that the Jews had lost their original language completely during their stay in Egypt, and as the original language was completely lost and Hebrew was a new improvisation, it not having originated from Sanskrit is understandable, and the same does not stand in the way of Jews having an Aryan origin.

The second factor is the absence of the cremation of the dead in the practices of the Jews. This was a widely practised custom of the Devs, whereas the Asurs did not practise it. There is, however, a passage in the Atharva Veda which shows that the Aryans in their past had several funeral practices. This is given below.

> They that are buried, and they that are scattered away, they that are burned and they that are set up raised—all those Fathers, O Agni, bring you to eat the oblation.
> (Atharva Veda, Kand—18, S-2, R-34)

This is a prayer to Agni to bring all the forefathers so that the offered oblations may be accepted by them. It also mentions the manner in which their funeral had been conducted, for which four practices have been mentioned. The first is burial, the second 'scattered away' which is for those whose dead body was immersed in a river, the third refers to cremation and the fourth 'that are set up raised' is for those whose funeral was in the manner of the Zoroastrians. It is evident that the Aryans had several funeral practices and that cremation emerged later, as it was not adopted by the Zoroastrians either. As the Jews were Devs who had migrated with the Asurs and had been separated from the main Dev population early on, the practice of cremating the dead did not go with them, as this seems to have emerged after they had parted away. It seems possible that the practice of cremation of the dead emerged as a consequence to the belief that the sacrificial oblation is taken to the gods by fire after it is burnt. Some people may have thought of applying the same principle to the body of their dead relative so as to send it to heaven. In any case, it appears to be a later development, because of which it is not found amongst the Jews.

Another major Jewish belief that comes in the way of them being Aryans is the concept of the Day of Judgement. There is not even a trace of this in the Vedic thought. In fact, the Vedic belief in the transmigration of the soul has significant contradictions with the concept of the Day of Judgement. On this point, it would of interest to examine the origin of the belief in the Day of Judgement because, unlike the New Testament wherein an explicit statement about it has been made at several places because of the impact of Paul, who, as a Pharisee, believed in it, the Old Testament does not speak of it. There are only a few stray references in Daniel and Isaiah about the Judgement of God that are quoted in support of this belief. In the older books of the Old Testament there is not even a trace. Evidently, the concept developed amongst the Jews much later. This is established also by the fact that several people who were ethnically of the same stock as the Jews did not believe in it. The earliest amongst these were the Samaritans. As mentioned before, the Jewish kingdom had split into two parts after Solomon. To the north was Samaria and to the south, Judea. Of the 12 tribes of Israel, 10 were in Samaria and were called Samaritans, while only two, Judah and Benjamin, were in Judea and were called Jews. The Samaritans did not believe in the Day of Judgement. It is, thus, evident that this belief was not prevalent amongst the Jews till the Samaritans broke away after Solomon. Later, in the times of Jesus, the accounts in the New Testament show that the Jews had two sects, the Sadducees and the Pharisees. Of these, only the Pharisees believed in the Day of Judgement, while the Sadducees rejected it. Later, it was during the Jewish revolt against Rome in Palestine in AD 66 that the rebels took control of Jerusalem and massacred the Sadducee elite, considering them to be collaborators of the Romans, which left only the Pharisees to shape the Jewish identity, because of which this became the sole Jewish belief.

It is, thus, evident that the concept of the Day of Judgement developed only amongst the Pharisees after Solomon. It finds no support from the Old Testament but has been propounded in the apocalyptic literature. Though the New Testament has incorporated one apocalypse as the Book of Revelation, the Old Testament has not included any of them. The concept, thus, developed amongst the Jews in their days of captivity in Babylon after Nebuchadnezzar had destroyed the temple at Jerusalem and taken them away as slaves. This is understandable, as the events had shattered all their beliefs by the destruction of their temple and desecration of the God, for whom the belief was that anyone entering His chamber would be burnt immediately. Some explanation had to be found for how and when God would punish the people who had offended Him and how and when those would be rewarded who had remained faithful to Him despite having suffered in life. Religion, essentially, keeps alive the hope of a better tomorrow. These were the people who had no hope for a better tomorrow in this life. They also had a burning rage against those who had harmed not only them but even the abode of God and had not been punished. Thus emerged the idea of a future when all the people who had committed atrocities would receive the severest possible punishment, while the believers would receive in plenty all the things that they desired in this life but could not get. The concept of the Day of Judgement is, thus, the creation of the Jews lamenting at their fate in Babylon and has no scriptural support from the Old Testament. This is further confirmed by the fact that it was the belief of the Pharisees alone. The word Pharas in several oriental languages is Persia and Pharisee is Persian. It was, thus, a belief that had been carried by the Jews who had returned from the Persian Empire. The concept of the Day of Judgement, thus, being a later development, does not negate the Aryan connection of the Jews.

The causes of the emergence of this belief amongst the

Jews in captivity in Babylon and the reasons for the success of Pauline Christianity in Rome amongst the slaves, the poor and the downtrodden were the same. All accounts show that the senate and the rich in Rome were influenced by Simon Magus and so were with the Christianity of the Apostles. To start with, it was only the slaves and the deprived people who became devoted followers of Pauline Christianity. It was the question of the capacity of the religion to keep alive the hope of a better future. All religions of the time promised a better future during the believer's life. For the slaves and the deprived of the Roman Empire, there was no better tomorrow. The promise made by all these religions was, thus, seen by them to be false. Paul promised a better future after death, at a time which could not be seen by the followers and so could not be known to be false. It is not necessary for religion to prove its promises to be true. It is enough if they cannot be proved to be false because after that faith takes over. Though Paul promised that the Day of Judgement would come within the lifetime of the people he was addressing, even after several centuries, when this promise had been seen to be false, faith has held the ground. The slaves and the deprived people of Rome at that stage could not have even known that it would not come within their lifetime, so this hope of a better tomorrow made them ardent followers of Pauline Christianity.

The next feature of the Jewish beliefs that does not seem to be in harmony with the Vedic thought is their monotheism compared to the perceived polytheism of the Vedas. That the polytheism of the Vedas is not real has been described in *An Aryan Journey* with the evidence emerging from the Rig Ved and other scriptures. They were monotheistic upto a certain stage when other divinities were brought in as a creation of the Supreme God or as His different expressions. The creation of these new divinities, however, did not dilute the monotheism at the philosophical level. However, at the ritualistic level, as the newly created divinities gained prominence, while the earlier Supreme God lost in importance, the religion began to appear to be polytheistic. The real Vedic concept, thus, has monotheism with one Supreme God with a large number of other gods who are believed to be His children. The same happened in Zoroastrianism wherein one has Ahur Mazda, the Supreme God, with a number of divinities who are His creation. However, as Ahur Mazda remained the central figure of worship, Zoroastrianism is understood to be a monotheistic religion despite the presence of so many divinities. Interestingly, the monotheism of Judaism is on the same lines. Though there is one God, there is mention of several other gods with Him. This has been stated by several writers. Some such statements are given below.

> Then Simon said 'I say that there are many gods, but there is one incomprehensible and unknown to all, and that He is the God of all these gods.'
> (*The Writings of the Early Church Fathers*, Vol. 8, Pseudo-Clementine Literature, Book II, Chapter 38)

> Why would you deceive the unlearned multitude standing around you, persuading them that it is unlawful to think that there are gods, and to call them so, when the books that are current among the Jews say that there are many gods?
> (*The Writings of the Early Church Fathers*, Vol. 8, Pseudo-Clementine Literature, Homily 3, Chapter 38)

> The law which frequently speaks of gods, itself says to the Jewish multitude, 'Behold the heaven of heavens is the Lord's thy God, with all that therein is,' implying that even if there are gods, they are under Him.
> (*The Writings of the Early Church Fathers*, Vol. 8, Pseudo-Clementine Literature, Homily 16, Chapter 7)

There are some gods of whom God is god, as we hear in prophecy, 'Thank ye the God of gods,' and 'The God of gods hath spoken, and called the earth.'
(*The Writings of the Early Church Fathers*, Vol. 9, Origen, Commentary on John, Book I, Chapter 34)

The true God, then, is 'The God' and those that are formed after Him are gods, images, as it were, of Him the prototype.
(*The Writings of the Early Church Fathers*, Vol. 9, Origen, Commentary on John, Book II, Chapter 2)

And so too, the Old Testament uses in the same way to correct the souls of the erring, by putting together in a way of comparison things that cannot be compared, as when it saith, 'Among the gods there is none like unto thee, O Lord.' And again 'There is no god like our God.'
(*The Writings of the Early Church Fathers*, Vol. 19, John Chrysostom, Homilies on Matthew, Homily 37)

In these passages, the writers are explaining and elaborating the belief of the Jews about God as stated in the Old Testament and other Jewish books. At several places, they have quoted the words of the Bible. They show that the monotheism of Judaism was similar to the monotheism of the Vedas, having one Supreme God with a large number of gods that were His creation and were under Him. In the Vedas, several of these gods have been named, which has created a separate identity for them. In the Bible, none of these gods have been given a name, because of which their identity has remained vague and, despite having been mentioned at several places, the monotheism of Judaism has remained unaffected.

Along with the monotheism of Judaism following the same pattern as that of the Vedas, their belief about the gods and their relationship with the Jewish people also has a marked similarity with the Vedic beliefs. The Aryans in Arjika had split into two groups over a religious dispute. The Vedic Aryans at this stage called themselves Devs and their rivals, Asurs. The Zoroastrian scriptures have also called them Daevas. Once these people moved out of Arjika to the delta of the river Amu Dariya, the word 'Dev' came to be used for God. Thus, the Vedic Aryans began to worship 'Devs', while they as a people were the children of Devs. The Zoroastrian scriptures have called them Daevas and Daeva worshippers at this stage. These Aryans retained the concept that they were children of Devs for a very long time and often aspired to become like the Devs. It is significant that the Jews had similar beliefs about themselves. The quest for God-like stature emerges from the following passage in the Bible.

> And the serpent said unto the woman, Ye shall not surely die:
> For God doth know that in the day ye eat thereof, then your eyes shall be opened, and ye shall be as gods, knowing good and evil.
>
> (Genesis 3:4–5)

The serpent tempts Eve to eat the fruit of the prohibited tree and promises that by doing so 'ye shall be as gods'. The belief that the Jews were children of gods has also been stated in the Bible. Two such passages are given below.

> I have said, Ye are gods; and all of you are the children of the most High.
>
> (Psalm 82:6)

> Jesus answered them, Is it not thus written in you law, I said, Ye are gods?
>
> (John 10:34)

This belief of the Jews that they were gods and that they were the children of God is identical with the Vedic belief at the stage when the Vedic Aryans were in Arjika and later in the delta of the Amu Dariya. They seem to have remained with the main Dev population in Amu Dariya area for some time, for which the belief that they were gods and the children of God went with them.

The next feature of the Jewish belief system that is not found in the Vedic thought is the concept of Satan. The Vedas have the Asurs, who are adversaries of the Devs and constantly at war with them. The concept, however, does not come close to the view of Devil, who is an evil entity opposing God. Zoroastrianism did develop a concept close to it, as they treated all Daevas as evil, with Angra Mainyu as their leader. Over time, Angra Mainyu became the creator of all evils in the world and began to resemble the Devil. The Devil, however, appears to be more of a Christian than a Jewish concept. It is very doubtful whether Judaism, at least in the early stages, had it in the way Satan is now projected. Mention of him is very scant and occurs only in the later books of the Old Testament. Any significant mention of Satan comes up only in the Book of Job, though there is a claim that in the Genesis, the serpent tempting Adam and Eve to eat from the Forbidden Tree was the personification of Satan. This does not seem likely because if it had been Satan, there would have been no reason for God to curse the serpent saying, 'Because thou hast done this, thou art cursed above all cattle, and above every beast of the field; upon thy belly shalt thou go, and dust shalt thou eat all the days of thy life: And I will put enmity between thee and the woman, and between thy seed and her seed; it shall bruise thy head, and thou shalt bruise his heal'. God has evidently cursed the serpent and all its future generations to suffer. If it had been Satan, it would make the serpent innocent, and God would have cursed an innocent creature.

There is no mention in the Bible when and how Satan was created. Two passages are claimed to be regarding Lucifer, and Satan is considered to be this fallen angel. These passages are not in the early books of the Old Testament and do not show that Lucifer became the Devil. Verses from the first of these passages are given below.

> For the Lord will have mercy on Jacob, and will yet choose Israel, and set them in their own land: and the strangers shall be joined with them, and they shall cleave to the house of Jacob. (1)
>
> And the people shall take them, and bring them to their place: and the house of Israel shall possess them in the land of the Lord for servants and handmaids: and they shall take them captives, whose captives they were; and they shall rule over their oppressors. (2)
>
> And it shall come to pass in the day that the Lord shall give thee rest from thy sorrow, and from thy fear, and from the hard bondage wherein thou wast made to serve, (3)
>
> That thou shalt take up this proverb against the king of Babylon, and say, How hath the oppressor ceased! The golden city ceased! (4)
>
> The Lord hath broken the staff of the wicked, and the sceptre of the rulers. (5)
>
> He who smote the people in wrath with a continual stroke, he that ruled the nations in anger, is persecuted, and none hindereth. (6)
>
> Hell from beneath is moved for thee to meet thee at thy coming: it stirreth up the dead for thee, even all the chief ones of earth; it hath raised up from their thrones all the kings of the nations. (9)
>
> All they shall speak and say unto thee, Art thou also become weak as we? art thou become like unto us? (10)
>
> Thy pomp is brought down to the grave, and the noise

of thy viols: the worm is spread under thee, and the worm cover thee. (11)

How art thou fallen from heaven, O Lucifer, son of the morning! how art thou cut down to the ground, which didst weaken the nations! (12)

For thou hast said in thine heart, I will ascend into heaven, I will exalt my throne above the stars of God: I will sit upon the mount of the congregation, in the sides of the north: (13)

I will ascend above the heights of the clouds; I will be like the most High. (14)

They that see thee shall narrowly look upon thee, and consider thee, saying, Is this the man that made the earth to tremble, that did shake kingdoms; (16)

That made the world as a wilderness, and destroyed the cities thereof; that opened not the house of his prisoners? (17)

All the kings of the nations, even all of them, lie in glory, every one in his own house. (18)

But thou art cast out of thy grave like an abominable branch, and as the raiment of those that are slain, thrust through with a sword, that go down to the stones of the pit; as a carcass trodden under feet. (19)

Thou shalt not be joined with them in burial, because thou hast destroyed thy land, and slain thy people: the seed of evildoers shall never be renowned. (20)

Prepare slaughter for his children for the iniquity of their fathers; that do not rise, nor possess the land, nor fill the face of the world with cities. (21)

For I will rise up against them, saith the Lord of hosts, and cut off from Babylon the name, and remnant, and son, and nephew, saith the Lord. (22)

That I will break the Assyrian in my land, and upon my mountains tread him under foot: then shall his yoke depart from off them, and his burden depart from off their shoulders. (25)

In the year that king Ahaz died was this burden. (28)

(Isaiah 14)

This is the only story of Lucifer in the Bible. Here, too, he is mentioned by name only in one verse wherein he has been called the 'son of morning' and is asked 'How art thou fallen from heaven'. It is by taking this single verse in isolation that Lucifer is considered to be an angel and to have fallen from heaven to become the Devil. Though his becoming the devil is not mentioned even here, if the entire story is taken into account, he does not appear to be even an angel but the king of Babylon who was killed. It would be wrong to consider the said verse in isolation, as Isaiah has narrated a story in the chapter and this verse is an integral part of it. He starts with a hope that the Jews would now be freed and will hold captive those very people who had kept them in slavery. He proceeds to mention that the king of Babylon had died and his sceptre had been broken. With his hatred, he says that hell was waiting for him. The further description is also of a mighty king who had earlier made the earth tremble and had destroyed the cities but had now been killed by the sword and did not get even a proper burial in his land. It also says that the Babylonian dynasty had ended and the Assyrians broken down. Isaiah mentions even the time of when this happened as 'In the year king Ahaz died'. This is evidently the account of a historical event, the defeat of the Chaldeans at the hand of the Persians and the end of the Babylonian dynasty, and not of an angel who had rebelled against God to be banished from heaven to become the Devil. Isaiah has used the name Lucifer for the Chaldean emperor and has metaphorically called his high status, heaven.

The second passage that is claimed to be a description of Lucifer is given below.

Son of man, take up a lamentation upon the king of Tyrus, and say unto him, Thus saith the Lord God; Thou sealest up the sum, full of wisdom, and perfect in beauty.

Thou hast been in Eden the garden of God; every precious stone was thy covering, the sardius, topaz, and the diamond, the beryl, the onyx, and the jasper, the sapphire, the emerald, and the carbuncle, and gold: the workmanship of thy tabrets and of thy pipes was prepared in thee in the day that thou wast created.

Thou art the anointed cherub that covereth; and I have set thee so: thou wast upon the holy mountain of God; thou hast walked up and down in the midst of the stones of fire.

Thou was perfect in thy ways from the day that thou wast created, till iniquity was found in thee.

By the multitude of thy merchandise they have filled the midst of thee with violence, and thou hast sinned: therefore I will cast thee as profane out of the mountain of God: and I will destroy thee, O covering cherub, from the midst of the stones of fire.

Thine heart was lifted up because of thy beauty, thou hast corrupted thy wisdom by reason of thy brightness: I will cast thee to the ground, I will lay thee before kings, that they may behold thee.

(Ezekiel 28:12–17)

This passage, which is claimed to be speaking about Lucifer and his banishment from heaven, is not about Lucifer even on the face of it. Ezekiel is cursing the king of Tyre and is prophesying that he would be cast out of the mountain of God. Tyre was a Phoenician kingdom, and the Phoenicians were very prosperous traders. All this is brought out in the passage and yet it is claimed to be speaking of Lucifer. Though it speaks of Eden, the garden of God, it is a figurative usage to mean prosperity, as the king of Tyrus is reported to be covered with diamonds, gold and all precious things. The Garden of Eden in the Genesis, in any case, was a simple place, where Adam and Eve, when they sought to cover themselves, had to resort to leaves. It did not have gold and diamonds. Ezekiel has proceeded, in his narrative, to prophesize in a similar manner the destruction of Zidon, which seems to be the other Phoenician city, Sidon, the Pharaoh of Egypt and others. Though it is evident that Ezekiel is speaking of the king of Tyre, even if it is admitted that this is a reference to Lucifer, it does not make him Satan, as God is reported to have said, 'I will cast thee to the ground, I will lay thee before kings, that they may behold thee'. The concept of Devil, as is found later, is not such a helpless creature.

The Christian writers have also noticed that the Hebrew scriptures do not bring out how Satan was created. This can be seen from the passage below.

> 'Since, then, you have honestly confessed, on the testimony of the scriptures that the evil one exists, state to us how he has come into existence, if indeed he has come into existence, and by whom, and why'. And Peter said, 'Pardon me, Simon, if I do not dare to affirm what has not been written.
>
> 'As nothing has been written as to how, and by whom, and why the evil one came into existence, we ought not to dare to assert more than the Scriptures'.
>
> (*The Writings of the Early Church Fathers*, Vol. 8, Pseudo-Clementine Literature, Homily 19, Chapter 3)

It is of interest that the word Satan in the Hebrew language means 'adversary'. It does not mean an evil creature or an adversary of God. At several places, it is found to be used for human adversaries also. In the light of this, a very significant statement made by Augustine reveals that the concept had its origin from the same belief as are in the Vedas.

And as if to point out the cause why they are the enemies of God's people, he adds, 'For Assur comes with them.' Now Assur is often used figuratively for the devil, 'who works in the children of disobedience,' as his own vessels, that they may assail the people of God.
  (*The Writings of the Early Church Fathers*, Vol. 8, Augustine, On Psalms, Psalm 83, Para 6)

The verse in the said psalm is 'Assur also is joined with them: they have helped the children of Lot. Selah.' Augustine has stated that the word 'Assur' is often used figuratively for the Devil. It appears that this was not a figurative use, to begin with, but was the actual statement, which in course of time became hazy. The Jews were referring to their human adversaries, the Asurs, who were opposed to the Devs, a word that had come to mean God, for which they have been called enemies of God's people and those who work in the children of disobedience. It thus appears that the concept of Devil was developed by Pauline Christianity. The Jews had only their adversaries, the Asurs, as the embodiment of evil on the same lines as the Asurs are projected in the Vedas. Later the same concept developed into a vague supernatural evil entity as human history was lost and got merged into mythological beliefs.

Unlike the Zoroastrians, the Kimmerians and the Vedic people, who had retained in their memory that in their remote past they lived in the Arctic Circle, there is nothing in the Bible to show that the Jews, too, remembered that they lived there. However, the only natural calamity remembered by them, as recorded in the Bible, could have happened only if they were living on ice like the rest who have remembered their stay in the Arctic Circle. This is the Great Deluge in which Noah saved himself and the rest of the creatures in his Ark. This story has to be taken as a record of a past event, as several cultures have it in their mythology. Though some may have taken it from others, yet so many people speaking of this is an indication of an actual happening, even if the reporting is distorted.

In the Bible, it is reported that God warned Noah of the coming deluge and asked him to make an ark, in which to place his family and all animals in pairs along with their food. Seven days later, it began to rain, which continued for 40 days and nights. With this, the entire land, including high hills and mountains, got submerged and remained submerged for 150 days, after which the water abated and in a few weeks land become dry. Noah and all animals that were in the ark made by him, came off to repopulate the earth again. It is obvious that if the intervention of God is kept out, what has been stated is not possible because neither can the entire earth be submerged by rain nor can all animals be brought on to an ark with enough food to survive for several months. However, if the supernatural is kept out, two things emerge from the narrative, one, that the entire surface on which people lived got submerged, and, two, despite that, humans and other animals were not wiped out. This is possible only if the people were living on ice like the people living in the Arctic Circle. These people seem to be living more to the south but still over the sea. With the receding of the Ice Age, the ice cover would have receded from the south, whereby a lot of area would have witnessed its melting. The ice on which these people were living for centuries would have melted and all known surfaces would have become water. This would have killed all the people and animals that were there. Some people on the fringes would have survived to carry the story. Over a period of time, it would not have been remembered that they were living on ice and the storytellers would have had before them the difficulty of explaining how the entire surface got submerged and how man and other animals survived despite it. As rain and floods were the only thing known that could submerge land, and as boat was the only thing known that could remain afloat in the waters, that is what has been imagined and a story has been woven. This story seems to be carrying the memory of the devastation caused due to the receding of the Ice Age and the melting of ice on which people lived.

All these points that have been derived from literary sources indicate that the Jews were Aryans and that they were Devs. Even those beliefs that do not match with the Vedic beliefs do not come in the way, as they are either later developments or had the same origin as the Vedic beliefs. However, a final statement cannot be made just on the basis of evidence from literary sources. It would be necessary to resort to other channels of information, especially genetics, to confirm this. The evidence from the literary sources is, however, strong enough to call for other sources to step in and share their findings.

BIBLIOGRAPHY

Aquinas, Thomas (2002). *Aquinas's Shorter Summa*. Manchester, NH: Sophia Institute Press.

Burrows, Millar. ed. (1986) *The Dead Sea Scrolls*. New York: Gramercy Pub. Co.

Dionysius. (2015) *Heavenly Hierarchy*. Edited by John Parker. Forgotten Books.

Dionysius. (2015). *Ecclesiastical Hierarchy*. Edited by John Parker. Forgotten Books.

Evagrius. (2015). *Kephalia Gnostika*. Translated by Ilaria L.E. Ramelli. Atlanta: SBL Press.

Hoffman, Joseph, ed. (1994). *Porphyry's 'Against the Christians': The Literary Remains*. New York: Prometheus Books.

John. (2008) *Ascent of Mount Carmel*. Edited by E. Peers. Radford, VA: Wilder Publications.

Kallistos. (1997). *The Orthodox Church*. Edited by Timothy Ware. London, England New York, N.Y: Penguin Books.

MacCulloch, D. (2009). *A History of Christianity: The First Three Thousand Years*. London, England: Allen Lane.

Pliny. (1991). *Natural History: A Selection*. Edited by J. Healy. London, England New York, NY,USA: Penguin Books.

Ranganathan, Shyam, trans. (2008). *Patañjali's Yoga Sutra*. London: Penguin.

Robinson, James M., ed. (1977). *The Nag Hammadi Library in English*. New York: Harper & Row.

Teresa. (2012). *The Way of Perfection*. Edited by E. Peers. Mineola, N.Y: Dover Publications.

The Holy Bible: King James Version. (1991). New York: Ivy Books.

The Holy Bible: New Living Translation. (2015). Tyndale House Foundation.

The Writings of the Early Church Fathers. (2014). Bible Study Tools.

Whitney, W.D., trans. (2009). *The Atharv Veda Samhita*. Parimal Publications.

INDEX

The Acts of the Apostles, 7, 8, 23, 24, 44, 48, 51, 53, 90, 119, 120, 122, 130, 131, 132, 133, 134, 135, 136, 137, 140, 141, 147, 148, 172, 174, 176, 178, 181, 209, 216, 219, 223, 230

Abraham, 12, 21, 72, 350, 351, 352, 353

Abrahamic races, 350, 353, 354, 355

Ahur Mazda, 365

Alexander, the bishop of Alexandria, 243, 248

Amu Dariya, 257, 353, 367, 368

Angra Mainyu, 368

animal sacrifice, 40, 187, 189

Antioch, 3, 4, 8, 9, 10, 25, 131, 138, 184, 185, 186, 187, 191, 192, 193, 196, 197, 215, 217, 230, 236, 239, 240, 244, 252, 253, 299

Apostolic Church, 10, 51, 53, 54, 91, 126, 150, 151, 152, 154, 157, 161, 163, 187, 188, 189, 193, 200, 203, 205, 206, 207, 213, 214, 217, 218, 223, 224, 227, 229, 231, 232, 238, 239, 247, 276, 277, 278

Arctic Circle, 256, 374, 375

Arian heresy, 41, 239, 240, 242, 243, 244

Arianism, 40

Arians, 40, 41, 242, 250

Arius, 231, 237, 238, 239, 240, 241, 243, 244, 245, 248, 249, 251, 252, 342

Arjika, 257, 353, 355, 357, 358, 359, 366, 367, 368

ark, 57, 374, 375

Aryan, xi, 256, 259, 335, 345, 350, 353, 354, 355, 356, 357, 358, 359, 361, 362, 363, 364, 366, 367, 368, 376

Assyrian Empire, 257

Assyrians, 258, 352, 353, 371

Asur Banipal, 257

Asur Hadden, 257

Asuristan, 257

Asurs, 257, 258, 350, 353, 355, 356, 357, 358, 359, 361, 367, 368, 374

Atharva Veda, 361

Atman, 261

Augustine, 40, 46, 47, 49, 50, 52, 62, 66, 70, 71, 72, 73, 166, 167, 250, 276, 279, 293,

304, 305, 306, 310, 316, 319, 329, 330, 331, 332, 333, 338, 357, 373, 374
Avesta, 256, 257, 356, 359

Babylon, 57, 59, 60, 61, 257, 350, 352, 353, 363, 364, 369, 370, 371
Babylonian Empire, 61
baptism, 35, 170, 209, 211, 216, 292, 299, 300
Barnabas, 3, 4, 6, 7, 8, 9, 10, 23, 135, 138, 140, 166, 184, 187
Bethany, 107, 109, 110, 121, 122, 125
Bethlehem, 62, 63, 64, 71, 173
Bishop of Crete, 32
Book of Revelation, 51
Brahm, 213
Brahma, 263, 264
Brahman literature, 259
the Bible, ix, 1, 2, 3, 8, 13, 41, 48, 49, 57, 61, 63, 67, 68, 69, 71, 76, 81, 84, 87, 90, 91, 92, 99, 120, 127, 129, 133, 141, 148, 164, 167, 170, 171, 174, 181, 183, 194, 195, 198, 205, 206, 207, 211, 269, 288, 308, 322, 323, 343, 345, 350, 359, 366, 367, 369, 371, 374, 375

Caesar Augustus, 62
Caesarea, 142, 144, 175, 176, 240, 241, 243, 244, 246
Caius, 202, 203

Carmelites or White Friars, 350
Catholic Church, 40, 229, 255, 278, 317, 318, 320, 331, 333
Celsus, 42, 72, 73, 126, 127, 160, 161, 290, 303, 316
Chaldeans, 56, 352, 371
Christian belief, 88, 115, 232
Christian doctrine, 237, 238, 290, 334
Christian literature, 7
Christian mystery, 296
Church Fathers, x, 3, 40, 41, 42, 43, 44, 45, 46, 47, 49, 50, 51, 52, 53, 54, 55, 65, 66, 67, 70, 71, 72, 73, 76, 78, 87, 90, 123, 126, 127, 130, 139, 140, 147, 149, 152, 153, 154, 155, 156, 157, 158, 159, 160, 161, 163, 164, 167, 168, 181, 183, 184, 185, 186, 188, 191, 192, 193, 194, 196, 199, 202, 209, 210, 212, 213, 214, 215, 216, 217, 219, 220, 221, 222, 223, 224, 225, 226, 228, 229, 230, 233, 234, 235, 239, 240, 241, 242, 243, 246, 248, 249, 250, 251, 252, 253, 267, 268, 269, 273, 275, 276, 278, 279, 280, 282, 283, 286, 289, 290, 291, 292, 293, 296, 297, 298, 302, 303, 304, 305, 306, 309, 310, 311, 315, 316, 317, 318, 327, 328, 329, 330, 331, 332, 333, 336, 337, 338, 339, 340, 341, 342, 348, 349, 357, 358, 359,

360, 365, 366, 373, 374
Church of James, ix, 41, 42, 51, 93, 217
Church of Paul, 43
Church of Rome, 171, 191, 193, 196, 197, 198, 199, 200, 201, 203, 255
Church of the Philippians, 27
circumcision, 3, 4, 7, 8, 9, 13, 27, 29, 32, 42, 49, 96, 187
consubstantial, 246, 247, 249, 250
Corinth, 16, 19, 146
Corinthians, 2, 15, 16, 17, 18, 19, 20, 21, 22, 93, 124, 134, 135, 136, 137, 139, 150, 165, 167, 254, 285, 286, 288, 294, 295
Council of Ephesus, 251, 253
Council of Nicea, 237, 245
Crucifixion of Jesus, 95, 99, 107, 108, 110, 114, 115, 123, 149
cycle of births and deaths, 89, 261, 262, 264, 307, 312, 315
Cyril, 50, 217, 218, 221, 223, 253
Cyril of Alexandria, 253

Daevas, 367, 368
Damascus, 6, 23, 24, 130, 131, 132, 133, 134, 135, 136, 137, 358
Daniel, 362
David, 48, 49, 62, 63, 64, 65, 66, 67, 69, 70, 71, 72
Day of Judgement, 30, 88, 102, 118, 125, 127, 180, 299, 300, 307, 308, 312, 316, 320, 359, 362, 363, 364
Dead Sea Scrolls, 91, 345, 346, 347, 348, 349, 356, 357
Devasthan, 257
Dev Asur Sangram, 359
Devs, 257, 258, 350, 353, 355, 356, 357, 358, 359, 361, 367, 368, 374, 376
the Devil, 82, 153, 283, 286, 371, 374
doctrinal differences, 2, 3, 10, 12, 34, 35, 40, 69, 169
dualism, 263, 265, 334, 335, 339, 343

Easter, 175, 176, 232, 233, 234, 235, 236, 237
Eastern Church/Orthodox Church, 40, 167, 168, 171, 185, 191, 204, 232, 253, 254, 255, 278, 306, 307, 321, 322, 331
Ebionites, 41, 42, 43, 44, 51, 53, 54, 65, 66, 69, 73, 168, 217, 218, 227, 243, 249
ecclesiastical council, 280
ecumenical Council, 238, 311
Egypt, 59, 63, 64, 68, 78, 228, 241, 272, 274, 275, 278, 302, 334, 345, 352, 360, 373
Elias, 91, 308
Elijah, 350
Emperor Claudius, 13, 146, 214, 219, 222

Emperor Constantine, 35, 207
Encratites, 43, 44
Ephesians, 2, 185, 187, 191, 288, 295, 296
Epistle of James, 11, 12, 54
Epistle to Philadelphians, 155, 315
Epistle to Polycarp, 155
Epistle to Smyrnaeans, 155, 188
Epistle to the Galatians, 22
Epistle to the Philippians, 26, 195
Epistle to the Romans, 15, 22, 196
Epistle to the Thessalonians, 29
Epistle to Titus, 31
Essenes, 90, 91, 345, 346, 347, 348, 349, 350
Eucharist, 168, 188, 189, 190, 299, 300
Euphrates, 60
Eusebius, the bishop of Nicomedia, 243, 246, 247
Ezekiel, 372, 373

Gabriel, 62, 72, 74
Galatians, 2, 6, 7, 8, 9, 10, 22, 23, 24, 25, 26, 135, 137
Galilee, 62, 64, 76, 93, 94, 95, 96, 97, 99, 100, 101, 103, 104, 107, 108, 109, 110, 113, 116, 118, 119, 120, 121, 173, 346
Genesis, 68, 350, 351, 352, 367, 368, 373

Gentile Church, 81
Gentiles, 3, 4, 5, 6, 7, 8, 9, 10, 11, 13, 25, 33, 35, 41, 47, 48, 53, 81, 96, 97, 132, 133, 135, 138, 159, 194, 219, 235, 271, 292, 295, 296
Gnostic Christianity, 78
Gnostic Christians, 300, 302, 309, 315, 324, 334
Gospel, 2, 42, 44, 45, 51, 53, 54, 61, 66, 69, 70, 71, 76, 80, 81, 93, 94, 97, 100, 103, 116, 118, 119, 125, 130, 173, 174, 188, 191, 192, 229, 230, 268, 277, 289, 301, 302, 308, 313, 324, 332, 339
Gospel of Luke, 51, 80, 125, 230
Gospel of Mark, 53, 61, 66, 80, 100
Gospel of Matthew, 42, 44, 51, 61, 66, 69, 93, 94, 97, 119, 173, 174, 229
Governor Felix, 142, 144
Governor Festus, 144
Great Deluge, 374

Herod, 54, 63, 64, 173, 174, 175, 176
the Holy Spirit, 35, 212, 217, 250, 297, 321
Hosius, 245, 246

Ignatius, 296
Ili River, 257
Immaculate Conception, 63, 64

Indus Valley Civilization, 258
Inferior God, 264, 334
interpolation, 51, 52, 53, 62,
  66, 69, 70, 80, 94, 95, 96,
  102, 115, 119, 121, 172, 173,
  176, 178, 197, 199, 209, 211
Irenaeus, 42, 43, 45, 65, 150,
  151, 191, 197, 198, 199, 200,
  212, 213, 214, 222, 223, 226,
  278, 282, 283, 289, 302, 303,
  309, 315, 327, 336, 339, 340,
  358
Ishwar, 263, 334, 335
Israel, 48, 49, 50, 58, 59, 63,
  81, 82, 105, 179, 180, 352,
  362, 369

Jacob, 48, 96, 369
Jerome, 54, 67, 68, 90, 147,
  149, 184, 228, 229, 270, 330
Jerusalem, 4, 5, 6, 7, 10, 14, 23,
  24, 25, 41, 42, 49, 50, 59, 61,
  62, 63, 66, 95, 104, 106, 107,
  108, 110, 116, 118, 119, 120,
  121, 122, 123, 124, 128, 130,
  131, 132, 133, 135, 137, 138,
  141, 142, 144, 145, 146, 173,
  176, 180, 208, 209, 217, 227,
  228, 243, 247, 362, 363
Jewish practices, 5, 10, 13, 25,
  26
Jewish scriptures, 68, 359
John, 7, 8, 9, 49, 50, 51, 52, 53,
  54, 55, 56, 59, 61, 66, 68, 72,
  75, 76, 77, 80, 81, 83, 84, 85,
  86, 87, 91, 95, 110, 111, 113,
  114, 115, 116, 118, 120, 121,
  122, 123, 139, 140, 166, 167,
  168, 169, 170, 171, 174, 175,
  177, 181, 184, 185, 186, 187,
  190, 194, 195, 208, 209, 210,
  230, 234, 236, 252, 253, 287,
  291, 298, 308, 312, 318, 319,
  329, 330, 332, 333, 341, 343,
  357, 358, 366, 367
John Chrysostom, 51, 53, 68,
  72, 76, 87, 139, 140, 184,
  194, 195, 210, 230, 298, 366
Joseph, 62, 63, 64, 65, 66, 67,
  69, 70, 71, 72, 73, 74, 75, 76,
  95
Judah, 48, 49, 50, 67, 362
Judaism, 3, 7, 10, 35, 42, 47,
  50, 89, 188, 236, 266, 268,
  274, 344, 345, 347, 365, 366,
  368
Judaizer, 3, 172
Judaizing the Gentiles, 3, 47,
  135, 138, 235, 271
Judas, 4, 77, 78, 84, 102, 132,
  289
Justin Martyr, 215, 222

karma, 261
kosher, 5, 8, 355

Lake Balkhash, 256
Law of Moses, 4, 5, 7, 8, 10,
  12, 25, 26, 29, 37, 40, 49, 50,
  141, 143, 187, 265
Lazarus, 85
Lucifer, 369, 370, 371, 372, 373

Magnesians, 185
Manicheans, 66, 170, 276, 305, 337, 338
Marcion, 45, 76, 151, 152, 212, 215, 217, 231, 303, 336, 337, 341
martyrdom, 130, 141, 146, 148, 149, 163, 164, 185, 197, 201
Mary Magdalene, 85, 92, 97, 98, 99, 101, 103, 104, 107, 109, 111, 112, 114, 115, 116, 117, 121, 122, 302
Mary the mother of James and Joses, 97, 99
Matthew, 42, 44, 48, 51, 52, 53, 61, 62, 64, 66, 67, 69, 70, 72, 74, 75, 76, 79, 80, 82, 83, 91, 92, 93, 94, 95, 96, 97, 99, 100, 101, 102, 103, 107, 108, 109, 110, 114, 115, 117, 118, 119, 121, 123, 128, 170, 173, 174, 189, 229, 265, 269, 271, 287, 288, 323, 366
Maya, 264, 335
Messiah, 61
Micah's prophecy, 64
moksha, 262, 307, 311, 312
monasticism, 229, 270, 271, 272, 276, 278, 279, 280, 281
monotheism, 359, 364, 365, 366
Montanist heresy, 198, 200
Moses, 4, 5, 7, 8, 10, 11, 12, 25, 26, 29, 37, 39, 40, 49, 50, 59, 105, 106, 109, 141, 143, 187, 265, 333

Mother of God, 251
Mount Olivet, 121, 122

Nag Hammadi Library, 77, 78, 275, 277, 278, 289, 301, 302, 308, 312, 313, 324, 325, 339, 348, 358
Nazareth, 62, 63, 64, 75, 97, 105, 179, 180
Nebuchadnezzar, 56, 57, 58, 61, 363
Nero, 130, 141, 147, 148, 149, 150, 164, 191, 193, 197, 202, 214, 223, 236
Nestorian Heresy, 251
Nestorius, 231, 251, 252, 253
New Jerusalem, 59
New Testament, 19, 189
Nicene Creed, 244, 247, 248, 250
Noah, 374, 375
non-dualism, 263, 265, 334, 335, 339, 343
Novation, 297, 299

Old Testament, 61, 63, 68, 355, 356, 357, 362, 363, 366, 368, 369
Oxus River, 257

Palestine, 241, 275, 350, 362
Parthian Empire, 131
Passion of Christ, 149, 188
Passover, 110, 116, 123, 233, 234, 235
Paul, vii, ix, x, 1, 2, 3, 4, 5, 6,

7, 8, 9, 10, 11, 12, 13, 14, 15, 16, 17, 18, 19, 20, 21, 22, 23, 24, 25, 26, 27, 28, 29, 30, 31, 32, 33, 34, 35, 36, 37, 39, 40, 42, 43, 44, 45, 46, 50, 51, 54, 57, 61, 69, 70, 72, 80, 81, 88, 90, 92, 93, 94, 96, 100, 101, 103, 120, 124, 125, 126, 127, 128, 129, 130, 131, 132, 133, 135, 136, 137, 138, 139, 140, 141, 142, 143, 144, 145, 146, 147, 148, 149, 150, 151, 158, 164, 165, 166, 167, 168, 169, 171, 172, 173, 176, 178, 179, 181, 182, 183, 184, 186, 187, 189, 191, 193, 194, 195, 197, 199, 200, 201, 202, 203, 205, 206, 207, 214, 218, 221, 222, 223, 227, 228, 234, 235, 236, 239, 249, 254, 255, 271, 285, 286, 288, 294, 296, 298, 299, 307, 323, 333, 334, 362, 364

Pauline Christianity, 3, 262, 307, 364, 374

Pauline Christians, 214

Pauline Church, ix, x, 3, 46, 51, 52, 61, 69, 88, 110, 125, 129, 148, 149, 150, 151, 152, 153, 154, 157, 158, 161, 162, 163, 164, 166, 167, 168, 170, 171, 172, 176, 179, 180, 183, 185, 186, 188, 189, 191, 193, 197, 200, 202, 203, 205, 207, 211, 213, 214, 217, 218, 224, 226, 227, 229, 232, 236, 238, 244, 245, 255, 259, 276, 277, 278, 279, 284, 294, 296, 300, 343

Pauline scriptures, 205, 206, 207, 218, 227, 229, 230, 231, 232, 237, 238, 239, 252, 254, 272, 306

Pauline theology, 116, 171, 176, 179, 182, 191, 196, 205, 206, 207, 218, 225, 227, 231, 232, 238, 239, 244, 247, 249, 254, 255, 270, 281, 321, 322, 334, 344

Pelegius, 251

Persian Empire, 363

Peter, 5, 7, 8, 9, 10, 15, 24, 25, 33, 46, 47, 51, 53, 54, 84, 96, 97, 104, 108, 109, 111, 113, 114, 115, 118, 119, 124, 129, 141, 148, 149, 150, 151, 158, 164, 166, 167, 168, 171, 172, 175, 176, 179, 180, 181, 182, 183, 184, 185, 191, 192, 193, 194, 195, 196, 197, 198, 199, 200, 201, 202, 203, 204, 207, 208, 209, 210, 211, 213, 214, 216, 219, 220, 221, 222, 223, 228, 229, 234, 235, 236, 247, 249, 254, 272, 277, 289, 290, 292, 299, 304, 306, 373

Pharisees, 4, 35, 78, 79, 82, 83, 85, 86, 89, 90, 91, 92, 101, 142, 143, 300, 345, 362, 363

Philip, 208, 209, 210, 211, 216, 219, 277, 308, 324

Philo the Jew, 228, 229, 270

Phoenicians, 360, 372

Phrygian heretics, 203
Porphyry, 72, 73, 74
presbyter, 153, 195, 198, 229, 237, 244, 245
prophecy, 59, 64, 66, 67, 68, 69, 285, 366
Prophet Isaiah, 68

Resurrection of Christ/Jesus, 18, 80, 101, 108, 111, 117, 237
Rig Veda, 356, 357
Roman Catholic Church, 317, 320, 331, 333
Roman Empire, 131, 144, 145, 146, 148, 164, 173, 176, 186, 231, 242, 364
Rome, 13, 61, 119, 130, 141, 142, 143, 145, 146, 147, 148, 149, 150, 151, 152, 153, 154, 161, 164, 171, 184, 185, 186, 187, 191, 192, 193, 194, 195, 196, 197, 198, 199, 200, 201, 202, 203, 207, 211, 212, 214, 215, 217, 218, 219, 220, 221, 222, 223, 229, 231, 236, 254, 255, 272, 278, 321, 362, 364

Sadducees, 79, 89, 90, 91, 142, 345, 362
Saint John of the Cross, 287
salvation, 10, 13, 35, 36, 39, 40, 47, 89, 182, 183, 225, 232, 249, 262, 264, 267, 307, 311, 312, 313, 315, 316, 317, 320, 321, 322, 326, 330, 331, 346

Samaria, 48, 49, 50, 120, 152, 208, 209, 210, 212, 217, 362
Samaritans, 47, 48, 49, 50, 96, 215, 362
Sankhya, 263, 265, 334, 335, 338, 339
Satan, 83, 133, 134, 150, 368, 369, 373
the Saviour, 77, 225, 233, 236, 266, 289, 290, 301, 325
Septuagint Version, 68, 69
sepulchre, 92, 93, 94, 97, 98, 99, 100, 101, 103, 104, 105, 107, 108, 109, 111, 114, 115, 117, 121, 123, 173, 316
Simon Magus, 151, 152, 186, 193, 200, 207, 211, 212, 213, 214, 215, 216, 217, 218, 219, 222, 223, 224, 225, 228, 231, 239, 245, 252, 282, 302, 357, 364
Solomon, 48, 49, 57, 362, 363
Son of God, 24, 36, 65, 70, 74, 77, 78, 83, 84, 88, 113, 116, 118, 127, 128, 129, 152, 161, 169, 206, 242, 248, 249, 251, 262, 296, 297, 299, 306
supernatural (conditions, occurrence), 61, 63, 164
Supreme God, 216, 263, 264, 297, 334, 341, 343, 364, 365, 366
Supreme Reality, 261
synagogues, 130, 131, 136

Tanakh, 68, 69, 346, 348

Tarsus, 131, 132, 144
Tertullian, 45, 46, 65, 68, 75, 76, 154, 163, 216, 224, 303, 310
Thomas Aquinas, 319, 320, 333, 357
Throne of Peter, 192, 204, 254
Timothy, 2, 5, 7, 8, 10, 28, 29, 30, 31, 32, 138, 139, 194, 271, 296, 321, 334
Trallians, 185
transmigration of soul, 88, 91
Trinity, 178
Turan, 258
Tyre, 74, 175, 372, 373

Upanishads, 213, 259, 260, 262, 263, 302, 322
Uzbekistan, 257

Valentinian Heresy, 198, 200
Valentinians, 163, 224, 226, 227, 291
Valentinus, 151, 152, 198, 200, 223, 224
Vedanta, 263, 265, 334, 335, 343
Vedas, 256, 257, 258, 259, 260, 263, 316, 331, 353, 356, 359, 364, 366, 368, 373, 374
Vedic beliefs, x, 345, 346, 349, 366, 376
Vedic literature, 259, 356
Vedic polytheism, 359
Vedic religion, 259, 260, 265, 281, 307, 322, 334, 344, 345, 347, 350

Vincent of Lerins, 244
Vistasp, 258

Western Church, x, 167, 171, 201, 232, 244, 278, 280, 281, 306
The Writings of the Early Church Fathers, 41, 42, 43, 44, 45, 46, 47, 49, 50, 51, 52, 53, 54, 55, 65, 66, 67, 70, 72, 73, 76, 87, 90, 126, 127, 130, 139, 140, 147, 149, 152, 153, 154, 155, 156, 157, 158, 159, 160, 161, 163, 167, 184, 185, 188, 191, 192, 194, 196, 199, 202, 210, 212, 213, 215, 216, 217, 219, 220, 221, 222, 223, 224, 225, 226, 228, 229, 230, 233, 234, 235, 239, 240, 241, 242, 243, 246, 248, 249, 250, 251, 252, 253, 267, 268, 269, 273, 275, 276, 278, 279, 280, 282, 283, 286, 289, 290, 291, 292, 293, 296, 297, 298, 302, 303, 304, 305, 306, 309, 310, 311, 315, 316, 317, 318, 327, 328, 329, 330, 331, 332, 333, 336, 337, 338, 339, 340, 341, 342, 348, 349, 357, 358, 359, 360, 365, 366, 373, 374

Yoga Sutra, 284, 285

Zidon, 373
Zoroaster, 258
Zoroastrianism, 258, 365, 368